Real-World Fractals

Real-World Fractals

Mark Finlay and Keith A. Blanton

M&T BOOKS

M&T Books
A Division of MIS:Press, Inc.
A Subsidiary of Henry Holt and Company, Inc.
115 West 18th Street
New York, New York 10011

Library of Congress Cataloging-in-Publication Data

Finlay, Mark
    Real world fractals : object-oriented fractal programming in C++ / Mark Finlay,
    Keith A. Blanton.
      p. cm.
    Includes index.
    ISBN 1-55851-307-8 : $39.95
    1. Fractals--Data processing. 2. Object-oriented programming.
    3. C++ (Computer program language) I. Blanton, Keith A. II. Title.
QA614.86.F56   1993
003'.7--dc20   93-29273
                                                                       CIP

96 95 94 93   4 3 2 1

Publisher: Steve Berkowitz   **Associate Publisher:** Brenda McLaughlin
Project Editor: Margot Owens Pagan   **Development Editor:** Christine de Chutkowski
Technical Editor: Steven Coy   **Copy Editor:** Laura Moorhead
Production Editor: Eileen Mullin   **Associate Production Editor:** Maya Riddick
Cover Design: Raquel Jaramillo

Dedication

To our family and friends who thought we would never finish this book, but put up with us anyway.

Acknowledgments

There are quite a few people who have helped make this book possible. First, and foremost, we would like to thank our families for their support when we needed it the most.

There are many behind-the-scenes folks who help create a book such as this one. We would like to thank our technical editor, Stephen B. Coy, for his timely and helpful advice. Thanks also to our editors, Christine de Chutkowski at M&T Books in San Mateo, Calif., and Margot Pagan at the new M&T Books with Henry Holt & Company. We would also like to thank our production editor Eileen Mullin for the fine job at designing the layout for the book and Raquel Jaramillo for the cover art.

IVEX Corporation in Atlanta, Ga., was extremely helpful in providing the terrain images shown in the color plates. We would like to thank IVEX for their permission to use the sample images. The IVEX visual system is used in flight simulators throughout the world due to its ability to provide detailed and accurate images of actual airfields with sub-inch resolution and texturing. The IVEX visual system is the first visual system to incorporate fractal texturing techniques for real-time display in flight simulation.

Iterated Systems, Inc. in Atlanta Ga. provided considerable support and material for the book on the topic of fractal image compression.

v

Iterated Systems has a number of commercial products based on the fractal compression fractal compression techniques described later in this book. Chapter 12 would not have been possible without their extensive cooperation and assistance. Dr. Michael Barnsley, CEO of Iterated Systems, also adds the following:

I hope you enjoy the commercial fractally compressed pictures which Iterated Systems, Inc. has provided. I believe that the resolution independence which is inherent in fractal technology will make the fundamental means by which images will be handled in the electronic domain for the future.

If you would like further information about commercial products based on fractal image compression you can contact Iterated Systems at:

Iterated Systems, Inc.
5550-A Peachtree Parkway
Suite 650
Norcross, Ga. 30092

In addition to direct help in creating this book, several kind vendors have supplied invaluable resources to help with creating the code and many of the images. We are very grateful to ATI Technologies for their contribution of an ATI Graphics Ultra Pro 24-bit graphics card for Windows and DOS. This graphics card is exceedingly fast and was exceptionally helpful in creating the images for the book. You can contact ATI about any of their products at the following address:

ATI Technologies Inc.
33 Commerce Valley Dr. E.
Thornhill, Ontario
Canada L3T7N6
(416) 882-2600

We also made extensive use of HiJaak PRO from Inset Systems, Inc. to perform screen captures and translate the generated images between different file formats. You can contact Inset Systems at:

Inset Systems
71 Commerce Drive
Brookfield, CT 06804-3405
(203) 740-2400

We are also very grateful to Cristina Palumbo at The MathWorks, Inc., for letting us evaluate and use copies of MATLAB® 4.0. MATLAB is a powerful mathematical and graphics analysis tool that lets you generate an amazing number of different types of plots. You can contact the folks at The MathWorks, Inc. at the following address:

The MathWorks, Inc.
24 Prime Park Way
Natick, MA 01760
(508) 653-1415

All of the software in the book was written using the Borland C++ version 3.1 development environment from Borland, Inc. All of the text for this book was written using Microsoft Word for Windows 2.0 from Microsoft Corporation.

Table of Contents

Why This Book is for You

This book is about putting fractals to work for you. Since the discovery of fractals by Benoit Mandelbrot, fractals have become an integral part of computer graphics. Fractals have been used to create some of the most realistic computer generated animation sequences in motion pictures and as the topic of innumerable books, calendars, magazines, and posters. However, most of the books about fractals you encounter deal with fractals only from the standpoint of computer graphics, that is, how to make pretty pictures with them. In this book, you will learn how to apply fractals to solve a wide range of problems including analyzing complex sets of equations, compressing data storage, and modeling natural phenomena. You will learn both the theory of fractals, the historical background behind the discovery of fractal curves, and many of the practical applications of fractal techniques.

The enclosed high-density diskette contains all of the source code for all of the C++ classes, libraries, and numerous demonstration programs. The source code in the book is written in C++ and makes extensive use of the object-oriented features of the C++ language to simplify creating your own programs. The book develops a logical class hierarchy of fractal objects, making it very easy to create new fractal objects built upon the basic fractal concepts of self-similarity, recursively defined curves, and iterated systems of equations. By employing the features of C++, generating fractal objects of any number of dimensions, drawing these objects on your screen, and adding your own enhancements is easy and straightforward.

Some of the topics covered in the book include:

◆   Developing an object-oriented graphics library that lets you manipulate two- and three-dimensional objects in an almost identical manner. With this hierarchal class structure, all of the graphics

1

objects can easily be scaled, rotated, and translated to any size or location on the screen.

◆ Developing a common set of fractal base classes for defining a tremendous variety of the classic fractal objects such as the Koch snowflake, Sierpinski Gasket, Menger Sponge, and many others. Using these base classes, you can create whole classes of new objects based on any combination of geometric shapes and recursive definitions.

◆ Introducing random variations into fractal objects to simulate natural phenomena ranging from trees to craters on the moon to clouds in a stormy sky.

◆ Exploring the Mandelbrot and Julia sets with a general purpose set of classes that let you study the Mandelbrot and Julia sets for any complex equation, not just the usual $z \rightarrow z^2 + c$ transformation.

◆ Using a simulation of Brownian Motion to model rough surfaces such as mountains, hills, and forests in a terrain model incorporating digital maps from satellites.

◆ Developing a set of classes demonstrating fractal image compression techniques. Fractal image compression can provide dramatic reductions in the amount of space required to store an image and is currently being employed in several different commercial programs.

◆ Introducing the study of chaos with new ways for analyzing complex sets of equations for dynamical systems.

You will need at least a 286 class PC system with a floating point coprocessor and an EGA or VGA graphics card and monitor. The source code has been developed using the Borland C++ version 3.1 development environment for DOS. Except for some specialized graphics routines, all of the code is designed to be as modular and portable to other C++ compilers and operating systems as possible.

Introduction

In your high school geometry and calculus classes, you learned about many different types of curves and shapes, such as the line, circle, ellipse, parabola, and others. These shapes all share a common basis; namely, they can be defined as the solutions of sets of either algebraic (like $x^2 + y^2 = r^2$) or differential equations. These shapes can be applied to representing the world around us. But there are no perfectly straight lines or smooth curves in any natural object. There are always irregularities and deviations from a purely mathematical curve. While these types of differentiable curves are useful approximations for modeling real objects, they cannot provide a complete model for an object.

As it turns out, there is a very rich class of nondifferentiable curves (curves that cannot be defined as solutions to a set of differential equations) that provide a more complete model of many naturally occurring shapes. Benoit Mandelbrot coined the term *fractal* to describe these curves. Fractal curves all share a property known as self-similarity, which means that subsets of the curve look like the whole curve when magnified. If you look around, you will see many types of objects that exhibit this property. Each branch of a tree generally looks similar to the parent branch to which it is attached. A cluster of stars in a constellation looks similar to clusters of galaxies. In this book, you'll learn how to create fractal models for many different types of objects, and you'll see how these models can be applied to solving many different types of problems that would be intractable using more traditional methods. The software provided with this book gives you the tools needed to explore the rich landscape of fractal geometry on your computer.

You've undoubtedly seen the many books with the intricate and beautiful pictures of fractal objects and complex equations, and yet you're probably wondering how these methods can be applied to solving real problems. Many books on programming fractal images exist already. There are now overwhelming numbers of picture collections in various books, magazines, and calendars of images that you can peruse, contemplate, and enjoy. In fact, this proliferation of images has generated renewed interest in general mathematics by graphically illustrating the inherent beauty, symmetry, and complexity of mathematical models. However, there are many direct applications of fractals that go far beyond pure mathematics. From simulation and virtual reality to signal processing and data compression to remote sensing and geographic modeling, fractal-programming techniques are being used increasingly in a wide range of applications.

While fractals provide a wealth of mathematical modeling tools, they are by no means the only ones available. In this book, you'll see how the concepts behind the development of fractals can be expanded into more general methods, referred to collectively as *procedural models*, which let you model a very wide variety of phenomena. You will see how your graphics display can be used both for showing intriguing images and as a terrific tool for visualizing and interpreting analytic results that could not practically be represented any other way.

The study of fractals has encouraged research into many different types of complex systems. Many types of natural phenomena—from modeling the interaction of atomic nuclei to colliding galaxies—are just too complex to model with the classical approach of trying to solve huge numbers of differential equations. Also, you are often only interested in the more qualitative, rather than purely quantitative, behavior of such systems.

As you'll see throughout this book, procedural models provide a very elegant and compact means of representing what would appear to be inordinately complicated systems. In fact, you'll see how complex behavior can be simulated by using a small set of rules for combining simple and, more importantly, well understood sets of transformations and iterated equations. By coding such models on the computer, you can view the results both statically (look at a picture) and dynamically (watch the system evolve on your screen) and then compare them to whatever system you are trying to understand.

In a very real sense, computers make the study of fractals and related mathematics possible. Because fractal curves are so complex, they cannot be drawn manually. Only a computer can perform the necessary calculations to draw a representation of a fractal curve. Fractal and procedural models are inherently recursively generated objects. For someone to efficiently render them on a computer requires the use of a language that intrinsically supports recursion. Until recently, the language of choice for fractals has been C. However, object-oriented programming languages and particularly C++ have become more available and offer powerful new features for fractal programming. The software for this book takes advantage of the object-oriented features of C++, producing both elegant and efficient code.

Since their initial use, fractals have been intimately tied to computer graphics. As such, almost all the code in this book is oriented toward displaying graphic imagery of one form or another. Many applications use fractal and procedural models to model three-dimensional data sets. So, there are both two- and three-dimensional graphics drawing routines included as part of the software in this book. The three-dimensional graphics package can be easily used and adapted to display a broad range of graphical objects, even beyond the many fractals presented in this book. Additionally, the software includes a volume-rendering package for visualizing clouds and other amorphous, three-dimensional data sets.

Using an object-oriented language such as C++ for fractal programming ties together two of the more recent trends in computer graphics: object-oriented programming and fractal modeling. C++ is a very good language for graphics, especially three-dimensional graphics because pictures are described in terms of objects already. A graphical object is manipulated in some way, such as by movement and rotation, to put the object on the screen. These types of operations represent the *methods*, in object-oriented terminology, for changing the object. You'll see many examples throughout the book that define graphical objects with fractal methods for generating a particular color, texture, or look of the object. Combining objects with fractals and procedural models is a powerful way of modeling many diverse types of systems and complex graphical environments.

What You Need

This book is written with a hands-on, try-it-for-yourself approach. So, you'll need access to a PC to try the demonstrations and play with the programs yourself. The complete source code for the software in this book is provided on the disk that accompanies the book. To effectively use the software, you must have experience with either C or C++ programming and be able to compile and execute C++ code on your PC. All the code development was performed using Borland C++, version 3.1, for MS-DOS. However, every effort has been made to remove all Borland-specific features from the code and to conform to the AT&T C++, version 2.0, standard. The small number of device-specific routines for the graphics card are provided in separate code modules that are easily adapted to other environments. To successfully run the demonstration programs, you must have a 286-class PC with a floating-point coprocessor or better. A standard VGA graphics card is also required. The software has been specifically adapted to work with the ATI Graphics Ultra Pro SVGA card to provide higher resolution displays and true 24-bit imagery. There is a demonstration program associated with all the chapters that describe the fractal-modeling techniques. The programs illustrate the various concepts and provide a working program example to show you how to create your own programs. Copy the sample programs and experiment with them to create new effects and enhanced demonstrations.

Organization of the Book

This book is organized into five parts. In Part I, you'll learn about all the various programming tools needed for the rest of the book. You'll learn how the study of fractals has progressed and why you need all these programming tools. Part II looks at the basic fractal methods in one and two dimensions. Part III examines how fractals can be generalized into procedural models that can be applied to more elaborate and useful models of various phenomenon types. In addition, Part III introduces the three-dimensional graphics module and shows how to create realistic models of terrain. Part IV explains how fractal and procedural models are used in a variety of applications ranging from simulation to digital-signal compression. Finally, in Part V, the future of procedural modeling is discussed with an emphasis on potential applications and problems that fractals may help solve.

Historical background

In Chapter 1, you'll learn about some of the developments that led to the discovery of fractals. As with all new concepts, the idea for fractals did not suddenly pop into someone's head. It is more a case of one thing leading to another. Since Mandelbrot initially coined the term *fractal*, there have been many contributors to fractal research, both in applying the fractal-modeling approach to solving various problems and in extending the basic concepts to encompass more applications. This chapter reviews these developments, leading you to today's state of the art advances.

Programming in C++

With the history of fractals in mind, we illustrate some of the C++ techniques used in creating the code for this book in Chapter 2. We assume you have at least some programming experience with C or C++. Chapter 2 describes the programming techniques and styles used for all the code provided on the disk that accompanies this book. In addition, Chapter 2 presents many useful programming practices that will help you produce cleaner and more readable code. As with any advanced programming language, C++ offers you many possible ways to implement a given algorithm. Chapter 2 suggests guidelines for you to follow that will aid you in adapting the code from this book to your own purposes. By following these guidelines, you will be able to produce both efficient and understandable code.

Fractal Graphics

While fractal algorithms are often interesting in general, their main appeal continues to be in creating pictures on screen. Chapter 3 describes the software tools for displaying both two- and three-dimensional graphics on your PC monitor. Each C++ function is presented with a brief description of its purpose and operation. A summary of all the available graphics functions discussed in each chapter is provided at the end of each chapter. In addition to supporting the demonstration programs found in this book, the graphics functions give you the tools for displaying your own two- and three-dimensional objects. By combining the tools found in the later chapters with the graphics-display functions, you can create a virtually unlimited number of elaborate pictures and dynamic simulations.

Affine Transformations

One of the key elements of all the algorithms discussed in this book are affine transformations, which are used just about everywhere because of their simplicity and generality. For instance, a graphical object can be translated, rotated, and scaled in a single step using a single transformation matrix. Many of the fractal algorithms can be easily described as repeated applications of various affine transformations. In Chapter 3, you will learn about the properties of affine transformations, how to use them, and how C++ provides a very compact and readable way of easily incorporating matrix operations into your code. Chapter 3 ends with a description of several utility functions that are useful in the more advanced algorithms.

Statistical Matters

One of the primary uses of fractal-modeling techniques is to recreate the seemingly random patterns found in nature. Statistical modeling is a key component in generating most of the fractal images you have probably seen. In Chapter 4, you will learn how to generate large numbers of uncorrelated pseudorandom numbers. The term *pseudorandom* refers to the property of these sequences that enables them to always be precisely recreated given the initial starting conditions used to generate the sequence. These random sequences are then used to generate random values that have a desired distribution, such as Gaussian (bell-curve distribution) or Poisson (random-point sampling). These "random" numbers are then used as input to create spectacular, realistic shapes and textures in both two- and three-dimensional images.

Fractal Curves

Now that you have all the software tools needed, you can begin creating fractal images. Chapter 5 starts with the simplest case: one-dimensional, or more accurately, single parameter fractals. The basic fractal concept of self-similarity, which is that a curve looks the "same" at different scales, is introduced and incorporated into various methods for generating fractal curves. The original definition of a fractal is presented with the *initiator* (starting shape) and the *generator* (rule for transforming the original shape). Building upon the basic definitions, you will see how the more general procedural models are defined, which lets you apply multiple rules and create complex shapes that are not strictly fractal, but are equally complex and intricate. You will also learn how to introduce randomness into the curves to create more natural looking shapes.

Affine transformations are used extensively to show how the combination of simple operations can produce images of great complexity and depth. In fact, many of the generator rules for creating the basic fractal curves can be viewed as the application of multiple affine transformations. You will also see how the generators can be extended to the non-affine cases to create even more complex and intricate curves. Finally, Chapter 5 concludes with a demonstration program that lets you interactively create your own fractal shapes on your display.

Solid Fractals

The basic initiator and generator method of creating fractals presented in Chapter 5 is expanded in Chapter 6 to let you to model fractal shapes composed of multidimensional solid objects such as the Sierpinski Gasket. While the focus of most fractal texts is on drawing fractal shapes, you'll also want to use fractal objects in other ways, such as modeling a process like diffusion. Chapter 6 introduces a C++ object class that lets you use fractal objects in a very general way in which drawing is just one of the ways you might use a fractal object. Furthermore, you'll see how deriving the fractal-object class from the graphics-object base class lets you combine fractal objects in ways that would be very difficult without the object-oriented benefits of C++. Chapter 6 concludes with a demonstration of the flexibility of the fractal-object classes by letting you interactively combine objects to create an endless variety of new shapes in different colors.

Modeling Nature

One of the main motivations for using fractal modeling is to simulate patterns and features found in naturally occurring objects. A classic example of such patterns is found in many types of plants. Each branch of a tree, for instance, often closely resembles its parent branch. This inherent self-similarity lends itself to using self-similar fractals to model plant growth from a single seed and plant evolution to create new types of plants. Chapter 7 looks at the research directed at creating accurate models of plant growth and plant evolution. By using a procedural modeling approach, you can—to a reasonable approximation—mimic many of the processes involved in growing plants, even in modeling how one seed can eventually cover an entire field with its progeny.

Plant structure, however, is only one small example of using fractals to model nature. In Chapter 7, you'll see other examples of two-dimensional fractals, such as distributing stars in a galaxy. As you'll see, there is a great diversity of images that can be created by fractal-modeling techniques. Furthermore, even within the same basic methods, the appearance can be substantially varied by adding random variations to the small set of controlling parameters in a model. The ability to produce so many types of images by specifying just a few parameters is one of the great appealing factors in using fractals. Chapter 7 ends with a demonstration program that lets you create a fractal forest silhouetted against a sky filled with fractal stars.

Complex Displays

The procedural models of the previous chapters provide one means of creating fractal curves. These are by no means the only method. In Chapter 8, your display screen is transformed into a map of the complex plane. Each pixel of the screen represents an initial complex number, z. Each value is then plugged into a simple equation to produce a new value, and the process is repeated. The equation-iteration process continues until a termination condition is reached. The number of iterations to reach this condition determines the color displayed on the screen at each pixel. By studying the behavior of the iterated sequences, you can learn about the overall features and stability of the system of equations being used.

Chapter 8 begins by presenting methods for displaying the Mandelbrot and complementary Julia sets. From there, you'll explore what happens as the iteration equations are altered, the termination conditions are varied, and the method for determining the displayed pixel color are changed. The effects of changing the iteration rules, even slightly, can have quite an astonishing impact on the displayed patterns. However, rather than simply creating esoteric patterns, you will see how the techniques used in generating these images lend themselves to modeling many types of real-world images. Chapter 8 ends with a demonstration program that lets you interactively view some interesting functions of the complex plane, including the Mandelbrot set and its complementary Julia sets.

Discrete Fractals

There are many ways to use recursive procedural models that, in all strictness, are not fractals. Still, such models can produce equally interesting and useful images and can be applied in situations in which a "pure" fractal might not be suitable. Chapter 9 looks at various methods for generalizing the fractal-drawing procedures to include more elaborate structures and recursive rules.

Most of the fractal models examined up until this point represent continuous patterns. In Chapter 9, you'll see some methods for dealing with quantized fractals in which only discrete values are generated. You'll see in Chapter 10 an example where discrete fractals (fractal curves that can take on only a small number of values at any point of the curve and are not necessarily continuous) provide a solution to a rather complex mapping problem.

Chapter 9 also introduces the problem of using fractals in curve matching. The classic curve-matching problem is to find the "best fit" of a curve that goes through, or at least near, a set of known points. In modeling random processes, you often want to create a curve that matches the fixed points, usually acquired by some external measurement. The curve itself represents some measured signal. The modeled curve must still have the random or fractal characteristics of the process creating the signal being measured. Chapter 9 shows several methods for creating such a curve in one dimension for both the continuous and discrete cases.

The Third Dimension

One key application of fractal modeling is creating the texture and appearance of three-dimensional objects. Two typical applications of three-dimensional fractal modeling are presented in Chapter 10. The first explores creating realistic models of terrain used for simulation, land management, and other geographic applications. The terrain model is then extended using the techniques presented in Chapter 9 to incorporate measurements of real terrain at low resolution with the higher resolution fractal terrain. This provides a very powerful technique for creating realistic models of actual places. Chapter 11 shows you how to use the three-dimensional rendering package provided with this book to create views of our newly created terrain.

Terrain modeling is essentially a two-dimensional fractal process. There are, of course, many three-dimensional objects that the terrain-modeling techniques do not address. For instance, the plant modeling presented in Chapter 7 can be easily extended to three dimensions to create very realistic models of trees. In Chapter 10, you will learn a method for modeling another phenomenon with which you are quite familiar, clouds. Instead of the more traditional polygonal modeling approach, clouds are modeled as three-dimensional collections of scaled spheres. This type of modeling is much more suitable for amorphous clouds than any type of polygonal model. Chapter 10 concludes with some examples of generating clouds.

Fractal Applications

Although these fractal models are useful constructs, you still have not seen any real applications of them. In this section of the book, you will discover ways in which fractal and procedural models are used to solve some vexing problems.

Life-saving fractals

As shown in Chapters 7 and 10, you often use fractal models to copy, or "create" natural phenomena. In Chapter 11, you will see how the fractal-drawing techniques are used in flight-simulation applications. The goal in a flight simulator is to recreate the environment that a pilot would experience in a real aircraft. The flight-simulator visual system attempts to produce as realistic a view as possible of the outside world to the pilot. Also, through such a visual system, pilots gain training about the specific airports that they will be using in the real world. So, the visual system needs to recreate the view that the pilot would see at the many airports around the world. Chapter 11 presents various rendering techniques in which fractal models are used to create simulated views of an airfield that are both realistic and consistent, whether the pilot is 20 miles away from the airfield or sitting on the Tarmac.

The techniques presented in Chapter 9 for discrete-valued fractals (fractal algorithms that choose from a small set of discrete values) are extended to two dimensions in order to generate a fractal map of an area. The technique of combining actual digitized data from a map with fractal-generated features provides a very compact means of representing a complex scene at all resolutions and scales.

In most applications, fractal modeling is used to either simulate the roughness of a surface by varying the height of the surface, as shown in Chapter 10, or by varying the texture of the surface by modulating the color. Chapter 11 shows you how to extend the modeling techniques to vary other attributes, such as transparency, luminance, and reflectivity, to create more realistic effects, such as painted stripes on runways or simulated skid marks. The fractal methods are then compared with alternative techniques such as photo texturing to show how the use of fractals can greatly reduce the amount of data that must be processed to generate such a scene.

Small is better

One of the more interesting applications of fractal modeling is its application in reducing the storage requirements for an image or, more succinctly, for image compression. Through the pioneering work of Dr. Michael Barnsley and Dr. Alan Sloan, fractal researchers recognized that images of self-similar structures, such as leaves and plants, could be created by repeatedly mapping a small set of points through affine transformations. This provides tremendous potential for reducing the storage requirements of such an image. Instead of storing an array of pixels, you only need to store a few starting points and the transformations to apply to those points. In Chapter 12, you will learn about the basic techniques for compressing and decompressing both one-dimensional signals and two-dimensional images.

Chaos

Over the last five years, the study of chaotic and nonlinear systems has greatly increased, primarily because of the availability of computer systems capable of processing the tremendous amount of data required to analyze such systems. In general, a *chaotic* system is one in which the output of the system is extremely sensitive to its input. For example, consider a marble balanced at the top of a hill. If the marble is moved in the slightest, it will quickly roll off the hill top. Which direction it rolls is subject to innumerable small events that are difficult, if not impossible, to predict.

Chapter 13 provides several examples of common chaotic systems and some of the techniques used to analyze them. Nonlinear and chaotic systems occur frequently in many applications, ranging from physics to medicine. Many of the more traditional analytic techniques, such as Fourier analysis, do not provide any real insight into the processes that generate the signal being studied. As you will see in Chapter 13, the study of chaos provides another approach to analyzing complex systems and explaining their behavior in, one hopes, more intuitive ways.

Future Applications

Chapter 14 looks at how the various fractal- and procedural-modeling techniques shown throughout the book might be adapted to other applications. You will also see how the methods are being adapted to other disciplines and how the analytic techniques are being improved.

Until recently, most of the development and advancement of fractal-modeling methods have been for improving the realism of computer-generated imagery. However, a new outlook is evolving in which previously intractable problems can be looked at from a different angle. The apparent complexity of a signal or an image can be the result of complex interactions, or repeated combinations of simple components. This is analogous to the observation that (almost) all the matter in the universe is ultimately composed of protons, electrons, and neutrons. The applications of fractals, procedural models, and chaos are searches for the component rules that govern complex systems. Fractals provide a promising approach to studying these problems created by the rich diversity of images and signals they are capable of generating, which often appear to conform to what you see in the real world.

The tools and demonstration programs provided in this book give you many different ways of exploring fractal processes for yourself. With the two- and three-dimensional graphics routines, you can create images of great complexity and beauty. The object-oriented approach in the design of the procedural-modeling routines let you adapt the software to many different applications. Our goal is to show you that fractals aren't just for making pretty pictures any more; they can be applied to many sorts of problems. The whole field is still in its infancy, and there are still many discoveries and advancements to be made. Above all, as the wealth of literature on the topic indicates, fractals can be both fun and practical. So have fun with the software and keep generating all those pictures for books and calendars, but remember that those so-called pretty pictures are gaining more and more real applications every day.

Fractal History

Benoit Mandelbrot first popularized fractals in 1975 in his book *Les Objets Fractals: Forme, Hasard et Dimension* (translated into English in 1977 as *Fractals: Form, Chance, and Dimension*). In his book, Mandelbrot coined the term *fractal* to describe a class of recursively defined curves that produce images of both the real and surreal. Since the publication of this work, the study and use of fractals in computer graphics has exploded to the point that even the casual computer user has undoubtedly encountered fractal imagery in the form of logos, magazine covers, or computer art.

The great complexity and intricate structure of fractals makes them artistically appealing. However, there are many other uses for fractals that go beyond simply making pretty pictures. With fractal algorithms, you can create accurate models of plants, coastlines, mountains, and other natural objects that would be difficult, if not impossible, to model by other means. Fractals provide a way of storing the detailed structure of complex objects in a compact and efficient manner. The ability to store a detailed description of an object with a small amount of data makes fractals ideal candidates for storage-compression algorithms, such as the fractal-image compression techniques shown in Chapter 12. Investigations into fractals have led researchers to study related areas such as *chaos*, the seemingly random behavior of complex equations, and *complexity*, the study of how to characterize how complicated a system really is. This book shows you many of the uses for fractals and, more importantly, provides you with the programming tools to apply fractals to your applications. Before diving into the actual programming of fractals, it is useful to examine the history of fractals to learn how we arrived at where we are, and where to go from here.

In the Beginning

Like all good ideas, fractals did not just magically appear. Fractals are based on the works of many mathematicians and other scientists. Mandelbrot put the historical pieces together to discover some truly insightful mathematics, but there was much prior work that formed a solid basis for his own research. More than one hundred years prior to Mandelbrot's discoveries regarding fractals, several mathematicians studied curves and geometric sets that, at the time, were considered pathological exceptions to the notions of continuity and differentiability. Georg Cantor, who lived from 1845 to1918, was one such mathematician whose work on pathological sets paved the way for much of today's mathematics, including the development of modern set theory. Cantor pursued the study of set theory to gain a deeper and more rigorous understanding of properties such as continuity, closure, and compactness. He was motivated to examine these unusual sets in order to test the validity of these theories.

The classical view of a curve in the plane is to think of the points (x, y) on a curve as functionally related. The simplest type of curve is defined by plotting $y = f(x)$. More general types of one-dimensional curves may be created by introducing a parameter t, and writing x and y as functions of this single parameter. The functions $x(t)$ and $y(t)$ are either specified explicitly or as solutions to some set of differential equations. The prevailing opinion of nineteenth-century mathematicians and physicists was that any phenomenon could be described as the solution of a set of differential equations, however complex those equations might be. The scientist's task was to find the equations describing the particular system under study. The problem with this approach is that it can quickly lead to having to solve extremely difficult sets of equations, which is especially difficult without supercomputers to at least find approximate numerical solutions.

The efforts of Cantor and others were directed at showing that you can construct a myriad of other types of curves that cannot be described by a finite set of continuous differential equations. All these curves share one common feature: Their construction is defined by a recursive procedure. You start with an initial curve, such as a simple line segment, called the *initiator*. You then apply a rule or set of rules to generate the next stage of the curve. Each rule is called a *generator*. The generator rules are then applied to each copy of the initiator in the new curve. The process is carried on ad infinitum.

In effect, the construction of these curves is very similar to what you learned in high school geometry for constructing classical geometric objects such as equilateral triangles. In classical geometry, you follow a prescribed procedure using a straightedge and a compass to generate new shapes from a starting shape. For instance, you can construct an equilateral triangle from a single line segment. Cantor studied what happened if you performed the construction repeatedly with the restriction that each construction step generated new pieces smaller than the original. Every time you generate a new set of pieces, you apply the same construction rule to the new pieces and continue. Cantor was interested in the properties of the *limiting* figure; that is, the figure that results from carrying out this construction operation infinitely. As he and many others have found over the last hundred years, these limiting curves possess some very interesting properties, such as having a dimensionality greater than the pieces of which they are made and the ability to model complex processes like diffusion.

A few words about intervals

In the following discussions on the Cantor Set, you will see some special mathematical notation used to specify intervals on the line. An *open* interval is a set that contains all the points between two endpoints but does not include the endpoints themselves. An open interval is denoted by a definition like (a, b). For instance, $(0, 1)$ means the interval from 0 to 1 and does not include either 0 or 1. A *closed* interval contains its endpoints and is denoted by $[a, b]$. For instance, $[0, 1]$ contains all the points between 0 and 1, including both 0 and 1. You may also specify that only a single endpoint is included by using the notation $[a, b)$ (a is included; b is not) or $(a, b]$ (b is included; a is not). The distinction is necessary when defining complex sets like the Cantor Set to ensure that every point is properly accounted for; that is, a point is not included in two separate intervals.

The Cantor Set

One of Cantor's results was the definition of a set on the interval $[0, 1]$ that has uncountably many points but is not dense; this set is known as, naturally enough, the *Cantor Set*. A set is *dense* about a point, *x,* if any open interval about x contains points in the set (of course, x must not be in the set). For instance, any finite set of points from an interval is not dense within that interval because you can always find an interval that is smaller than the smallest distance between two of the points. An *uncountable* set is one for which there is no one to one correspondence between the members of the set and the positive integers, meaning there is no way to enumerate the members of the set. There are uncountably many points in any interval of the real line, for instance. Finding a countably infinite subset for an interval is not difficult. The sequence *1/n* for all integer values of *n* greater than 0 is a countably infinite subset of the interval $[0, 1]$ that is not dense, except around point 0. But defining an uncountably infinite subset is more difficult. The Cantor Set is defined by a simple recursive procedure:

1. Take the interval $[0,1]$ and remove the middle-third interval of $(1/3, 2/3)$. This leaves the two intervals $[0, 1/3]$ and $[2/3, 1]$.

2. Repeat the process again on the remaining two intervals. The Cantor Set is the set of points that are never removed.

Figure 1–1 shows an example of the successive points remaining after several iterations of the process. A horizontal line is used to highlight the sets of points belonging to the set at each stage. Note that the set becomes more disconnected at each stage. While it is certainly not obvious at first glance, you can see that the Cantor Set contains uncountably many points, meaning that a one-to-one relationship between the interval [0,1] and the points in the Cantor Set exists. With a little more effort, you can also construct some interesting functions with the Cantor Set, such as the Devil's Staircase shown in Figure 1–2.

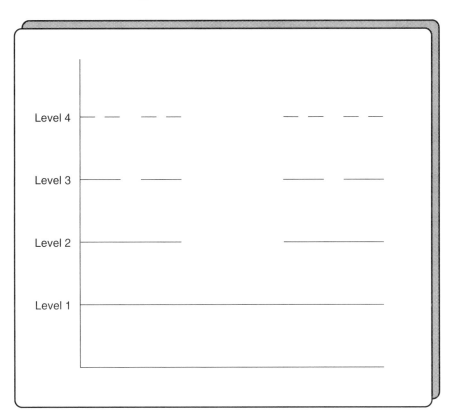

Figure 1–1. The Cantor Set created by removing the middle third of each interval.

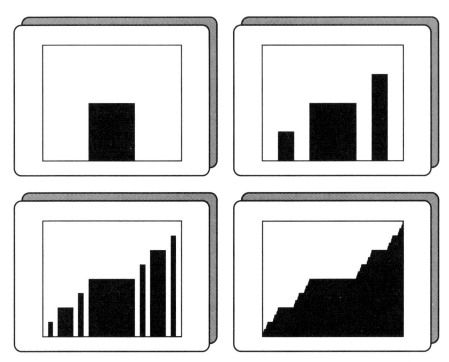

Figure 1–2. Devil's Staircase constructed by assigning appropriate heights to the horizontal lines from Figure 1–1.

The Devil's Staircase is recursively constructed using the same procedure as for the Cantor Set. Each time an interval is removed, you draw a horizontal line between the two endpoints of the interval. The height of the line is determined as follows: If you are at recursion level k, and you are removing interval l, then the height of the horizontal line is $(2*l – 1) / 2^k$. At the first level, for instance, the interval from 1/3 to 2/3 is removed, and is drawn at height 1/2. At the second level, the interval [1/9, 2/9] is removed and drawn with height 1/4 and the interval [7/9, 8/9] is removed and drawn with height 3/4. This process is continued indefinitely. The resulting curve is a fractal curve that is continuous, but is "flat" at most places because it was constructed entirely out of horizontal line segments. If you perform the construction process for any finite number of recursion levels, you are left with a set of disconnected horizontal segments. It is only in the infinite limit that you actually end up with a continuous curve that rises smoothly from 0 to 1, but has no non-horizontal pieces.

The geometric properties of the Devil's Staircase and other similarly constructed curves are often much more complex than the curves you are probably most familiar with from algebra and calculus. The Devil's Staircase is a complex structure, but you will see in Chapter 8 that it is easy to generate a program to draw this and many other recursively defined curves on your display.

While there are many interesting properties and variations of the Cantor Set, our primary interest in this type of function is in its unique properties it possesses:

1. While these curves have quite complex structures, they can be represented in a very compact way, simply by storing the initiator (usually a simple geometric shape like a line segment) and the generator rule for constructing the curve.

2. These curves more accurately represent the detailed and intricate shapes and surfaces found in natural objects than the collections of the relatively smooth curves found in classical geometry.

3. The curves are recursively defined and generally have no simple, closed-form representation (that is, representable in the form $y = f(x)$) and therefore cannot be drawn using traditional plotting methods.

By their very definition, these curves are difficult to draw, much less to analyze because of their recursive definition. In Cantor's time, recursive curves were generally considered anomalous mathematical oddities that had no physical counterpart and, thus, did not merit further study. This is an understandable attitude considering that at the time, there was really no good way to draw these curves, let alone use them in an analysis of some problem. In a real sense, the advent of computer graphics was an essential development before these types of curves could be effectively studied.

Other Examples

Some notable examples of other types of recursively defined shapes are the Koch Curve (also known as the snowflake curve), named after Helge von Koch, and the Sierpinski Gasket, named after Waclaw Sierpinski. You have undoubtedly seen many examples of each of these in one form or another in books, magazines, and calendars of fractal images. They both follow the same basic rules; for instance, they both start with an initial shape and then apply a transformation rule to generate the next stage.

To create the Koch Curve, you start with a line segment and apply the generator shown in Figure 1–3. The curve is generated by starting with a hexagon and applying the generator to each side of the hexagon. The Sierpinski Gasket starts with a triangle, as shown in Figure 1–4, and uses a procedure very similar to that for the Cantor Set, namely, dropping out the central triangle. In both cases, the process is carried on ad infinitum to reach the final figure.

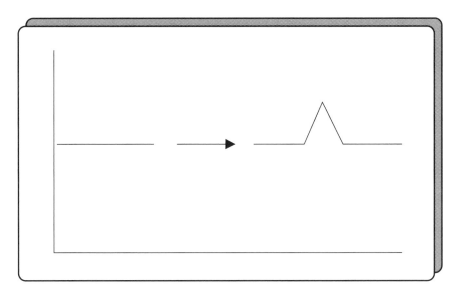

Figure 1–3. Generating the Koch Curve, also known as the snowflake curve.

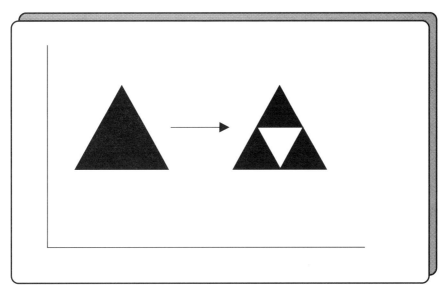

Figure 1–4. Generating the Sierpinski Gasket.

Note the difference between the two objects in that the Koch Curve is generated by replacing a one-dimensional shape with another one-dimensional shape. As you can see in Figure 1–3, the generator is always scaled so that it can exactly replace each line segment. Note that the generator is 4/3 longer than the original line segment. You will see in Chapter 5 that the ratio between the size of the generator and initiator is intimately related to the dimensionality of the resulting curve. Unlike the Koch Curve, the Sierpinski Gasket uses two-dimensional areas for its definition. The Sierpinski Gasket is essentially a two-dimensional version of the Cantor Set.

It is easy to see how many variations of these objects can be created by using different initiators and generators. However, the Koch Curve, Sierpinski Gasket, and their endless variations, all have at least one thing in common, a property known as self-similarity. With *self-similarity,* if you take a portion of the curve and magnify it by an appropriate amount, you get an identical copy of the curve. For the Koch Curve, you can take any segment and magnify it by three to get a copy of the curve. The Sierpinski Gasket uses a magnification factor of two, because each stage divides a triangle in half both vertically and horizontally. Self-similarity is an intrinsic property of recursively generated objects, such as those in this book, because of the way the object is constructed.

In order to perform a useful recursion step, the generator must transform the object into smaller copies of itself. The operation is then repeated for each copy. Furthermore, the generator must perform the replacement at the same location and orientation as the piece it is replacing. In the snowflake curve, for instance, each side of the polygon is replaced by the generator oriented at the same angle as the polygon side. Similarly, the Sierpinski Gasket may be viewed as taking a triangle and making three copies of it that are positioned within the original triangle. The same operation is then applied to each of the newly created triangles. Each step of this process is an *affine transformation* (a transformation consisting of a combination of rotation, scaling, translation, or reflection) of the initiator. This observation leads to an elegant way of specifying a generator, namely, as a series of affine transformations that are applied to the object. The later chapters of this book explain how affine transformations provide a very powerful means for generating fractals in many applications.

Making Space

Recursively defined curves such as the Koch Curve challenged many tenets of nineteenth-century mathematics. One of the most revolutionary concepts introduced by these curves was to change the intuitive notion of what constitutes a dimension. Most people tend to think of a one-dimensional curve simply as a graph in a plane. Such a curve has no "thickness," so it seems natural that such a curve could never "fill" an area of the plane. A curve is said to "fill," or cover, an area if you can prove that the curve passes through every point (x, y) within the square. Unfortunately, the simple notions of dimension vanish when dealing with curves of infinite length. In 1890, the Italian mathematician Giuseppe Peano presented a paper containing the definition of a continuous curve that fills a unit square in the plane. The method of constructing this curve is shown in Figure 1–5.

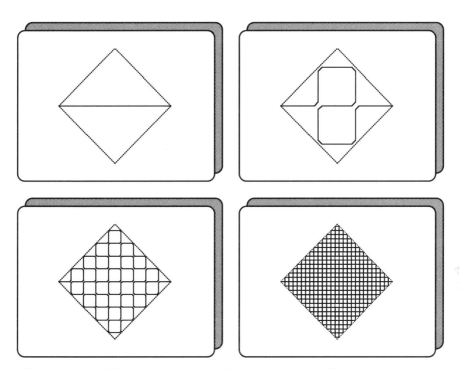

Figure 1–5. Initiator, generator, and several iterations for generating the plane-filling Peano Curve.

There are many possible variations on this basic method of construction. This original plane-filling curve is called the Peano Curve. The basic curve-construction method can easily be extended to any number of finite dimensions. So, the Peano Curve can fill a cube in three dimensions as well as the square in two dimensions. You normally think of a one-dimensional curve as being unable to fill multiple dimensions. The Peano Curve and its many variations demonstrate that this intuitive notion is untrue for many of the fractal and recursively defined curves. Furthermore, just as Cantor showed that there are many ways to define sets, Peano showed that there are many types of related curves that are easily constructable for defining sets, even if difficult to draw because they may have unusual properties, such as being continuous without being differentiable as well as being able to fill a multidimensional space. These properties are very different from those of the curves and shapes normally encountered in your high school calculus class.

The notion of mathematical dimension has been completely altered by the efforts of mathematicians such as Peano, Cantor, and Sierpinski. The result today is that there are now several definitions of what a dimension is, and the one to use depends on the particular problem of interest to you. Our primary interest is in what Mandelbrot termed the fractal dimension. Chapter 5 examines this concept in more detail, but for now, simply note that *fractal dimension* is a measure of the inherent complexity of a curve. For example, the fractal dimension of the Peano Curve is two, which indicates its plane-filling properties. By themselves, however, the results of these researchers still seem quite esoteric and not very applicable to solving real-world problems.

Nature Takes Its Course

Mandelbrot's primary contribution to the field of mathematics was his recognition that these recursively defined shapes actually occur quite frequently in nature. In his book *The Fractal Geometry of Nature*, he points out many examples of naturally occurring fractals. From modeling galactic clusters to studying the leaves and branches of a tree, many natural objects appear to be composed of collections of smaller objects that, to some degree, are similar to the larger object. In many species of trees, for instance, the structure of a branch looks very similar to the structure of the whole tree. If you look around, you'll see many other examples in all sorts of different objects.

A fractal is a geometric entity that exhibits self-similarity at all scales. For instance, you can continuously magnify the Sierpinski Gasket by two and always end up with the same figure. Similarly, you can magnify the Koch Curve by three to get a new copy of the curve. All fractal objects possess a discrete self-similarity scale factor. Nonfractal objects do not possess such a scale factor. If you zoom in on a portion of a smooth nonfractal curve, such as a circle, parabola, or line, for instance, the portion you zoom in on will appear smoother and straighter. If you zoom in enough, the magnified portion will appear as a straight line. A nonfractal object always has a magnification limit beyond which there is no further structure in the curve to see, as shown in Figure 1–6. Fractal objects have no such magnification limit; no matter how much you zoom in, you will always see more structure and detail in the curve.

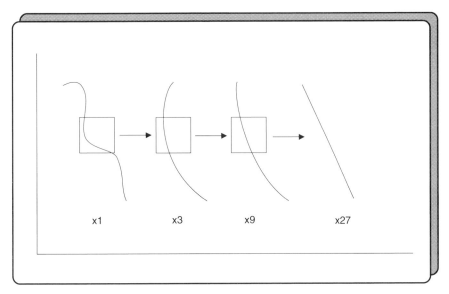

x1   x3   x9   x27

Figure 1–6. Zooming in on a smooth nonfractal curve eventually produces lines with no detail or structure.

Fractals in nature generally will not satisfy the criteria that they are self-similar at all scales. If you zoom in enough on a plant, you will eventually reach the level of the molecules composing the plant, which certainly will not possess the same spatial structure as the plant. However, many objects do exhibit self-similarity over several orders of magnitude in scale. This large range of scales makes such objects quite suitable for modeling with fractals.

Unlike the rigid geometric fractals of the Koch Curve, natural objects are not strictly self-similar; that is, the object is not composed of smaller objects that are exact copies of itself. Mandelbrot introduced the idea of statistical self-similarity as a more general and realistic model of objects in nature. In a *statistically self-similar* object, the pieces that make up the object have the same general structure as the overall object, but vary randomly from an exact scaled-down copy. From a modeling standpoint, this means that the generator of the fractal is randomly altered at each level of recursion. The variations must be small enough to still keep the generator looking roughly the same. For instance, you can create an interesting variant of the Koch Curve by randomly changing the height of the generator. The overall curve still generally looks like the Koch Curve, but it now possesses a more random appearance characteristic of natural objects. An example of a statistically self-similar Koch Curve is shown in Figure 1–7.

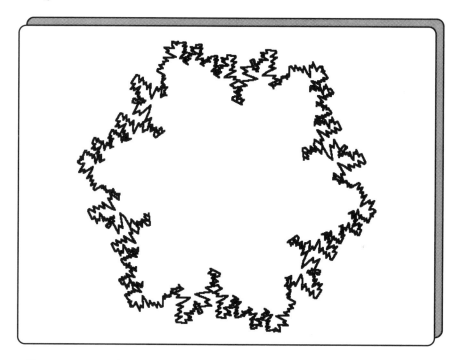

Figure 1–7. Koch Curve, or snowflake curve, with random variations in the height of the generator.

You will see many examples throughout this book of statistical self-similarity. The beauty of this approach to modeling complex objects is that it breaks (the term *fractal* is derived from Latin verb *frangere* meaning to break) a complex object into more manageable pieces. For instance, if you were given a drawing of the Sierpinski Gasket without any other information and told to write a program to draw it on the screen, you might find it difficult to do so. The fractal-modeling approach provides a means of examining and manipulating otherwise intractable types of objects.

On a more fundamental level, the fractal structure found in living organisms corresponds well with the genetic coding rules of growth and evolution. Dr. Alvy Ray Smith, former president of Pixar, Inc., an offshoot of Lucas Film Productions, explored this idea extensively by modeling the growth and evolution of plants. An organism starts from a beginning cell (the initiator), such as the seedling of a tree. The genetic code within the seed provides the instructions (the generator) for replicating cells and growing the organism. By simply repeating the genetic instructions for each cell, the organism grows in a naturally fractal, or at least recursive, manner.

Storing an initiator and a set of generator rules is a more compact way to store a complex structure than trying to encode a complete description of what the end result should be. This approach also lets the individual cells adapt to their environment as they grow. Clearly, the fractal model described so far is still a simplistic one, but through the discussion on modeling plants in Chapter 7, you'll see how very complicated structures become when you simply add more rules (more genetic codes) and trigger different rules at different stages of development.

Fractals and Computer Graphics

As we've already pointed out, it is difficult to draw recursive curves by hand. In the precomputer era, the works of M.C. Escher represent some of the most interesting explorations of recursively defined shapes. Many of his drawings demonstrate the endless possibilities for creating images with limitless detail. However, Escher's abilities to see these types of images and to transfer them to paper or wood were quite unique. Without an easier method for drawing such shapes, it is quite difficult for the average mathematician, artist, or scientist to visualize and explore the possibilities presented by fractal objects.

The popularity of fractal modeling today is entirely due to the availability of fast computers and computer graphics. A computer is the only practical means of drawing fractal models in a realistic amount of time. As you will see in the later chapters, the computer is ideally suited to drawing these shapes by using recursively defined procedures. More important, the computer lets you easily explore variations by allowing relatively interactive control of the parameters governing a fractal.

One of the main reasons for the success of Mandelbrot's work were the efforts of his co-worker Dr. Richard Voss, whose images of clouds, terrain, and other shapes provided some of the first examples of how fractal- and procedural-modeling techniques could be used to create very realistic models of natural shapes. As with so many other developments in the sciences, once people saw the results, interest in the techniques used to create the pictures grew rapidly.

It is not surprising that fractal modeling is used so extensively in computer graphics today. One of the overriding goals in computer-generated imaging is to create as realistic an image as possible. Prior to the introduction of fractal-drawing techniques, most computer-generated images looked very artificial. Object surfaces tended to appear unnaturally smooth and shiny or to look very polygonal. Various texturing techniques, such as adding random noise, were used to help alleviate this problem; however, these methods, although an improvement, still did not accurately reproduce natural-looking textures.

Levels of Detail

To see why many computer-graphics applications need fractal and procedural models, consider the problem of producing a perspective view of a grassy field. Most three-dimensional rendering programs require a list of polygons to draw. To draw the grassy field, you would have to define polygons for all the grass in the field, or define a grass texture. Typically, the position of every blade of grass is unimportant; you simply want the overall appearance of grass. Furthermore, you do not want to model, and subsequently draw, every blade of grass if you are one mile away. But you might like to draw individual blades of grass if the camera is sitting on the grass. You are stuck between modeling every blade for the close-up picture, or having far too many polygons for the far away picture.

What you're lacking is a method for generating just the right number of grass blades, depending on your distance from the field. Fractals solve this problem by providing a model that can be evaluated at any desired level of detail, without requiring huge amounts of storage for unused polygons. For any given view, you evaluate the fractal model recursively until a level is reached in which adjacent grass blades cannot be resolved by the display device. If the view is far away, you don't need to recursively evaluate the fractal very far. But if the view is close up, then you evaluate the model to the point at which individual grass blades are generated. By using various statistical techniques, you may add random offsets to the fractal model in order to mimic natural variations. Assuming the random offsets are small compared to the size of the fractal generators, the overall structure that makes the image look like grass remains with suitable randomness to make it appear more realistic.

Fractal Compression

As you'll see in later chapters, fractal and procedural models provide a very compact way of defining a complex structure. A model of the Sierpinski Gasket, for instance, can be stored as a series of three affine transformations (matrices) and a starting triangle (three vertices). By adding appropriate controls to include random variations, you can create a huge variety of textures and shapes from a very small set of defining parameters. This observation led Dr. Barnsley and Dr. Sloan to develop the concepts of and various methods for fractal compression. The idea is straightforward. If you can find the initiators and generators to define a particular object, you only need to store these few pieces of information rather than the entire model of the object. Chapter 12 provides a more complete description of fractal-compression techniques and the significant benefits they produce.

Chaos

One problem caused by the widespread use of computers is the implicit assumption that the answers that the computer produces are correct.

Whenever you perform a floating-point calculation, the computer is only using an approximation to the actual numbers. There is always some loss of precision and accuracy, no matter how many bits are used to store the number. In most calculations, this is often insignificant. However, these precision errors can cause great problems in highly complex calculations, or more commonly, in iterated calculations. An iterated calculation is one in which the output of a calculation is used again as the input to the same calculation. The iteration proceeds for a certain number of cycles or until some desired convergence is reached. A simple example is the following computation of x^{10}. One way to compute x^{10} is as follows:

```
float x, y;

y = 1.0;
x = 10.0;
// Compute x^10
for(i=0; i<10; i++)
  y *= x;
```

The output of the multiply operation, y, is used as the input for each pass of the *for* loop. The problem with this method is that errors accumulate each pass. The more passes, the more errors in the final result; until finally, the result becomes essentially meaningless. The problem of losing precision in calculations has tended to be overlooked until recently, as computers have become powerful enough to run complex systems of equations through millions of iterations.

Given that the problem of using finite precision arithmetic is not going to disappear, the next best thing is to characterize how sensitive a system is to its input. To do this, you must ask, How much does the output change as a function of deviations in the input? And the answer to that is it can change by quite a lot. Furthermore, for even relatively simple systems, the output can vary wildly for very small variations in the input and in ways that seem totally random and unpredictable. The study of chaotic systems, or *chaos*, is an attempt to characterize this type of behavior and to see if in fact there are predictable patterns in a chaotic system. The hope is that chaotic systems will possess some overall structure that can be used to predict their behavior, in much the same way that a fractal object has an overall structure in the midst of great complexity.

Fractal Programs

Fractals are an important tool not only for making pretty pictures, but for creating realistic and useful models of the world around us. The discovery of some esoteric "exceptions" to the standard notions of dimension have changed our way of looking at the world. These mathematical oddities provide a rich class of mathematical objects with unusual and useful properties for modeling the complex world around us. Most things in nature are built from smaller building blocks that tend to look just like the larger object, just as a child looks like his or her parent or a sapling looks like the mighty oak (as long as it's an oak sapling, of course). It is therefore natural to describe such objects by a recursive-procedural model that exploits the commonality between the complex object and its component pieces. All fractal programs have some recursively defined procedure that provides a prescription for making a scaled-down copy of the original object. You will see many examples of recursive procedures throughout the programs in this, and almost any other, fractal book.

Fractals are appealing from a programming standpoint because the computations involved with rendering fractals can be made very efficient. As we mentioned earlier, the computer is ideally suited for computing recursive algorithms. Many of the algorithms can be coded using affine transformations, requiring a minimum number of computations to generate these complex surfaces. Fractal algorithms can be incorporated in on-the-fly calculations of the shape and texture of an object because of this innate efficiency. The rendering software can easily take advantage of this to only render as much as it needs to any desired level of detail. This provides a powerful modeling capability that is repeatedly exploited in the algorithms presented in this book.

Programming fractal models is an interesting exercise because it is both fun and produces some amazing results from what appear to be very simple tools. The next three chapters provide the background methods and programming tools you will need to use in the rest of the programs found throughout this book. Chapter 3 will be especially useful for familiarizing yourself with affine transformations. You will use affine transformations throughout your programs, both for drawing objects on your display and for implementing the fractal algorithms. In the next chapter, you will learn about the object-oriented methods used in the software for this book and some general C++ programming guidelines that you should find helpful. As you'll see, C++ makes programming fractals (and many other things) easier and the code much more understandable. With the C++ tools in place, you can quickly move on to exploring the many worlds of fractals and to creating fractal programs of your own.

C++ Programming Techniques

Cand C++ are the programming languages of choice for almost all graphics-related programming. This is primarily because of the abundance of software already available and, more importantly, already debugged for almost all computer platforms and display devices. Until the last five years, C was the principal program-development language for graphics. However, object-oriented programming is now recognized as the preferred method for casting an algorithm into a program.

In this book, we assume that you are already familiar with C programming and that you have at least been exposed to C++. Even with a common programming language, everyone develops his or her own style of coding and developing algorithms. In this chapter, you will see the programming guidelines and practical considerations used in developing the software for this book. The methods presented here are not intended as absolute rules that should always be followed. Anyone who has been programming for any length of time learns that there are always exceptions to any programming rule. Instead, this chapter will aid you in understanding why the code in this book looks and functions the way it does, as well as offer some guidelines on how to create your own C++ programs.

Object-Oriented Programming

The C++ programming language is an object-oriented extension to C. The term *object-oriented* refers to the notion that a program is made up of *objects* that possess two major attributes: the data that defines what they hold and the functions associated with the object to manipulate that data or interact with other objects. C has always possessed the first attribute with C structures. A structure lets you refer to a group of related data as a single entity. A C program is defined as a series of functions that take passed arguments and return a computed value. A function may access the data within a structure by accessing the individual member elements. However, the data in a structure is really only half of what you need to use the structure. The other half consists of the functions that take the structure and perform some action based on the data, or change the data of the structure based on other arguments.

Typically, many of the problems in a C program come about when functions manipulate the data elements of a structure directly. For instance, you may have a structure that is stored as part of a linked list. If another function corrupts the pointers defining the linked list, then the list is destroyed. In effect, every function that uses this structure must be coded with the method for processing the linked list. If you then decide to change the structure from using a linked list to using an array or a more complicated list structure, then you must change every function that accesses the structure to know about the change. Changing all the functions is not only a lot of trouble, it will very likely introduce programming errors.

The object-oriented approach to programming takes a different view of functions. The primary entity in an object-oriented program is, not surprisingly, an object. The object not only has the data stored in it, like the C structure, but it also has functions defined as part of the object. The functions associated with the object are often referred to as *methods*. The methods for an object should define all the interactions of any other objects or functions with the object. In C++, the methods for an object are called *member functions*, and are declared in the definition of each object class. In general, your program will not directly access the data elements of the object, but will manipulate them using the appropriate object methods. By explicitly controlling the methods through which your program can access the object data, you greatly reduce the chance that your program can corrupt the object structure.

Furthermore, an object-oriented approach makes programs considerably more modular in nature. Think of an object as a black box. The object's methods define the input and output to the black box. The data elements of the object define how it works internally, and should generally be of no interest to anything but those internal functions. By accessing the object only through its methods, you can change the internal structure of the object without having to change any other programs. As long as the methods appear the same—even if their implementation has changed completely—any outside programs using this object do not have to change.

Suppose you have a set of data stored in a linked list, for example. In C++, you would define a linked-list class that defines how the linked list operates, that is, how to access a particular element of the list, how to add or delete an element, how to find out if the list is empty, and so forth. To manipulate your data, you define a new class that is derived from this linked-list class. Your new class can now use all the functions of the linked-list class without having to bother with any of the details of the linked-list class implementation.

Now, let's say you decide that a doubly linked list would be a better approach for storing the application data. But you have already developed many functions that use the structure you have currently defined. With C++, this poses no problem at all. You change the base class to use a doubly linked-list storage method. By redefining the methods of the base class, you do not need to make any changes to your derived class. So, your application does not need to know any of the details as to how the list is implemented. It simply uses functions, such as *getNext()* and *getPrevious()*, to get elements of the list independent of the implementation.

You will see many examples of base classes being used in this way for derived classes throughout the software in this book and in virtually any C++ application. However, C++ also offers a number of additional C enhancements to aid in programming and maintaining an application.

The C programming language has been in use for about 20 years. As people have developed ever more complex programs, the shortcomings of C have become more apparent. C++ is not only an attempt at adding object-oriented features to C, but it also addresses some of the limitations of C. In particular, C++ provides the following benefits:

◆ C++ provides strong type checking of function arguments. The arguments passed to a function must have their type declared both in the definition of the function and in the header file that defines the function. While it may seem painful to always have to make these argument declarations, it saves time and grief by letting the compiler ensure that all functions are called with valid arguments.

◆ A C++ class may be derived from other classes. So, you can create new classes that have all of the attributes of the base class. As in the linked-list example discussed previously, your program does not need to know how the base class is implemented, only how to access the methods of the base class.

◆ A new type of passed value, the *reference*, lets you pass a pointer to an argument implicitly. This provides more natural looking code for many types of functions. In addition, a function may return a reference as the return value. Referenced variables may be used as *lvalue*, that is, the function call may appear on the left-hand side of an expression. As you will see, this feature can be very useful when defining overloaded functions.

◆ The C operators, such as +, −, *, /, and so on, may be redefined to work with your data types. This feature can easily be overused, but it can greatly increase the readability of your code. You will see several examples of this in the definitions of the complex, vector, and matrix classes in Chapters 3 and 4.

◆ A relatively new addition to C++, the *template*, provides an extension to the C-macro capability. Instead of defining a C macro to perform a C function, you create a template that describes the function. The compiler then uses this template to create an appropriate function for the type of arguments you pass. In addition, templates may be used to define whole classes of objects that use different data types. An example of using templates is presented in Chapter 3 with the definition of the vector and matrix classes.

This list is by no means complete. C++ introduces many new programming features that are more thoroughly covered in the references listed in the bibliography. As with any programming language, many of these new features must be used in practice before they can be appreciated.

The primary advantage of C++ over other object-oriented languages is that C++ is a superset of American National Standards Institute (ANSI) C. The compatibility of C++ with C is one of the primary reasons for the current success of C++. There are several other object-oriented languages that predate C++, but they all mandate that you must learn the new language to gain any benefit. By contrast, an experienced C programmer can use the new features of C++ in a gradual way, without having to learn an entirely new and unfamiliar language.

Using C++ for graphics programming of fractals, or any other types of graphics, has several advantages over other object-oriented languages and implementations, including:

◆ It is a very popular programming language and is rapidly growing into the language of choice for many PC applications. There are many compilers, development tools, and books available to assist you in developing programs.

◆ If you are conscientious, you can create very efficient code and still maintain the elegance and maintainability provided by a high-level language. C++ provides the ability to explicitly define functions for inline-code expansion, if desired.

◆ There are many software packages and applications available for you to use once you have mastered the techniques presented in this book. You will find many more graphics applications and fractal programs based on C++ in the coming years as more programmers become familiar with the language.

As previously mentioned, knowing the syntax and grammar of a programming language is only a part of learning how to create effective programs. Let's now look at some of the methods used in coding the software of this book to create readable, modular, and above all, working programs.

Headers and Modules

Just as in C, C++ source files are divided into two basic types, header files and module files. Because C++ is upward compatible with C, you use standard C header files, usually with an *.h* file extension, and C module files, with a *.c* file extension. The modules represent the source code of your program. To avoid confusing C and C++ code, C++ modules are stored in files with a *.cpp* extension, and C++ header files are stored with an *.hpp* extension.

Most of the effort in C++ programming is in creating your classes. You will find that once you properly structure your classes, creating and using the member functions is very straightforward. Many of the example programs in this book are surprisingly short because all the work is done by the class member functions. Most of the source files are organized as a header file defining a particular class and an associated module file (same name, *.cpp* extension) that defines the non-inline member functions for those classes.

While no general rules really exist for how to organize source files, you should try to keep each source module down to a reasonable size. Don't try to put each function in a separate module or put all your functions in the same file, unless it is a very simple program. One useful rule of thumb is to keep all your function definitions to a single page in length.

This makes them easy to catalog when printed and forces you to think about breaking complex functions into manageable pieces.

Header Files

There is usually an *.hpp* header file corresponding to each C++ module file. Each header file provides definitions for the following:

◆ class definitions;

◆ constant symbols and template definitions; and

◆ function prototypes.

The general structure of a standard header file is shown in Figure 2–1. C++ class definitions are an extension of C *struct* definitions. C++ provides the same macro capability as C with the *#define* directive. In addition, C++ provides the capability to create safer and more flexible inline-function definitions with the template facility.

Unlike C, C++ requires prototypes for all functions. Instead of just declaring the return data type of a function, the function prototype also declares what type of each argument to use. This gives the compiler the ability to check all the uses of the functions throughout your program and report any argument-mismatch errors (wrong number of arguments or wrong data type) at compile time. Function argument-mismatch errors are a common cause of problems in many C applications. So although it may seem like a lot of extra work at first to do this, the benefits are well worth the effort.

Listing 2–1. Structure of a C++ header file.

```
#if !defined(HEADER_HPP)      // You can also use the
                              // equivalent #ifndef statement
// Use the name of the module, like MYLIB in place of the name
// header here

#define HEADER_HPP     1
```

```
/*****************************************************************/
/*

    header.hpp

    Programmer(s):      Who gets blame if program doesn't work?

    Purpose:            Why did you spend time on this?

    Revision History:   Who changed it right before the
                        demonstration?
*/

// A header file should be able to stand on its own; that is,
// it should include all the other header files it needs
// to work all on its own.

#include <stdlib.h>     // Put all headers needed by this module
#include <windows.h>


/*****************************************************************

    constANTS for defining module wide constants
    Using const for these symbols is preferred because the
    compiler can perform better type checking


*****************************************************************/

const    long MAXBUF    1024
const    long MAXSIZE   65536


/*****************************************************************

    Typedef declarations

*****************************************************************/

typedef         float           angle;

// A common use of typedef is to define symbolic names for
// template classes. This makes it very easy to change the
```

```
// storage
// method and type for a class.

typedef RWFvec_2DVector<float> RWFmodule_Vector;

/*************************************************************

    Class Definitions

*************************************************************/

class RWFmodule_Point {
    private:
    float x, y;
    protected:
    public:
    // Define the constructors and destructors
    RWFmodule_Point(void)        {x = 0; y = 0;};
    // A constructor with different arguments
    RWFmodule_Point(float xp, float yp) {x = xp; y = yp;};
    // Destructor
    ~RWFmodule_Point(void)       {};
    // Copy constructor
    RWFmodule_Point(RWFmodule_Point &p) {x = p.x; y = p.y;};

    // Utility functions

    // Note that these are all defined as inline functions
    // because the function is defined immediately following
    // its declaration

    void getXY(float &xp float &yp)   {xp = x; yp = y;};
    float getX(void)                       {return x;};
    float getY(void)                       {return y;};
    void setXY(float xp, float yp)    {x = xp; y = yp;};
    void setXY(RWFmodule_Point &p)    {x = p.x; y = p.y;};
};

// Example of derived class
class RWFmodule_Circle : public RWFmodule_Point {
    private:
```

```
      float radius;
      protected:
      public:

      // Define the constructors and destructors
      RWFmodule_Circle(void)    {radius = 1;};
      ~RWFmodule_Circle(void)   {};
      // The copy constructor for the base class is
      // automatically called
      RWFmodule_Circle(RWFmodule_Circle &c)
       {c.radius = c.radius;};

      void move(RWFmodule_Point &p);
   };


   /*************************************************************


      Function Declarations and Prototypes


   *************************************************************/


   extern RWFmodule_Point &RWFmodule_Print(void);
```

Class Definitions

The *.hpp* header files are even more crucial in C++ than they are in C. You must not only define all the data structures for the classes defined in this particular header, but you must declare all the member functions (methods) for each class. A typical class definition should look like the following:

```
class myClass {
 private:           // Members accessible only to the class
 int a, b;
 float c, d;

 protected:         // Members accessible to derived classes
 public:            // Members accessible by everybody
                    // Generally, limit public members to the
                    // methods
```

```
myClass(void);// Declare a constructor
myClass(myClass &mc);    // Declare a copy constructor
~myClass(void);          // Destructor

void getInteger(int &a1, &a2){a1 = a; a2 = b;};
}; // End of definition
```

The scope qualifiers, *private, protected*, and *public*, set the access level of the class members to the outside world. A *private* element can only be accessed by member functions of that particular class. Other functions cannot directly access *private* elements, thus, preventing them from inadvertently altering them. *Protected* members can be accessed by any derived classes. This is useful when you have a set of classes that need to access a common item from the base class. *Public* members can be accessed by any function. In general, you should try to make all the data members *private* or *protected* and make the member functions *public*. If you find that you need too many public data members, then you probably need to rethink how you have defined your classes.

It is a good practice to list the three types of data elements, *private, protected*, and *public,* even if you do not have any assigned data elements or functions. Listing all three qualifiers lets you easily determine the level of access of any particular member.

Create and Destroy

Three standard member functions are defined in the example class declaration of *myClass*. These correspond to the *constructor*, the recipe for creating a new object of the class; the *copy constructor*, a special constructor that creates a new object from an existing one; and the *destructor*, for destroying the class. These three functions should always be defined, even if they don't do anything initially. As your classes become more complex, you'll almost always find that you need to perform some sort of initialization when an object is created and some special action when the object is destroyed.

The use of constructors and destructors usually causes considerable confusion when you first start using C++. Whenever a class is created, all the data elements in the class definition have their respective constructors, if defined, called. For instance, suppose you define a second class as follows:

```
class secondClass {
 private:
 myClass mc;
 protected:
 public:
 secondClass(void);
 ...              // Define new member functions
};
```

Whenever an object of type *secondClass* is created, the constructor for *myClass* is called first, followed by the constructor for *secondClass*. So, the *secondClass* constructor need not initialize *myClass* as it has already been accomplished.

Whenever a *secondClass* object is deleted, the *secondClass* destructor is called first, followed by the destructor for *myClass*. So, the constructors and destructors of a class generally do not have to worry about creating and destroying the individual data elements.

One of the principal uses of constructors and destructors is in handling data that has been allocated in the heap and is referenced by a pointer. Let's create a new class, *thirdClass*:

```
class thirdClass {
 private:
 myClass *mc;
 protected:
 public:
 thirdClass(void)     {mc = new myClass;};
 ~thirdClass(void)    {if(mc) delete mc;};
 ...                  // Define other functions
};
```

In this example, the reference to *myClass* is through a pointer. This data will not be automatically allocated. The constructor for *thirdClass* is defined to create the data for us. The *new* operator allocates the data for *myClass* from the heap and then calls the *myClass* constructor. Because the data is stored via a pointer, it will not be deallocated automatically when a *thirdClass* object is destroyed. The *thirdClass* destructor is, therefore, defined to delete the *myClass* object pointed to by the data member *mc*.

The use of constructors and destructors illustrates the different philosophy used in creating C++ classes as opposed to C structures. When defining C structures, you usually end up storing pointers to other structures, as in the definition of *thirdClass*, so that you can gracefully initialize and later delete those structures. This requires you to create unique function names to create and destroy each structure, such as *myClassCreate()* and *myClassDelete()*. This is unnecessary in C++. Instead of using a class pointer, you simply declare an instance of the class directly, as was done in the definition of *secondClass*. The structure will be created according to the rules specified in the constructor for that class. Similarly, each data member within a class is destroyed according to the rules in its respective destructor. In many cases, this eliminates the need to carry around pointers to other objects. The use of constructors and destructors helps ensure that objects are always created and destroyed correctly; objects created and destroyed incorrectly are very common and annoying problems in most C applications.

Running on Overload

Another useful feature in C++ is the ability to define functions with the same name, but passed different arguments. This is referred to as *function overloading*. When the compiler scans a source module, it attempts to match each function call with a corresponding function prototype from a header file. A function is defined both by its name and by the number and type of its arguments. The compiler generates a unique function for each combination of argument names and numbers. Overloading function names is quite a useful feature and, as such, is also easily misused.

One common use of function-name overloading is in the definition of member functions. Recall the *RWFmodule_Point* function shown in the header-file listing of Figure 2–1. You might want to specify a new position of a point by either passing an explicit *x* and *y* location or by passing another point. In either case, both functions perform the same operation but with different data types. It makes sense to use the same function name to indicate that the same operation is performed. For this example, the position of the point is moved to the location specified by the argument(s) passed to *setXY()*.

Function overloading also gives you the ability to keep function names simple while avoiding name collisions with other objects. In graphics applications, for example, it is necessary to create classes describing graphical objects like points, lines, circles, and so forth. You often want to perform certain common operations, such as moving, rescaling, and drawing objects. C++ lets you define a function, such as *move()*, *rescale()*, and *draw()*, for each object. You can then perform the desired operation for an object simply by a call such as *object.draw()*. Then, whenever you need to draw an object, you simply call its *draw()* function, which is a much easier name to remember.

Virtual Functions

The C++ virtual-function facility lets you go even further in overloading function names. A virtual function is simply a placeholder for a function. A class that is derived from this base class may provide a new definition for any virtual function defined in the base class. So far, this is no different from ordinary function overloading. The difference occurs when you use pointers to a base class. A pointer to a base class may be used to point to any base-class object or to an object derived from that base class. Consider the following two declarations:

```
class base_object {
 private:
 protected:
 public:
```

```
    virtual void draw(void);
};

class circle : public base_object {
 private:
 protected:
 public:
 void draw(void);
};

base_object *obj;
circle    *circ;

circ = new Circle;
obj = circ;

...

obj->draw();
```

The *circle* class is derived from the *base_object* class. The pointer *obj* is assigned to point to a newly created *circle* object. When the call to draw the object is made with *obj->draw()*, the *draw()* function for the circle is called. This is very useful when you have a list of different kinds of objects all derived from one base class. For each *base_object* pointer, the appropriate function is called, depending on the specific object to which it points. This typically eliminates the need for big *switch()* statements or function pointers to select the appropriate function to apply to a given object.

You will see several examples of virtual functions in the graphics code described in Chapter 3.

Overloaded Operators

In addition to overloading standard C-type functions, C++ lets you overload the *operator* functions, such as +, *, −, and /. Almost every standard operator can be overloaded. In fact, you are already quite

familiar with this facility within C itself. C already lets you add variables of different data types, performing the appropriate data-type casting as needed. C++ gives you direct control to adapt the operators to any classes you like.

However, you must be careful when overloading an operator. Consider one of the simplest examples, the complex class available with Borland C++. The overloaded + operator for adding two complex numbers can be defined in one of two ways:

```
Complex operator + (Complex &z1, Complex &z2)
{
  Complex zout;

  zout.x = z1.x + z2.y;
  zout.y = z1.y + z2.y;

  return zout;
};
```

or

```
Complex
Complex::operator + (Complex &zadd)
{
  Complex zout;

  zout.x = x + zadd.x;
  zout.y = y + zadd.y;

  return zout;
};
```

In the first case, the function is a nonmember function of two arguments that is declared as a *friend* of the *Complex* class so the function can directly access the data members *x* and *y*. In the second case, the operator is declared as a member function of a single argument. In general, it is preferable to declare binary operators as *friend*s, especially if the operator is symmetric like + and −. An overloaded binary operator declared as a member function can only use the syntax of *<class> <operator> <argument>*. So, the operator would only be over-loaded if the class argument is the first argument. The software in this book generally adopts the convention of declaring binary operators as *friend* functions, and defines the operator for each possible order of the arguments, in case the arguments are of different types (for exam-ple, to allow adding a *float* and a complex number together). There are, of course, occasions that you would like to restrict the order in which the operator can be used, such as with the = operator. In these cases, you should declare the operator as a member function.

You should also note that the operator function is performing consider-ably more operations than might be initially apparent. For instance, the + operator, as previously shown, performs the following actions each time it is called:

◆ calls the *Complex* constructor to create *zout;*

◆ adds the *x* and *y* components;

◆ calls the *Complex* copy constructor to copy *zout* to whatever takes the result of the addition; and

◆ calls the *Complex* destructor to get rid of *zout.*

Of course, the *Complex* constructors and destructors are very simple, but with more complicated classes, these operations might take consid-erably longer than you might realize. Things are even more involved with a simple statement such as the following:

```
Complex a, b, c;
c = a + b;
```

Now, the result of *a + b* must also be copied into *c*. If the = operator has not been overloaded for this class, then elements of the structure are simply copied. Otherwise, the overloaded = operator is used. In either case, a lot of operations are executed to evaluate this seemingly simple expression.

One way to get around this limitation is to be sure to overload the various *in-place* operators, such as +=, *=, −=, and so forth. For example, you can create the += *Complex* operator as follows:

```
Complex &
Complex::operator += (Complex zadd)
{
  x += zadd.x;
  y += zadd.y;

  return *this;
};
```

Now the expression $c = c + z$ can be performed much more efficiently by using $c += z$. The += operator, as defined in this example, eliminates the need to create and destroy a temporary variable.

An overloaded operator should always return the data type of its class. This lets you use binary expressions in any context, such as passing an argument. You should also try to restrain the tendency to overload too many operators. You can easily get caught in the situation of making the code less readable because it is too succinct and compact. As shown in the previous example, a lot of operations are implicitly performed by overloaded operator functions.

Passing References

The += operator, as defined in the example, also avoids copying the result as its return value. Instead, it returns a reference to itself. A *reference* is, in effect, a pointer to an object. A reference can be used in the same way as a declared object. In particular, you can use a returned reference as an *lvalue*; that is, it can appear on the left-hand side of an = operator. In this example, the += operator returns a pointer to the object that can be used in subsequent operations if necessary. In general, an in-place member function (a function that modifies the object) can return a reference to the object. The nonmember function + operator (the first example of the *Complex* operator +) cannot return a reference to *zout* because *zout* is destroyed after the function returns. It must therefore return a copy of *zout*.

Also, note that the examples pass their arguments via a reference. Passing an argument by a reference is effectively the same as the common C method of passing pointers. By using the reference argument, the arguments are not copied to temporary variables to be used by the function internally. You will almost always want to pass any class argument by reference, just as you would pass a structure pointer—rather than the structure—to a C function.

In addition to reducing the argument passing overhead, it is often useful to declare function arguments that you wish to modify as reference arguments. Suppose you want a function to modify each of its two integer arguments, for instance. In C, you would define the function as:

```
void func1(int *x, int *y)
{
 int resultx, resulty;
 /* Process the args, and set the return values */
 *x = resultx;
 *y = resulty;
}
```

func1() is then called with arguments such as *func1(&x1, &y1)*. In C++, you can make a more natural definition of this type of function as:

```
void func1(int &x, int &y)
{
 int resultx, resulty;
 // Process the args, and set the return values
 x = resultx;
 y = resulty;
}
```

You may then call the function simply *func1(x1, y1)*. Either function syntax will work, but the second is a little more elegant.

Static Variables

The keyword *static* is used to declare variables that are retained even after a function exits. If the static declaration is made inside a function definition, then the variable will be retained after the function returns, just like a global variable. The variable may, however, only be used by that one function. If a static variable is declared at the beginning of a module, outside any function definition, then the variable is available to every function in the module. A static variable still refers to only one memory location. So, if function *foo1()* changes it and then calls function *foo2()*, *foo2()* will see the changed value. Using global variables can be quite tricky if the variable is set in multiple places in the program.

One good use for *static* variables within a function is to initialize pointers. In the following code segment, for instance, we define a temporary variable:

```
void process_circle(Circle &c)
{
  static Circle *temp_circle = NULL;

  if(temp_circle == NULL)
    temp_circle = circleCreate(0,0, 1.0);

<rest of function>
}
```

When *process_circle()* is called the first time, the static variable *temp_circle* will point to *NULL*, usually defined as *(void *)* 0 or just 0. This will then force it to create the temporary circle by calling the *circleCreate()* function. The variable *temp_circle* may then be used as temporary storage or for whatever purpose you intended. Whenever *process_circle()* is called again, *temp_circle* will not be *NULL*, and so it will not bother creating it again. This saves the execution overhead of having to create and destroy the temporary circle each time *process_circle()* is called. This can be quite important for time-critical applications such as image animation.

Similarly, you can eliminate the extra overhead of creating and deleting storage in operators such as *Complex +*. Consider the following new definition of the + operator:

```
Complex
Complex::operator + (Complex &zadd)
{
  static Complex zout;

  zout.x = x + zadd.x;
  zout.y = y + zaddout.y;

  return zout;
}
```

In this example, the temporary variable *zout* is not deleted when the function returns. Furthermore, *zout* does not need to be created for subsequent calls to the + operator. This removes some of the computational overhead of the + operator. However, you must be careful about using static variables in this manner. With more complicated classes, the constructor for the class may do more than just allocate space for the structure. It might be critical to make sure the return value—in this case *zout*—is properly initialized before continuing with the rest of the computation. By using a static variable, *zout* retains the value it had at the end of the previous computation, which can cause disastrous results for certain types of classes.

In general, you should avoid using global variables. Globals have their applications, such as keeping track of global-state information to avoid having to pass unnecessary extraneous arguments to all your application functions. But this can be avoided by putting all the global information into a class definition and using appropriate member functions to get the information needed by an application. Global variables should be treated as variables that are only modified during program initialization or when a major change of program state has occurred that affects most of the modules. Otherwise, create an appropriate structure to contain your state information and pass it to the functions that need to use the information.

The Zen of Macros

The C macro capability provides a powerful (sometimes too powerful, as you can easily create macros with hard-to-find programming bugs) means of defining symbolic constants and creating inline expressions. A macro is processed by simple substitution. As the compiler scans a source file, any macro name that is encountered is replaced with the definition of the macro. The expression is then compiled normally. There are two basic types of macros :

```
#define PI                  3.14159   /* Defining parameters */
/* Inline function */
#define MAX(x,y)            ((x) > (y) ? (x) : (y))
```

The first type is the basic means for defining any particular constants you might want to use. However, in C++ there is an even better way to define such constants, via a *const* declaration. The advantage of using *const* is that it defines the data type of the parameter, and thus allows the compiler to perform better type checking. For instance, you should define any program limits, such as maximum array sizes, time limits, and so on, using *const* declarations. You can then change it later if necessary and, more importantly, the symbolic name gives you a better indication of what the constant was meant to signify. For instance,

```
const    long MAX_ARRAY_SIZE   1000

double array[MAX_ARRAY_SIZE];
```

is much better than:

```
double array[1000];
```

It is even more useful when a limit or constant is a more complex expression, for example:

```
const float PI           3.14159
const float RAD_TO_DEGS 180. / PI
```

Another common use of *#define* is in providing optional compilation control by employing the *#ifdef/#endif* directives. This gives you the flexibility to compile modules differently, depending on which environment you are using, such as between MS-DOS and MS-Windows or between different compiler manufacturer's implementations of C++. So, you can retain some environment-specific features without having to make code changes when compiling under different environments.

Useful Directives

You can use the *#ifdef* directive to solve the annoying problem of including header files multiple times. Suppose header file *foo1.hpp* includes header file *foo2.hpp*, for instance. In your main module, *foo.cpp*, you include *foo1.hpp* and *foo2.hpp*. Without the proper precaution, you would receive lots of multiply-defined-structure definitions, macro definitions, and so on when you tried to compile *foo.cpp*. The problem is that *foo2.hpp* is included twice. To avoid this, use the following in all your header files:

```
#ifndef <HEADERNAME>_HPP
#define <HEADERNAME>_HPP        1
    .
    <rest of header file>
    .
#endif
```

where <HEADERNAME> is usually the name of header files, such as *FOO1* and *FOO2* in this example. Notice that our convention is to capitalize the entire name of the header file in the *#define* and *#ifdef* statements. While not required, this helps avoid possible conflicts with the header filename elsewhere. With this technique, the header-file definitions will only be included once, regardless of how many times you included it. You can also have all your header files cross-reference one another without causing massive conflicts. This technique is used by all the system header files, such as *stdio.h* and *sys.h*, to avoid the multiple-definition problem.

C++ Templates

The second main use of macros is to define simple inline functions. The syntax is very similar to defining a normal function, except that there are no data-type declarations. However, the current versions of C++ remove almost all of the need for this type of macro by replacing them with C++ templates. A *template* is a recipe for creating either a function or a class. The template acts as a prototype to tell the compiler how to create a function with specific data types. By using the C++ *inline* directive, you can get the same benefit of inline code substitution as you can with a C macro.

For instance, the function *MAX(x,y)* is usually defined in C as follows:

```
#define MAX(x,y)        ( (x) > (y) ? (x) : (y))
```

This definition is fine but can lead to problems if the arguments *x* and *y* are different data types. The equivalent *template* definition for *MAX()* is:

```
template<class T1, class T2>
inline T1 MAX(T1 &x, T2 &y)
{return((x > y) ? x : (T1)y);}
```

This particular version of *MAX()* always returns a result with the same type as the first argument, *x*. You can, of course, make it return whatever type you wish. If the argument *y* cannot be cast as the same type as *x*, then you will receive a compiler-error message to that effect. The compiler uses the template to create new functions that match the arguments you pass in a given invocation of the function.

In addition to defining template functions, you may also create template classes. For instance, you might want to create a list class for different types of data. One way to do this is with a template:

```
template<class T>
class rwfSimpleList_Template {
 private:
```

```
    protected:
    public:
    fSimpleList_Template *next;  // Pointer to next element
    T data;                      // Data element
    };
```

This template creates a list element of data type *T*. To create a list of type *int*, you would use a *typedef* such as:

```
    typedef rwfSimpleList_Template<int>  rwfSimpleList_int;
```

By using this class template, you can now create lists of any desired data type. All the classes created from the same template will have exactly the same functions and operations. The only differences will be in the data types they store. Template classes should be used whenever you have a class that you wish to adapt to different data types. You will see a more practical example of class templates in the definition of the vector and matrix classes in Chapter 3.

Naming Conventions

In order to avoid conflicts with other graphics packages and with your own routines, we've used standard naming conventions for all the classes and functions of software in this book. As you use more software libraries, you will inevitably find that someone else has created a class called *Circle* or *Point* or a function called *DrawCircle()*. Most of the functions in the software are member functions of the various classes, so names are kept relatively simple within the class definition. Any standardized naming convention always makes the names longer and sometimes less intuitive. But this is much better than having to change your source code later to avoid conflicts with some terrific new library you just purchased.

The conventions are that we've used are reasonably straightforward. All the class names have the following syntax:

```
    class RWF<module>_<Name> {
      private:
```

```
protected:
public:
};
```

Each class name begins with an uppercase *RWF* (for real-world fractals, of course). The *<module>* name is an abbreviation for the module file in which the function is defined. For instance, the vector classes all begin with *RWFvec_*. The *<Name>* portion is a name describing the particular class, such as *RWFvec_2DVector*.

To help distinguish template-class names, the word *template* is appended to the class-template definitions. Specific instances of templates are always declared in a *typedef* statement such as:

```
typedef RWFvec_2DVectorTemplate<int> RWFvec_2DVectorInt;
```

By declaring template classes in this manner, you can easily change the data types used for a specific instance simply by changing the data type used in the *typedef* statement.

To distinguish function names from class names, all nonmember functions begin with a lowercase *rwf_*, such as *rwf_randGaussian()*. The rest of the function name is indicative of the purpose and operation of the function.

For More Information

This chapter provides some rules and guidelines on using C++ to create an application. It certainly does not cover all aspects of C++ programming. Because of the increasing popularity of the C++ language, there are a number of texts available explaining C++ coding styles and practices in more detail. Some recommended sources are the following:

Goodwin, Mark. *Serial Communications in C and C++*. MIS:Press, Inc., 1992.

Goodwin, Mark. *User Interfaces in C and C++*. MIS:Press, Inc., 1992.

Goodwin, Mark. *User Interfaces in C and C++ for OS/2, Version 2.0.* MIS:Press, Inc., 1993

Ladd, Scott Robert. *Applying C++.* M&T Books, 1992.

Ladd, Scott Robert. *C++ Components and Algorithms.* M&T Books, 1992.

Nelson, Mark. *Serial Communications: A C++ Developer's Guide.* M&T Books, 1992.

Oualline, Steve. *C Elements of Style.* M&T Books, 1992.

Siegal, Charles. *teach yourself... C.* MIS:Press, Inc., 1991.

Sprott, Julien C. *Strange Attractors.* M&T Books, 1993.

Stevens, Al. *C++ Database Development* MIS:Press, Inc., 1992.

Stevens, Al. *teach yourself... C++,* 3rd Edition. MIS:Press, Inc., 1992.

Fractals on Display

Now that you have seen some of the coding styles and techniques used for the software in this book, it is time to apply these methods to fractal programming. The first thing you will need is a graphics library that lets you display images and graphics on your screen. In the next chapter, you will learn about our C++ library for displaying both two- and three-dimensional graphical objects. You will also see how C++ templates are extensively used to create a very compact and efficient set of routines for manipulating vectors and matrices of multiple data types. With these library routines, you'll be able to begin your exploration of fractals and their many applications and see the results on your screen.

Graphics for Fractals

The popularity of fractals is almost entirely because of the beautiful and intricate graphic images you can create with them. Current literature on computer graphics is filled with color images of fractal figures, and this book is no exception. As pointed out in Chapter 1, computer graphics are essential to understanding and applying fractals to model a phenomenon because the computer is the only practical means for generating and visualizing such complex and intricate figures. It is therefore essential to have a suitable graphics library for drawing fractal objects.

In this chapter, you'll learn how to build an object-oriented graphics package based on a set of primitive graphics routines, such as those provided in the BGI library of Borland C++. The C++ graphics classes developed in this chapter let you work easily with either two- or three-dimensional fractal objects. In addition to the graphics classes, this chapter also provides three other important classes: a vector class, a matrix class, and a flexible container class for storing arrays of arbitrary objects. All the graphics and fractal routines developed throughout the book make extensive use of the vector, matrix, and table classes to create readable, efficient, and maintainable code.

Matrix and Vector Fun

Many of the fractal algorithms you'll see later in the book are based on repeated applications of affine transformations to scale, rotate, and translate objects. An *affine* transformation of the vector *v* generates a new vector *v'* by multiplying *v* by a matrix. Each coordinate of the transformed vector *v'* is a linear combination of the coordinates of *v*. The most important feature of affine transformations is that you can represent any combination of transformations by a single matrix.

Multiple transformations can be stored as a single matrix using matrix multiplication to combine the individual transformations. This property makes matrices a compact and efficient means of representing a transformed object. One of the great benefits provided by C++ is the ability to overload the normal arithmetic operators with your own definitions. By overloading operators such as + and * to accept vectors and matrices as operands, you can create more readable source code that lets you write algorithms in a more natural mathematical notation.

Vectors

Vectors are primarily used to define a set of coordinates, such as an (*x*, *y*) point on the screen or a an (*x*, *y*, *z*) point in space. You'll primarily use two- and three-dimensional vectors, although the vector class can actually handle any number of components. The basic vector class is called *RWFvec_Vector*. This class stores a vector of *float* values. However, *RWFvec_Vector* is actually defined from the *RWFvec_VectorTemplate* template class using a *typedef* statement. The definition of *RWFvec_Vector* is simply:

```
typedef RWFvec_VectorTemplate<float> RWFvec_Vector;
```

You can use a similar *typedef* to create vectors of *int*, *long*, *double*, *Complex*, or whatever data type you like. All the normal vector operations, such as addition, subtraction, dot product, and so on, work in the same manner as they do for the *float* vector type. The ability to create class templates is a big advantage of C++ over C because you only have to maintain and debug the single template class, instead of maintaining separate classes for each different vector data type you might want to use.

Working with vectors is quite easy. To create a two-dimensional vector, you declare the vector with the following statement:

```
RWFvec_Vector vec(2);
```

This statement uses the *RWFvec_Vector* constructor to create a two-element vector of *float* values. Of course, you can create a vector of any number of dimensions by replacing the two in the previous statement to the number of desired dimensions. All the elements of the vector are initialized to zero when the vector is created. You must be sure to specify the number of dimensions for a vector whenever you declare one. In almost all respects, you can use a vector the same way as you would a single *float* variable. Most of the arithmetic operators are defined for vectors via their normal mathematical definition. For instance, + and -, respectively, add and subtract the vector elements. You can access the individual vector components as if the vector were an array, by using the overloaded subscript operator *[]*. So, *vec[0]* refers to the first element, *vec[1]* to the second element, and so on.

In addition to using the arithmetic operators with vectors, you can also easily manipulate vectors and scalars. For instance, you can add a constant to each component of a vector with an expression like the following:

```
RWFvec_Vector vec1(3), vec2(3);

vec1 = 3.0; // Set all elements of vec1 to 3
vec2 = vec1 + 2.0; // Add 2 to all elements of vec1
```

You may freely mix vector and scalar operands in an expression. The effect performs an operation, such as addition and subtraction, between the scalar and each component of the vector. Also note that the = operator has been overloaded as well, so that you may set two vectors equal to one another or set a vector equal to a scalar, which sets all components of the vector equal to the scalar quantity. The only requirement when using these operators is that all the vectors in an expression must have the same number of dimensions, otherwise undefined results can occur.

In addition to the +, –, and = operators, the incremental operators += and –= have been overloaded as well, so you can increment a vector the same way you would any scalar quantity. When you want to simply increment a vector by another vector or scalar, the expression v += $vinc$ is more efficient than the equivalent statement $v = v + vinc$. The reason for the increased efficiency is that whenever the expression $v + vinc$ is evaluated, the + operator must create a temporary vector to store the result, and then destroy the temporary when the operation is completed. With the += operator, the temporary is not needed because the vector itself may be used for storage.

Specialized vector operations

One quantity you'll probably be interested in is the length of a vector, usually denoted by the notation $|v|$. The length of a coordinate vector is the distance from the coordinate to the origin. This quantity is just the square root of the sum of the squares of each coordinate. For the *RWFvec_Vector* class, the member function *length()* returns the length of the vector.

Two common vector operations you'll encounter are the scalar dot product and the vector cross product. The *scalar dot product* between two vectors simply multiplies each pair of coordinates from the two vectors and sums all the products together. The resulting quantity has a number of useful properties, the primary one being the relationship illustrated in Equation 3–1.

$$v_1 * v_2 = \sum_{i=1}^{n} v_{1i} * v_{2i} = |v_1||v_2|\cos\theta \qquad \textit{(Equation 3–1)}$$

The relationship shown in Equation 3–1 states that the dot product is equal to the product of the lengths of the vectors multiplied by the cosine of the angle between the vectors. One result of this equation is that you can quickly tell if two vectors have an angle less than 90 degrees if the dot product is greater than zero, equal to 90 degrees if the dot product is exactly zero, or have an angle greater than 90 degrees if the dot product is less than zero. You'll see this relationship exploited extensively in the later chapters when drawing three-dimensional fractals. You can compute the dot product between two vectors in your code simply by using the * operator, as shown in Equation 3–1. Note that the length of a vector is equal to the square root of the vector dot product.

The vector cross product is useful in three-dimensional graphics applications. The *vector cross product*, denoted as *v1 x v2*, takes two vectors and generates a third vector perpendicular to the vectors *v1* and *v2*. Equation 3–2 shows how the coordinates are computed for three-dimensional vectors. The length of the cross-product vector is equal to $|v1|*|v2|*\sin\theta$. If the length of the cross-product vector is zero, then the two vectors are parallel to one another. Frequently, the cross product is used to generate a direction vector perpendicular to a plane figure, such as a polygon.

$$x' = v1[1]*v2[2] - v1[2]*v2[1]$$ *(Equation 3–2)*

$$y' = v1[2]*v2[0] - v1[0]*v2[2]$$

$$z' = v1[0]*v2[1] - v1[1]*v2[0]$$

The *RWFvec_Vector* member function *cross()* computes the cross product of one vector with another. To generate *v1 x v2*, you use the expression *v1.cross(v2)*.

In addition to using vectors to store coordinates, you can also think of a vector as representing a direction in space. These vector types are called *direction vectors*. In many graphics applications, you construct a direction vector simply by subtracting one coordinate vector from another. The resulting direction vector is then said to *point* from one point to another, defining a particular direction. It is often convenient to normalize a direction vector so that it always has unit length. The *RWFvec_Vector* member function *normalize()* performs this function. If the vector has length zero (all elements of the vector are zero), then it is not normalized.

Table 3–1 provides a summary of all the member and *friend* functions associated with the *RWFvec_Vector* class. The same functions are available to any vector class created from the *RWFvec_VectorTemplate* template class. A C++ *friend* function is a normal function that has the same type of direct access to the data elements of a class as member functions do.

Table 3–1. *Friends* and member functions for the *RWFvec_Vector* class

Member Function	Description
float & operator [] (unsigned int i)	Returns the *i*th element of the base vector Because this returns a reference, you may use it on the left-hand side of an =.
int size(void)	Returns the dimension of the vector
RWFvec_Vector operator (+ or –) (RWFvec_Vector &v1, RWFvec_Vector &v2)	Returns the sum (or difference) of *v1* and *v2*
RWFvec_Vector operator (+, –) (RWFvec_Vector &v, float s)	Adds (or subtracts) the scalar *s* from all elements of vector *v*
RWFvec_Vector & operator (+=, –=) (RWFvec_Vector &v)	Adds (or subtracts) the vector *v* from the base vector and stores the result back in the base vector
RWFvec_Vector & operator (+=, –=) (float s)	Adds (or subtracts) the scalar *s* from all elements of the base vector and stores the result back in the base vector
RWFvec_Vector & operator = (RWFvec_Vector &v)	Copies the vector *v* to the base vector
RWFvec_Vector & operator = (float s)	Sets all elements of the base vector to the scalar *s*
*float operator * (RWFvec_Vector &v)*	Returns the dot product between the base vector and vector *v*

Table 3–1. *continued*

Member Function	Description
RWFvec_Vector operator * *(RWFvec_Vector &v1, float s)*	Returns a new vector where each element is the product of the corresponding element in *v1* multiplied by the scalar *s*
RWFvec_Vector &operator *= (float s)	Multiplies the elements of the base vector by the scalar *s* and stores the result back in the base vector
float length(void)	Returns the length of the base vector
RWFvec_Vector &normalize(void)	Normalizes the base vector. The result is stored in the base vector.
RWFvec_Vector cross(RWFvec_Vector &v)	Returns the vector *(*this) x v*, the cross product between the base vector and *v*. This should only be used for two- or three-dimensional vectors.

Matrices

The principal reason for using vectors in this book is to represent the coordinates of an object such as a line, polygon, or multidimensional fractal. As explained earlier, most of the transformations used by the fractal algorithms involve affine transformations. Any affine transformation of a point, such as rotation, scaling, or translation, can be computed by multiplying a coordinate vector by a transformation matrix. For instance, the equation for a two-dimensional affine transformation is shown in Equation 3–3.

$$\begin{pmatrix} x' \\ y' \end{pmatrix} = \begin{pmatrix} m_{00} & m_{01} \\ m_{10} & m_{11} \end{pmatrix} \begin{pmatrix} x \\ y \end{pmatrix} + \begin{pmatrix} xoff \\ yoff \end{pmatrix} \qquad \text{(Equation 3–3)}$$

The transformation is defined by six coefficients: the four elements of the multiplying matrix and the translation vectors (*xoff*, *yoff*). Each

element of the matrix is identified by the row (first index) and column (second index) of its location in the matrix. The matrix M multiplies the column vector using the standard rules for matrix multiplication, as shown in Equation 3–4.

$$x' = m_{00}*x + m_{01}*y + xoff \qquad \textit{(Equation 3–4)}$$

$$y' = m_{10}*x + m_{11}*y + yoff$$

Each row of the matrix transforms the column vector by multiplying one element at a time and summing the results. You can easily generalize this type of transformation to n dimensions by using an $n \times n$ matrix and vectors of n elements. The ith transformed coordinate is the result of computing the dot product of ith row of the matrix with the original vector. After performing all the multiplications, you then add in the offset vector, as shown in Equation 3–4.

It is more compact to express a transformation with a single matrix, rather than the combination of a matrix and an offset vector. You can do this by adding an additional row and column to the multiplying matrix and by adding an extra element to each vector that's equal to one. In effect, you have added an extra dimension to all the computations to automatically incorporate the offset vector. The new vector coordinates, with the extra 1 carried with every vector, are called *homogeneous coordinates*. By using homogeneous coordinates, you can now represent the entire transformation with a single matrix, as shown in Equation 3–5.

$$\begin{pmatrix} x' \\ y' \\ 1 \end{pmatrix} = \begin{pmatrix} m_{00} & m_{01} & xoff \\ m_{10} & m_{11} & yoff \\ 0 & 0 & 1 \end{pmatrix} \begin{pmatrix} x \\ y \\ 1 \end{pmatrix} \qquad \textit{(Equation 3–5)}$$

Both the vector and matrix classes use homogeneous coordinates. So, an *n x n* matrix is actually stored with *n+1* rows and *n+1* columns, as shown in Equation 3–5. The *(n+1)st* column stores the translation offset. Any affine transformation of *n*-dimensional vectors can be represented by a matrix in the form of Equation 3–5.

The principal reason for using matrices is to simplify the computation of multiple-coordinate transformations. You can combine any two transformations simply by multiplying their respective matrices. It is easy to show that the result of the matrix multiplication is another affine transformation. Many of the fractal algorithms involve repeatedly applying the same transformation matrix to a set of coordinates. With affine transformations, you do not have to compute the transformed coordinates each time the transformation is applied. You only need to maintain a single matrix and multiply the transformation matrix by the current matrix. This greatly reduces the amount of storage and the amount of computation that must be performed when generating complex fractal figures.

In exact analogy to the vector classes, the *RWFmat_Matrix* class represents a matrix of *float* coefficients. There is also the base-template class *RWFmat_MatrixTemplate* to create matrices with other data types as coefficients. You will only need the *RWFmat_Matrix* type for the software in this book, however. Although you only need square matrices for the code in this book, you can create matrices with whatever dimensions you like using code statements such as the following:

```
RWFmat_Matrix mat1(2,2); // Create 2 x 2 matrix
RWFmat_Matrix mat2(2);   // Also creates 2 x 2 matrix
```

The matrix is initialized to the identity matrix (all are zero except for the diagonal elements, which are set equal to one) when the matrix is created. In this example, the matrices are declared as 2 x 2, but are actually stored as 3 x 3, with the extra row and column added to support homogeneous-coordinate transformations. The matrix-data structure actually stores the coefficients as rows of *n*-dimensional vectors. Furthermore, the subscript operator *[]* has been overloaded for the *RWFmat_Matrix* class so that you can access any row of the matrix as a *RWFvec_Vector* vector. So as in the previous example, *mat1[0]* refers to the top row, *mat1[1]* the second row, and so on. *mat1[0]* is a valid *RWFvec_Vector* vector, and you can use any of the associated member functions for the vector class. In particular, you can access any of the coefficients in a row using a statement such as *mat1[i][j]*, which references the coefficient in the *i*th row and *j*th column. Thus, you can directly refer to the elements of the matrix

as if the matrix were a simple two-dimensional array. By internally structuring the matrix class as a series of row vectors, the code for multiplying a vector by a matrix is simply:

```
RWFmat_Matrix mat(2,2);
RWFvec_Vector vec(2), vecout(2);


...
// Multiply the vector vec by the matrix mat
int nrows = mat.numRows();
for(int i=0; i < nrows; i++)
  // mat[i] is the vector for the ith row
  // The ith element is just the dot product
  // between this row and vec
  vecout[i] = mat[i] * vec;
```

The internal data structures of the vector and matrix classes are basically the same as the similar structures you might create in C. The main difference with the C++ classes is that you can overload the binary operators to greatly simplify the use of vectors and matrices. Additionally, by defining appropriate constructors and destructors, you can treat vectors and matrices just like any other data type, freely declaring them as needed. As an example of the difference, consider the following C code to multiply a vector by a matrix:

```
// In C, it's best to return data pointers
RWFvec_Vector *yourfunc(RWFmat_Matrix *m)
{
RWFvec_Vector *a, *b;

/* Create three-dimensional vectors */
a = RWFvec_Create(3);
b = RWFvec_Create(3);

/* Now create the matrix */
m = RWFmat_Create(3, 3);

/* Now set the elements */
RWFvec_Set(a, 0, 1.0);   /* Element 0 */
```

```
RWFvec_Set(a, 1, 1.0);  /* Element 1 */
RWFvec_Set(a, 2, 1.0);  /* Element 2 */

/* And so forth */
...

/* Get the result */
RWFmat_MultiplyVector(m, a, b);

/* Don't forget to get rid of a */
RWFvec_Delete(a);
return b;
}
```

With the C++ vector and matrix classes of this chapter, the function *your-func()* becomes:

```
RWFvec_Vector yourfunc(RWFmat_Matrix &m)
{
RWFvec_Vector a(3), b(3);     // Calls the constructor
                              // automatically

a = 1.0;        // Assign all elements to 1.0

b = m * a;      // Overload the * operator to do the
                // multiply
// Also, note that the = operator is overloaded as well
// to ensure that the correct data is copied to b

return b;       // Returns a copy of b using the vector
                // copy constructor
// Also, the temporaries a & b are automatically deleted
// on exit
}
```

Using the enhanced features of C++, you can make your programs look more like you actually wrote out the equations in mathematical notation. The differences between C and C++ are even more evident when more complicated operations are used, such as multiplying by several matrices or adding many vectors together.

Specialized matrix operations

The *RWFmat_Matrix* class can handle any number of dimensions, but for the purposes of this book, you will almost exclusively use two- and three-dimensional matrices for coordinate transformations. For two dimensions, any affine transformation can be treated as a combination of four basic transformations: translation (add an *x* and *y* offset), scaling (scale the coordinates by *x* and *y* scale factors), rotation (rotate about the origin), and reflection (change the sign of either *x*, *y*, or both). The same four operations apply to three dimensions as well, except you must include rotation about any of the three axes, rather than just a single rotation angle. You will typically want to apply these operations one step at a time. For instance, to move an object on the screen, you must apply a translation to the object's transformation matrix. To change the size of the object, you can simply scale its corresponding transformation matrix. The *RWFmat_Matrix* provides member functions to make applying these basic transformations simple. Let's look at the *translate()* member function; all the other member functions (*scale()*, *rotate()*, and *reflect()*) have a nearly identical calling sequence.

The *translate()* member function comes in two flavors. The first version specifies a translation by passing an *RWFvec_Vector* as an argument. The matrix is translated by the values stored in the passed vector. You must pass a vector that has the same dimension as the matrix, otherwise the matrix is not changed. To simplify the processing of two- and three-dimensional matrices, a second method is provided so you may call *translate()* with either two *float* arguments (two-dimensional matrix) or three *float* arguments (three-dimensional matrix). The matrix is offset using the scalar arguments. In the case of two dimensions, the arguments represent *x* and *y* offsets; for three dimensions, the arguments represent *x*, *y*, and *z* offsets. You may use either version of *translate()*, depending on the particular needs of the program.

The member functions *scale()*, *rotate()*, and *reflect()* work in an almost identical manner to *translate()*. Because two-dimensional rotation only requires a single angle and three-dimensional rotation requires three angles, *rotate()* accepts either one or three arguments with angles specified in degrees. For the three-dimensional case, the angles represent rotation about the *x*-, *y*-, and *z*-axes respectively. The *reflect()* member function is a little different in that it will take *int* arguments that are either 1 or –1, indicating either to reflect (–1) a particular coordinate, or not to reflect (1). You should note that you can accomplish the same effect as *reflect()* by using negative scale factors with the *scale()* member function. The following code segment illustrates how to use these member functions to perform a series of transformations.

```
RWFmat_Matrix mat(2, 2);

// mat starts as the identity matrix
mat.scale(2.0, 3.0);          // Scale by 2 in x, 3 in y
mat.rotate(45.0);             // Rotate by 45 degrees
mat.translate(100.0, 100.0);  // Move to (100, 100)
```

The order of the transformations is quite important. Each time you use one of the member functions, it multiplies the current matrix from the left-hand side, as shown in Equation 3–5. The resulting matrix from the example code segment would be quite different if the same operations were performed in the reverse order, starting with the call to *translate()*.

A number of other matrix member functions are provided. (The complete list is in Table 3–2.) The most useful of these functions are the overloaded * operator, which lets you multiply a vector by a matrix, returning a transformed vector; the overloaded * operator, which lets you multiply two matrices; and the *identity()* member function, which simply sets the matrix back to the identity matrix (all are zero except for diagonal elements, which are set to one). You'll find as you read through the text and examine the source code that the vector and matrix classes make the software more compact and easier to understand.

Table 3–2. *Friends* and member functions for the *RWFmat_Matrix* class

Member Function	Description
RWFvec_Vector & operator [] *(unsigned int i)*	Returns a reference to the *i*th row vector of the matrix. Because this returns a reference, you may use this value just like any other *RWFvec_Vector*.

Table 3–2. *continued*

Member Function	Description
int nrows(void), int ncols(void)	Returns the number of rows and columns of the matrix, respectively. This size does not include the extra row and column for processing homogeneous coordinates.
RWFmat_Matrix operator (+ or –) *(RWFmat_Matrix &m1,* *RWFmat_Matrix &m2)*	Returns the sum (or difference) of matrices *m1* and *m2*. The matrices are added on an element by the element basis.
RWFmat_Matrix operator * *(RWFmat_Matrix &m1, RWFmat_Matrix &m2)*	Multiplies matrices *m1* and *m2* in the order *m1*m2*
RWFmat_Matrix & operator (+=, –=) *(RWFmat_Matrix &m)*	Adds (or subtracts) the matrix *m* from the base matrix and stores the result back in the base matrix
RWFmat_Matrix & operator *= *(RWFmat_Matrix &m)*	Left multiplies the base matrix by the passed matrix *m*. The result is stored back in the base matrix.
RWFmat_Matrix & operator = *(RWFmat_Matrix &m)*	Copies the matrix *m* to the base matrix
RWFvec_Vector operator * *(RWFmat_Matrix &m, RWFvec_Vector &v)*	Transforms vector *v* using matrix *m* and returns a new vector
RWFvec_Vector & operator *= *(RWFvec_Vector &v)*	Transforms the vector *v* using the base matrix. The result is stored back in vector *v*.
RWFmat_Matrix & identity(void)	Sets the matrix back to the identity matrix
float determinant(void)	Returns the determinant of the matrix

Table 3–2. *continued*

Member Function	Description
RWFmat_Matrix & translate (RWFvec_Vector &v)	Translates the matrix using the vector *v*
RWFmat_Matrix & translate(float xoff, float yoff)	Translates a two-dimensional matrix using the passed offset values
RWFmat_Matrix & translate(float xoff, float yoff, float zoff)	Translates a three-dimensional matrix using the passed offset values.
RWFmat_Matrix & scale(RWFvec_Vector &v)	Scales the matrix using the coefficients in vector *v*
RWFmat_Matrix & scale(float xscale, float yscale)	Scales a two-dimensional matrix using the passed scale values
RWFmat_Matrix & scale(float xscale, float yscale, float zscale)	Scales a three-dimensional matrix using the passed scale values
RWFmat_Matrix & rotate(float angle)	Rotates a two-dimensional matrix through the angle *angle*. The angle is measured in degrees with positive angles corresponding to counterclockwise rotation.
RWFmat_Matrix & rotate(float xangle, yangle, zangle)	Rotates a three-dimensional matrix about the *x*-, *y*-, and *z*-axes respectively
RWFmat_Matrix & reflect(void)	Changes the sign of all axes
RWFmat_Matrix & reflect(int axis)	Changes the sign of the specified axis. If *axis* is zero, then the first coordinate is changed; if *axis* is one, then the second coordinate is reflected, and so forth.

Graphic Objects

You now have a nice set of utilities for manipulating vectors and matrices. The next task is to draw objects on the screen. At this point, we assume you are familiar with basic graphics functions, such as drawing points, lines, and polygons. The Borland C++ BGI graphics package provides a complete set of tools for performing the basic graphics functions, as do many other graphics packages. Many of the references listed in the bibliography describe computer-graphics algorithms in much greater detail than is possible or necessary in this book. We have provided an object-oriented graphics interface to the standard-procedural graphics calls that greatly simplifies the process of drawing objects on screen.

Almost all the graphics packages you have probably encountered are procedurally based: You call functions to draw something on the screen. In this section, you'll read how to take a different approach with object-oriented graphics. Computer graphics is, in fact, an ideal paradigm for object-oriented programming generally. Most graphics drawings are composed of objects. For instance, a typical CAD drawing consists of lines, circles, ellipses, text, and various other kinds of graphical objects. You normally want to operate on either a single object or groups of objects to move, resize, rotate, or perform some other action.

The standard way of storing and processing these objects would be to store the objects in some complex database structure, and then write functions, such as *draw_world()*, that draw all the objects in the database. In effect, *draw_world()* must scan the entire database and call the appropriate procedure to draw each object, using the equivalent of a *switch()* statement to select the correct drawing procedure. Any time you want to add a new object type, you must modify *draw_world()* to include the new function to draw the new object.

A different way to write the *draw_world()* function is for each object to know how to draw itself. Each object therefore has its own *draw()* function. All the *draw_world()* function has to do is to call the *draw()* function for each object in the database. This approach makes it much easier to introduce new objects into the database. The *draw_world()* function does not have to know anything about the objects in the database; all the objects are assumed to know how to draw themselves. The easiest way to see how this works is with a simple example.

The *RWFgraph_Point* class is a very simple graphics object that represents a single pixel on the screen. When you declare an *RWFgraph_Point* object, you can specify its initial location on the screen as a set of integer *x*- and *y*-coordinates. There are two basic member functions needed to draw the point, *setColor()*, which sets the drawing color, and *draw()*, which actually draws the point on the screen. You can draw a point on the screen with the following code segment:

```
RWFgraph_Point p1(100, 100);

rwf_graphInitialize(0);    // Initialize graphics
p1.setColor(WHITE);        // Draw in white
p1.draw();
```

All the other graphics objects are nearly as simple to use. Because graphics objects have many common attributes, such as drawing color, position, orientation, and size, it is natural to create a base class containing all the common attributes. Specific objects are then derived from the base class. The class *RWFgraph_Object* serves as the base class for all graphics objects. Table 3–3 lists all the public member functions for a two-dimensional *RWFgraph_Object*. As you'll see, the *RWFgraph_Object* supports both two- and three-dimensional objects with equal ease.

Table 3–3. Member functions for the *RWFgraph_Object* graphics base class

Member Function	Description
void setColor(int color)	Sets the drawing color to the passed value. This value is normally treated as a palette index.
void setColor(int red, int green, int blue)	Sets a specific RGB value to draw with
void draw(void)	Draws the object on the screen

Table 3–3. *continued*

Member Function	Description
void move(float xoff, float yoff)	Moves the object by an amount *xoff* horizontally and *yoff* vertically
void scale(float xscale, float yscale)	Scales the object by *xscale* vertically and *yscale* vertically
void rotate(float angle)	Rotates the object by the specified angle. *angle* is in degrees, with a positive angle corresponding to counterclockwise rotation.
void setMatrix(RWFmat_Matrix &mat)	Sets the object's transformation matrix equal to the passed matrix
RWFmat_Matrix getMatrix(void)	Returns the object's current transformation matrix
*RWFgraph_Object & operator * (RWFmat_Matrix &m, RWFgraph_Object &object)*	Multiplies *object*'s transformation matrix by the passed matrix *m*. This has the same effect as the code statement: *object.setMatrix(m * object.getMatrix());*
*RWFgraph_Object & operator *= (RWFmat_Matrix &m)*	Multiplies *object*'s transformation matrix by the passed matrix *m*. This has the same effect as the code statement: *object.setMatrix(m * object.getMatrix());*

Two-dimensional objects

The main function you'll find of interest in Table 3–3 is, of course, *draw()*, which actually puts something on the screen. However, you'll notice several functions in Table 3–3 that let you move the object or change its size or orientation. All graphics objects have an associated transformation matrix. This matrix defines the position, size, and orientation of the object on the screen. Whenever an object is drawn, all coordinates defining the object are transformed using the transformation matrix to convert the original object coordinates to actual screen coordinates. The *draw()* routine for each object must perform the transformation whenever the object is drawn.

The member functions *setMatrix()* and *getMatrix()* let you set and retrieve the transformation matrix directly. You can therefore use any of the standard matrix functions directly, such as *identity()* or multiplying by another matrix, on the transformation matrix of a graphics object. The fractal-drawing routines of the following chapters use this capability extensively to generate a transformation matrix and then apply it to an object.

For the purposes of the software in this book, you only need a few graphics objects. You have already seen the point class *RWFgraph_Point*. It only carries two data values, its pixel coordinates. The member functions *setCoord()* and *getCoord(),* respectively, set the current position or retrieve it. You may pass either a single argument referencing a two-dimensional vector to *setCoord()* or two separate arguments, a direct *x*- and *y*-location. If you pass two *float* values to *getCoord()*, it will return the current position in those variables. If, however, you call *getCoord()* with no arguments, it returns a two-dimensional vector containing the current position. This method of calling *getCoord()* is quite useful when you need to transform the current position with a matrix.

The next step up from the point class is the *RWFgraph_Line* class, which represents a line drawn between two points. The member functions *setFirst()* and *setEnd(),* respectively, set the starting and ending point of the line segment. As with *setCoord()* and *getCoord()*, you may pass either two arguments of *x* and *y* or a two-dimensional vector containing the starting points. The constructor for *RWFgraph_Line* lets you specify both the start and end points by declaring the line with four arguments. If you declare an *RWFgraph_Line* with no arguments, a unit line segment from (0,0) to (1,0) is created.

The next class is the *RWFgraph_Polyline* class. This class defines a connected set of line segments, stored as an array of points. The polyline is

drawn simply by drawing connecting lines between each successive pair of points. The subscript operator *[]* is overloaded for this class, such that *polyline[i]* returns the *i*th point of the polyline as a *RWFgraph_Point* object. So, you can use references such as *polyline[i].setCoord()* to set the coordinates of the *i*th point of the polyline or *polyline[i].getCoord()* to retrieve the current position. The member function *numPoints()* returns the number of points in the polyline.

The following code segment shows a simple example of how to create a polyline defining a unit square (sides of length one):

```
RWFgraph_Polyline poly(4);    // Initially contains five points

// Define a unit square
poly[0].setCoord(0, 0);
poly[1].setCoord(1, 0);
poly[2].setCoord(1, 1);
poly[3].setCoord(0, 1);

// Now center the square at the origin
poly.move(-0.5, -0.5);
```

The *RWFgraph_Polygon* class is almost identical to *RWFgraph_Polyline*. The only difference is that *RWFgraph_Polygon* represents a closed figure by connecting the last point with the first. The first point is actually stored twice, once at the beginning and once at the end of the list of points. An *RWFgraph_Polygon* has all the same member functions as *RWF-graph_Polyline*.

The final graphics object is provided primarily for variety. The *RWFgraph_Circle* object defines a circle. The constructor for this object lets you specify the center position and radius. If you do not pass any arguments, a unit circle centered at (0,0) is created. By using the *scale()* member function, you can turn the circle into an ellipse by scaling the *x*- and *y*-axes differently. The member functions *setRadius()* and *setCenter()* let you explicitly set the radius and center of the circle, although in most cases it is actually more desirable to use *scale()* and *move()* to perform the equivalent operations on a unit circle.

Table 3–4 lists all the basic two-dimensional graphics objects along with their specialized member functions. You'll see many examples of how to draw with these objects and how they are used to define fractal objects in the next several chapters.

Table 3–4. The basic two-dimensional graphics-object classes and their associated member functions. All these objects are derived from the *RWFgraph_Circle* class, and therefore have the same member functions, as shown in Table 3–3.

Class Name	Member Functions	Description
RWFgraph_Point	*RWFgraph_Point(float x, float y)*	Constructor for RWFgraph_Point. Sets the initial position to (*x*, *y*).
	void setCoord(float x, float y)	Sets the coordinates of the point to the passed values
	void setCoord(RWFvec_Vector &v)	Sets the coordinates of the point to the values in the passed two-dimensional vector
	void getCoord(float &x, float &y)	Returns the coordinates of the point to the passed variables
	RWFvec_Vector &getCoord(void)	Returns the coordinates of the point as a two-dimensional vector

Table 3–4. *continued*

Class Name	Member Functions	Description
RWFgraph_Line	*RWFgraph_Line(float x1, float y1, float x2, float y2)*	Constructor for *RWFgraph_Line*. Sets the line segment to run from (*x1, y1*) to (*x2, y2*).
	void setFirst(float x, float y)	Sets the first point of the line segment
	void setEnd(float x, float y)	Sets the last point of the line segment
	void setFirst(RWFvec_Vector &v)	Sets the first point using a two-dimensional vector
	void setEnd(RWFvec_Vector &v)	Sets the last point using a two-dimensional vector
RWFgraph_Polyline	*RWFgraph_Polyline(int npoints)*	Constructor for *RWFgraph_Polyline*. This creates a polyline of *npoints* points.
	RWFgraph_Point & operator [] (unsigned int i)	Returns a reference to the *i*th point of the polyline as an *RWFgraph_Point*
RWFgraph_Polygon	*RWFgraph_Polygon(int npoints)*	Constructor for *RWFgraph_Polygon*. This creates a polyline of *npoints* points.
	RWFgraph_Point & operator [] (unsigned int i)	Returns a reference to the *i*th point of the polygon as an *RWFgraph_Point*

Table 3–4. *continued*

Class Name	Member Functions	Description
RWFgraph_Circle	*RWFgraph_Circle(float x, float y, float radius)*	Constructor for *RWFgraph_Circle.* This creates a circle centered at (*x, y*) with a radius of *radius.*
	void setRadius(float radius)	Sets a new radius for the circle
	void setCenter(float x, float y)	Sets a new center for the circle
	float getRadius(void)	Returns the current radius of the circle
	void getCenter(float &x, float &y)	Returns the current center of the circle

Three-dimensional objects

The graphics object described so far let you draw two-dimensional objects on the screen. However, the same classes can define three-dimensional objects as well. All the objects are defined by series of coordinates, which are stored as vectors. You can just as easily store three-dimensional coordinates with a *RWFgraph_Vector* as you can store two-dimensional coordinates. So all the previous classes may use three-dimensional vectors wherever two-dimensional vectors are used, such as in the calls to *setCoord()* and *getCoord()*. Furthermore, the functions *setCoord()*, *getCoord()* and the constructors for the *RWFgraph_Point*, *RWFgraph_Line*, *RWFgraph_Polyline,* and *RWFgraph_Polygon* classes have been overloaded to accept three *float* arguments of *x*-, *y*-, and *z*-coordinates to specify initial positions. In almost all respects, you can treat three-dimensional objects the same way you would treat two-dimensional ones.

Transforming three-dimensional objects is as easy as the two-dimensional ones. The *RWFgraph_Object* member functions of *move()*, *scale()*, and *rotate()* are all overloaded to accept three arguments for three-dimensional objects, instead of just the two arguments shown in Table 3–3.

Table 3–5 shows the additional three-dimensional member functions for *RWFgraph_Object*.

Table 3–5. Specialized three-dimensional member functions for the *RWFgraph_Object* class. These functions have no effect if the object is already defined as a two-dimensional object.

Member Function	Description
void draw(RWFgraph_ViewGeometry &vg)	Draws a three-dimensional object in perspective using the passed viewing-geometry structure
void move(float xoff, float yoff, float zoff)	Moves the object three spaces by an amount (*xoff, yoff, zoff*)
void scale(float xscale, float yscale, float zscale)	Scales the object in all three axes by (*xscale,yscale,zscale*). You use this function to change the size of the object.
void rotate(float xangle, float yangle, float zangle)	Rotates the object about the three coordinate axes

By default, an object is considered two-dimensional unless you either use a three-dimensional constructor (such as *RWFgraph_Point(float x, float y, float z)*) or you explicitly set the parameters of the object to three-dimensional coordinates. When you create a *RWFgraph_Polygon*, for instance, the object is considered two-dimensional. If, however, you use *setCoord()* with any of the three arguments or pass a three-dimensional vector, then the polygon is considered three-dimensional. The internal transformation matrix is automatically adjusted to the proper number of dimensions. The member functions to set three-dimensional coordinates are the same as those presented in Table 3–4, with the only difference being that you pass three coordinates instead of two to functions like *setCoord()*.

The one major difference between two- and three-dimensional objects is in the *draw()* member function. Notice that the *draw()* function in Table 3–5 requires an argument, namely a structure that defines the perspective viewing geometry. To draw three-dimensional objects on your two-dimensional screen requires specifying the geometric layout shown in Figure 3–1. The simplest way to think of the viewing geometry is as if you were positioning a camera to take a picture of the three-dimensional object. You must specify where the camera is located, what direction you are looking, and the field-of-view (the field-of-view effectively defines the type of camera lens you are using, which can be anything from a wide-angle to telephoto lens). Additionally, you can specify the lighting conditions for the scene. You can also specify what part of the screen the image should be drawn. (By default, the entire screen is used.) The *RWFgraph_ViewingGeometry* class lets you define a viewing geometry to use in drawing three-dimensional objects. Table 3–6 lists all the member functions for the *RWFgraph_ViewingGeometry* class.

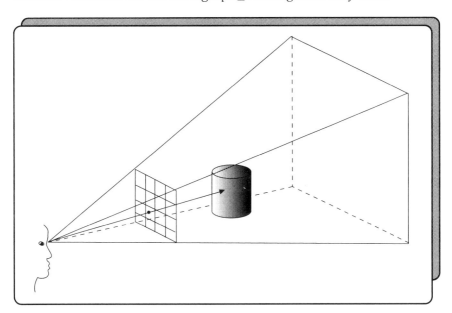

Figure 3–1. Geometrical setup defining the perspective viewing geometry for three-dimensional objects.

Table 3–6. Member functions for the *RWFgraph_ViewingGeometry* class

Member Function	Description
void setEyepoint(float x, float y, float z)	Sets the location of the camera in three-dimensional space. The default location is (0, 0, 0).

Table 3–6. *continued*

Member Function	Description
void setEyepoint(RWFvec_Vector &eyepoint)	Sets the location of the camera in three-dimensional space
RWFvec_Vector getEyepoint(void)	Returns the current eyepoint position
void setEyeDirection(RWFvec_Vector &dirvec)	A vector that points in the direction you want to look. The default-view direction is (1,0,0).
RWFvec_Vector getEyeDirection(void)	Returns the current eyepoint direction
void setFOV(float xfov, float yfov)	Set the field-of-view angles. These angles are measured in degrees. Large angles create a wide-angle lens effect (large perspective changes), while small angles create a telephoto effect (small perspective changes).
void setOrientation(float angle)	Sets the orientation angle of your view. A nonzero value rolls the view about the view-direction vector.
float getOrientation(void)	Returns the current orientation angle.
void setScreen(int x1, int y1, int x2, int y2)	Sets the output on the screen to the specified location, where (*x1, y1*) is the upper-left corner and (*x2, y2*) is the lower-right corner. By default, this is initialized to be the entire display screen.
void getScreen(int &x1, int &y1, int &x2, int &y2)	Returns the current output screen rectangle in the passed variables

Table 3–6. *continued*

Member Function	Description
RWFvec_Vector getProjectedCoordinates (RWFvec_Vector &v)	Transforms the passed-coordinate vector into the three-dimensional screen coordinate system in which *z* measures the distance from the eyepoint to the passed coordinate vector *v*.
void setLight(RWFvec_Vector &dirvec)	Sets the direction of the global light source. In effect, this sets the position of the sun.
void setLightAttributes(float ambient, float contrast)	Sets the effective ambient (minimum) light levels and the amount of lighting contrast

The three-dimensional version of the *draw()* function projects the object to the screen using the standard perspective-projection techniques (for a complete description of this technique, refer to Chapter 6 of the book *Computer Graphics: Principles and Practice*, which is included in this book's bibliography). *draw()* handles the coordinate transformations, "backface" removal (does not draw an object that faces away from the eyepoint), clipping, and the final perspective transformations to generate a two-dimensional object to draw on the screen. So as you can see, three-dimensional drawing is a natural extension of the two-dimensional object-drawing routines. You'll see extensive applications of three-dimensional graphics objects for drawing fractal terrain and clouds in Chapters 10 and 11.

The graphic-object classes are greatly simplified by the use of the vector class to store coordinates and the matrix class that perform transformations. With these classes, it is quite easy to combine two- and three-dimensional objects into an intuitive set of graphics classes, as you can see from the great similarity of the member functions for the two cases. Because of their common calling conventions, there are really very few functions you need to remember to create complex graphics objects in either two or three dimensions.

Device independent graphics

One of the design goals for the software in this book is to ensure that the programs can be run on as many different systems as possible without rewriting the code. The *RWFgraph* class library uses the Borland C++ BGI package to actually draw the objects, but you can easily adapt the same objects to other graphics libraries by simply modifying the *draw()* member functions for each object. All the graphics software in this book uses the graphic-objects library, so the programs work with most other graphics packages. There are, however, several global functions listed in Table 3–7 that are used by the programs in this book. All these functions can be found in the *rwfgraph.c* module.

Table 3–7. Global graphics functions.

Function	Description
void rwf_graphInitialize(int mode)	Initializes the displays and sets the display mode to the passed value. This function performs the same operation as the BGI function *initgraph()*.
void rwf_graphSetPaletteIndex (int index, int red, int green, int blue)	Sets the specified palette index to the passed RGB value
void rwf_graphEraseScreen(void)	Erases the entire screen
int rwf_graphGetMaxX()	Gets the maximum *x*-coordinate for the display mode. The screen is (*rwf_graphGetMaxX()* + 1) pixels wide, or horizontal.
int rwf_graphGetMaxY()	Gets the maximum *x*-coordinate for the display mode. The screen is (*rwf_graphGetMaxY()* + 1) pixels long, or vertical.
void rwf_graphClose(void)	Releases the display. Equivalent to the BGI function *closegraph()*.

Although the graphics classes are easy to use, they do not represent very complicated objects. In the following chapters, you'll learn how to create new fractal objects that are derived from *RWFgraph_Object*. The most common way to create an object, however, is to define an object as a collection of the more primitive graphic elements. Three-dimensional models, for instance, are usually defined as collections of polygons. An example of such a model is the cube, which is defined as having six four-sided polygons. You might then want to take an element like the cube and use it to build even more complicated models. Figure 3–2 illustrates this idea in two dimensions. To create models built from more primitive components, you need a common way of storing multiple objects in a table that can be treated as a single graphics object. This leads to the final object class of this chapter, the table class.

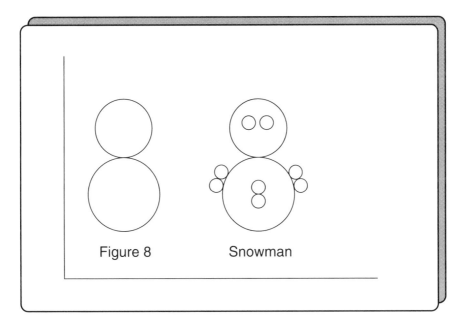

Figure 3–2. You can define a figure eight as two adjoining circles, as shown on the left. You can then create more elaborate objects by combining multiple figure eights, as shown on the right.

A Simple Table

As your final class for this chapter, we present a generic container class for storing multiple related items in a table, similar to a C array. Creating and maintaining lists of objects in a typical C program is usually painful (or at least mildly annoying) because you must redefine the table-management routines for each object type you might want to keep in the table. Several of the fractal objects in the later chapters, for instance, need to store an array of matrices. Other objects require lists of graphics objects such as polygons.

There are many ways to define such a list, but with the C++ template, you can define your own container classes, or a structure for holding a group of related objects, to create a table that can hold any type of object. So, your table-management routines are only defined once in the template. Furthermore, you can easily change how the table is stored without affecting any of the programs that use the template-table class. To your program, a table always looks like a simple array, even though the table might be internally stored as an array, a linked list, a tree, or some other structure. The table class takes care of all the mundane list-management chores, such as creating new elements as needed, deleting the structures when the table is destroyed, and maintaining the order of elements in the table.

The basic table-template class is *RWFlist_SimpleTable*. You create a table to hold a specific kind of object with *typedef* declarations, similar to the way *RWFvec_Vector* is declared. You can declare a data type to hold a table of matrices with a declaration of the form as follows, for instance:

```
typedef RWFlist_SimpleTable<RWFmat_Matrix>
        RWFlist_MatrixTable;
```

Accessing an element in the table is made simple by overloading the subscript operator *[]*. This lets you get individual elements as if they were stored in a simple array. So, you can always get the *i*th element of a table with the expression *table[i]*. (This returns a reference to the *i*th element.) In most respects, you treat an *RWFlist_SimpleTable* exactly like an array.

But unlike an array, the table class automatically manages the size of the array for you, creating new elements as needed. The *size()* member function returns the number of elements in the table.

Whenever you access an element of the array with the subscript operator, the table checks to see if the index is less than the current table size. If the index is greater than the current table size, the table class automatically extends the table to contain enough elements to access the element at the specified index. The *setMaximumSize()* member function lets you set the maximum number of entries allowed in a table. If you try to access elements beyond this maximum size, an error is generated and your program is terminated. The dynamic-allocation capability of the table class lets you easily add new elements to a table. The following code segment, for instance, creates a 10-element table of three-by-three matrices:

```
RWFlist_MatrixTable mtable; // Creates a 0 length table
RWFmat_Matrix m(3, 3);

for(i=0; i < 10; i++) {
  mtable[i] = m;
  m.scale(0.5, 0.5, 0.5);  // Scale the matrix by 1/2
}
```

In this example, there is no explicit size set for the table. The size is determined by the last access to the table, which in this case was the index value nine. An *RWFlist_SimpleTable* stores copies of objects, so you can use the same object to assign elements, just as if the table were stored as an array. When the table is deleted, all the individual elements are deleted as well by calling their respective destructors. You may also use the member function *reset()* to reset the table size back to zero.

The source file *rwflist.hpp* contains the complete definition of the *RWFlist_SimpleTable* class template. The definition is actually fairly simple, taking advantage of the C++ capability to overload the subscript operator and return references that can be used on the left-hand size of an =. Table 3–8 lists all the member functions for the *RWFlist_SimpleTable* template class.

Table 3–8. Member functions for the *RWFlist_SimpleTable* template class.

Member Function	Description
TYPE & operator [] (unsigned int i)	Returns the *i*th element of the table. If the table is not big enough to contain the *i*th element, it is extended to the maximum size possible.
int size(void)	Returns the current number of elements in the table.
void setMaximumSize(int n)	Sets the maximum table size possible. (The default maximum size is 100 elements.)
int getMaximumSize(void)	Returns the maximum size setting for the table.
void reset(void)	Resets the table to zero elements. All the current elements of the table are deleted.
void remove(unsigned int i)	Deletes the *i*th element of the table. The size of the table is reduced by one.
void swap(int i, int j)	Swaps the *i*th and *j*th element of the table. A temporary table-data type is used to perform the swap.

As an example of how to use the *RWFlist_SimpleTable* class, let's consider the problem posed at the end of the previous section—defining a new graphics entity as a collection of other graphics objects. This problem can now be easily solved with the *RWFlist_SimpleTable* class. By using the following statements, you can define two different types of tables, one as a table of objects and the other as a table of pointers to objects:

```
typedef RWFlist_SimpleTable<RWFgraph_Object *>
        RWFlist_ObjectPtrTable;
```

This declaration defines a table of pointers to *RWFgraph_Object* objects. You can store pointers to any of the primitive graphic objects derived from *RWFgraph_Object* in this table. You only need the the following code to draw the objects in the table:

```
RWFlist_ObjectPtrTable otable;

for(int i=0; i < otable.size(); i++)
  otable[i]->draw();
```

With a slight change to the definition of *RWFlist_ObjectPtrTable*, you can make it a true graphics object of its own, with all the same member functions as an *RWFgraph_Object*. To create any new graphics object, you derive the new class from the *RWFgraph_Object* class. You can do the same thing with a table of objects. So as you can see, the table of objects becomes a new graphics object with the following declaration:

```
class RWFgraph_ObjectList : public RWFgraph_Object,
                            public RWFlist_ObjectPtrTable
{
};
```

This definition uses the multiple-inheritance feature of C++ to create a new class that is a combination of both the base-graphics class and the table class. *RWFgraph_ObjectList* has the member functions of both *RWFgraph_Object* and *RWFlist_ObjectList*. To complete the class, you need only define the *draw()* member function for the list of objects. The two-dimensional *draw()* member function for this class is defined as follows:

```
void RWFgraph_ObjectList::draw(void)
{
  RWFmat_Matrix temp_matrix;
  RWFgraph_Object *optr;

  for(int i=0; i < size(); i++) {
    // Get the pointer to the ith object
    // Because this is an RWFlist_SimpleTable, you can
    // use [] to access each element.
```

```
        optr = (*this)[i];
        // Composite each object's matrix with the matrix
        // for the entire list.
        temp_matrix = optr->getMatrix();
        // tmatrix is the private matrix for the
        // RWFgraph_Object class
        optr->setMatrix(tmatrix * temp_matrix);
        optr->draw();
        // Restore the object's original matrix
        optr->setMatrix(temp_matrix);
    }
}
```

The three-dimensional *draw()* function is similarly defined. With the *RWFgraph_ObjectList* class, you can now combine any collection of graphics objects into a single object. If you transform this object, all the objects in the table will be transformed together. For instance, you can define a cube once, store it as a *RWFgraph_ObjectList* of polygons, and then use the cube just like any other graphics object. Furthermore, you can create new objects that are composed of collections of *RWFgraph_ObjectList* objects. So, you can create a stack of cubes as another *RWFgraph_ObjectList*, in which each element of that list is the "cube" object. With this single additional class, you can create a truly hierarchical graphics database, thanks to the multiple-inheritance capabilities of C++.

Graphic Conclusions

With the tools in this chapter, you now have an elegant and straightforward means of manipulating vectors and matrices that you can use to create and draw both two- and three-dimensional graphic objects, and to create multiple-objects tables of any data type. By exploiting the operator-overloading and multiple-inheritance capabilities of C++, these classes are very easy to use when compared to their C equivalents. With the C++ template capability, you need only define complex structures such as the dynamic *RWFlist_SimpleTable* class once, and then use the same structure with all your different data types.

Affine transformations and graphics are essential tools in the study of fractals. Making the tools both intuitive and easy to work with helps not only with understanding the algorithms, but in creating reliable software quickly. You'll see many examples in the following chapters of how to use these classes to greatly simplify the coding of various fractal algorithms. In the next chapter, you'll learn a conundrum: how to generate random numbers in a controlled and predictable manner. With the tools of this chapter and the random-number generator of the next chapter, you'll be ready to begin exploring the fractal universe.

Probability, Statistics, and Random Numbers

O ne of the primary uses of fractal modeling techniques is to recreate the seemingly random patterns found in nature. Modeling such features requires the ability to generate long sequences of "random" numbers. However, to consistently reproduce a given fractal curve, you do not want to to use truly random numbers. Instead, you would like to create a reproducible sequence in which given the same starting point, you always generate the same sequence. In this chapter, you will see how to generate such random sequences in a very controlled and portable manner. You will also learn how to generate random sequences according to a prescribed distribution, such as the normal distribution (or bell-curve distribution), the Poisson distribution, and several others. You will then see how these various random-number generators are applied in several applications and in fractal programs in particular.

Not Quite Random

In a strict sense, computer-generated random numbers are not really random at all; rather they are generated using completely deterministic methods. Each time the random-number routine is called, the next returned random number is generally a function of or, in some way, dependent upon the previously generated value, or values. Because of this functional dependency, computer-generated random numbers are referred to as *pseudorandom*, meaning that they are not truly unpredictable. Furthermore, such sequences are inherently reproducible because if you start with the same input or initial value, you generate the same sequence.

While predictability and reproducibility may seem odd attributes for a random-number generator, they are, in fact, essential features for fractal programming. Consider the Koch Curve, or snowflake curve, presented in Chapter 1. One way to introduce randomness into this curve is to vary the height of the generator at each recursion step. To produce a consistent drawing independent of the drawing scale, the same height for the generator must be used each time a particular segment is replaced. Consider Figure 4–1. In the first recursion step, each side of the hexagon is replaced by a generator with a random-height displacement. In the second step, the sides are again replaced by copies of the generator. If you wanted to zoom in on a piece of the curve, it is important that your drawing program generate the same random heights for each generator as in the unmagnified view. If the random sequence is not reproducible, then the curve would appear different each time it is redrawn as different random-height variations are introduced. Drawing consistent fractal curves requires a mechanism for introducing random variations in a very controlled fashion.

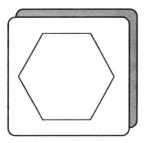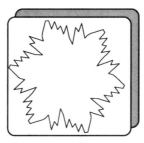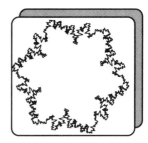

Figure 4–1. Generating a random snowflake curve. By processing the sides of the curve in the same order, you can use a pseudorandom-number generator to recreate the same generator heights at each recursion level.

Often, it is unimportant that a random-number generator be truly random. The important feature you need is for the sequences to be free of any apparent pattern. Technically, this means that the output of the random-number generator should be a sequence of statistically uncorrelated numbers. Practically, this means that the sequence should not have an obvious pattern, such as periodically repeating itself with a relatively short period. The main requirement from your application program is that the sequence appears totally random and any patterns in the sequences do not manifest themselves in objectionable ways. Generally, any type of short-period periodicity in the random-number generator will show up in any application that needs lots of random numbers, such as a fractal program. It is therefore best if you minimize any of these artifacts of computer-generated random numbers.

Uniform Randomness

There are two basic requirements for a pseudorandom-number generator. First, it must be able to generate a sequence of uncorrelated numbers without obvious patterns; and, second, it must be able to entirely reproduce any sequence given the same starting value. Let's begin with generating the simplest type of sequence, one in which the random numbers are uniformly distributed.

A *uniform* distribution is one in which for a given range, any number in that range is equally likely to occur. Consider the problem of generating uniformly distributed numbers in the range from 0.0 to 1.0. The function used in the software that accompanies this book is called *rwf_randRand()*. Using this function, you can generate uniformly distributed random numbers for any desired range from *a* to *b*, with the following expression:

```
x = (rwf_randRand() * (b - a)) + a;
```

The standard C library provides two functions for random-number generation, *srand()* and *rand()*. *srand()* takes a single integer value as an argument. This passed value is referred to as a *seed*, and is used to initialize

the random-number generation. By using the same value for seed, you get the same sequence of random numbers, thus, satisfying the second criteria. The *rand()* function is the actual random-number generator and returns random values of type *int* ranging from 0 to *RAND_MAX*, where *RAND_MAX* is a constant normally defined to be the largest positive value for a variable of type *int*. You generate random numbers in the range from 0.0 to 1.0 using an expression such as:

```
x = rand() / (float)(RAND_MAX + 1.0);
```

On most systems, *rand()* is not a very good random-number generator to generate truly uniformly distributed values. It uses a method known as *linear congruential generation* to generate each successive value. The algorithm is simply:

```
next_val = (a*prev_val + c) % m
```

Each time *rand()* is called, it generates the next value using the previous value. Whether the values *a*, *c*, and *m* are used depends on the particular implementation and hardware used. This computation is very fast, requiring only one multiply, one add, and one modulus operation. However, this method often produces less than ideal results, especially if the constants *a*, *c*, and *m* are poorly chosen. However, it would be nice to retain the efficiency of this basic approach.

One way to improve the basic method is not to use *rand()* directly to generate the random number, but to use it to generate an index into a precomputed table of random numbers. Each time you access an entry in the table, you replace the entry by calling *rand()* again. Thus, you are effectively using *rand()* twice, once to select a random table index and once to replace that entry of the table after the entry is used. This approach removes virtually any periodicity of the *rand()* routine by buffering accesses through the table. The implementation used for *rwf_randRand()* is shown in Listing 4–1.

Listing 4-1. Listing for *rwf_randRand()* and *rwf_randRandSrand()* using table lookup to remove periodic artifacts from the system-supplied *rand()* function.

```
#define rwf_randRand_TABLE_SIZE 101
#define rwf_randRand_INITIAL_SEED 3030303L

// These are known to both rwf_randRandSrand() and rwf_randRand()
static int first_time = 1;
static float ran_table[rwf_randRand_TABLE_SIZE];
static float last_rand;

float rwf_randRand(void)
{
 int index;

 if(first_time)
  rwf_randRandSrand(rwf_randRand_INITIAL_SEED);

 index = NINT(rwf_randRand_TABLE_SIZE * last_rand);
 last_rand = ran_table[index];
 ran_table[index] = rand() / (RAND_MAX + 1.0);

 return last_rand;
}

void rwf_randRandSrand(unsigned long iseed)
{
 srand(iseed);
 for(int i=0; i < rwf_randRand_TABLE_SIZE; i++) {
  ran_table[i] = rand() / (RAND_MAX + 1.0);
 }
 last_rand = rand() / (RAND_MAX + 1.0);
 first_time = 0;
}
```

Notice that *rwf_randRand()* is nearly as efficient as *rand()*, requiring only one additional scaling and indexing operation in addition to a call to *rand()*. *rwf_randRand()* produces very acceptable sequences of uncorrelated, uniformly distributed random numbers. It is the basis for all the random-number generation used throughout the software listed in this book.

Other Distributions

Now that you have a set of routines for generating uniformly distributed random numbers, the next feature you need is the ability to generate random sequences with other types of distributions. Recall from your long forgotten probability course that a distribution is characterized by its *density* function. For a continuous variable, the density function $p(x)*dx$ represents the probability that a random variable will take on a value between x and $x + dx$. To find the probability that a random variable will take on a value between a and b, you evaluate the integral of $p(x)$ from a to b:

$$Prob(a \leq x < b) = \int_a^b p(x)\, dx \qquad \textbf{(Equation 4–1)}$$

For the uniform distribution generated by *rwf_randRand()*, $p(x) = 1$ for $0 \leq x < 1$, and $p(x) = 0$ for all other values of x. What you would like is to be able to generate any desired distribution using the uniform distribution computed by *rwf_randRand()*. So assume that you have a desired density, $p(y)$. You want to find the invertible function $G()$, such that the random variable $Y = G(X)$ has the probability density $p(y)$, where X is uniformly distributed in the interval $[0, 1]$. The probability that Y is between a and b is the same as the probability that X is between $G^{-1}(a)$ and $G^{-1}(b)$. Because X is uniformly distributed, this probability is simply $ABS(G^{-1}(b) - G^{-1}(a))$. Using this result leads to Equation 4–2.

$$\int_a^b p(y)\, dy = |G^{-1}(b) - G^{-1}(a)| \qquad \textbf{(Equation 4–2)}$$

Because Equation 4–2 is true for all a and b, then $G^{-1}()$ is the integral of $p()$ (or, possibly, $-G^{-1}()$ if $G()$ is a decreasing function). Therefore, $G()$ is the inverse of the integral of $p()$, as shown in Equation 4–3:

$$G(x) = (\smallint\, p(x)\, dx)^{-1} \qquad \textbf{(Equation 4–3)}$$

The function you need for $G()$ is the inverse of the integral of the desired density function $p(x)$. Note that if $p(x)$ is a decreasing function, then you use $-p(x)$ to get the proper sign in the integral. While this is quite a useful result, it can still lead to problems in some cases. Particularly in the instance when there may not be a closed-form solution for the integral of $p(x)$ and even if there is, there may not be a simple way of finding the inverse function. However, there are still many cases that can be solved using Equation 4–3.

The exponential distribution has $p(x) = e^{-x}$, for instance. The integral of $p(x)$ is $-e^{-x}$. Because e^{-x} is a decreasing function, you must actually integrate $-e^{-x}$, yielding e^{-x}. The inverse function yields $G(x) = -ln(x)$. Thus, you can create a routine to generate exponentially distributed random sequences with code such as the following:

```
float rwf_randRandExponential(void)
{
 double x;

 x = rwf_randRand();
 return (-log(x));
}
```

The two distributions used most frequently in this book are the uniform and normal, or Gaussian, distributions. You already know how to generate uniformly distributed sequences. Let's see how to generate normal distributions using the uniformly distributed random sequences from *rwf_randRand()*.

Normal Distributions

A plot of the standard normal distribution is shown in Figure 4–2. It is the familiar bell-shaped curve that appears throughout any study of probability and statistics. Normal distribution occurs so frequently, primarily as a result of the central-limit theorem, which states that the sum of any large number of independent observations of a random variable, such as a person's height, water temperature, intelligence, and so on, will tend toward a normal distribution. It is therefore reasonable to use normal distributions to introduce randomness into a computer model, fractal or otherwise. Chapter 9, for instance, introduces terrain modeling in which random terrain heights are introduced during the fractal computations. In the absence of other criteria, it is reasonable to assume that the variations in height are normally distributed. You will see many examples throughout the book of how normal distributions are used to introduce these variations.

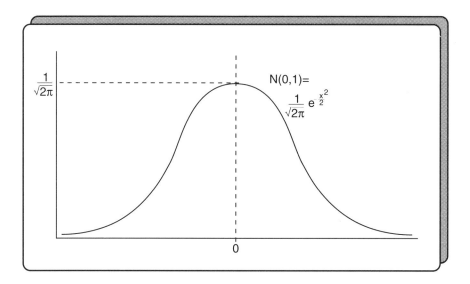

Figure 4–2. Plot of the standard normal, or Gaussian, density function.

The standard normal distribution has the density function shown in Equation 4–3. In general, a normal distribution is characterized by two parameters, the mean, or average value, and the variance σ^2. The standard deviation is just σ, the square root of the variance, and provides a measure of how far you expect the random variable to deviate from the mean. The standard normal distribution has a mean of 0 and a standard deviation of 1. Let's first see how to generate random sequences using the standard normal distribution, and then how to turn those sequences into ones with an arbitrary normal distribution.

$$p(x) = (1/sqrt(2*\pi))*e^{-(x*x)/2}$$

(Equation 4–4)

Unfortunately, the function shown in Equation 4–4 cannot be integrated. You therefore cannot use the method shown in the previous section to find a suitable function $G(x)$, as was done for the exponential distribution. Instead, you must take a different approach and use a bona-fide trick to find an appropriate transformation.

Joint Distributions

Consider the following function:

$$p(x,y) = [(1/sqrt(2*\pi))*e^{-(x*x)/2}] * [(1/sqrt(2*\pi))*e^{-(y*y)/2}]$$

(Equation 4–5)

Equation 4–5 represents the joint density of two independent, normally distributed, random variables X and Y. In polar coordinates, you have $R = r^2 = x^2 + y^2$, and $\theta = atan(y/x)$ (in which θ is just the angle the point (x, y) makes with respect to the x-axis on a two-dimensional plot). Then $p(x, y)$ can be rewritten as:

$$p(R, \theta) = (1/(2*\pi))*e^{-R/2}$$

(Equation 4–6)

Now, if x and y are uniformly distributed from −1 to +1, and you only consider the points (x, y) inside the unit circle, then R is uniformly distributed as well. (This is an exercise left to the reader!) The question now becomes: What function of R has the exponential density function $p(R,\theta)$? This particular problem was solved previously: The answer is $G(R) = -2*log(R)$ (the additional factor of −2 occurs because there is an $R/2$ in the exponent instead of just R). θ is uniformly distributed from 0 to $2*\pi$.

But where does this get you? First, you can generate a uniformly distributed R from two uniformly distributed random variables, say $v1$ and $v2$, as $R = v1^2 + v2^2$. Next, you can generate the desired joint distribution $p(R, \theta)$ by replacing R with $G(R) = -2*log(R)$. From Equation 4–4, both of the Cartesian coordinates x and y are independent Gaussian-random variables. The final calculations are shown in Equation 4–7.

$$x = \sqrt{G(R)} * cos(\theta) = \sqrt{(-2*log(R))} * (v1/\sqrt{R}) = \sqrt{(-2*log(R)/R)} * v1$$

$$y = \sqrt{G(R)} * sin(\theta) = \sqrt{(-2*log(R))} * (v2/\sqrt{R}) = \sqrt{(-2*log(R)/R)} * v2$$

(Equation 4–7)

Note that the *cos()* and *sin()* terms are replaced with the $v1/\sqrt{R}$ and $v2/\sqrt{R}$ respectively. These substitutions are made by using the equations $x = r * cos(\theta)$ and $y = r * sin(\theta)$, where θ is uniformly distributed. While it seems rather convoluted (because it is), this method leads to a very efficient routine for generating normally distributed random sequences as shown in Listing 4–2.

Listing 4–2. The function *rwf_randRandGaussian()* returns normally distributed random sequences by using uniformly distributed polar coordinates.

```
// Return standard normally distributed random
// numbers

float rwf_randRandGaussian(void)
{
  static int need_newvars = 1;
  static float factor, v1, v2;
  float result;

  if(need_newvars) {
   float r = 1.1;
   while (r >= 1.0 || r == 0) {// Find radius < 1.0
    v1 = 2.0*rwf_randRand() - 1.0;
    v2 = 2.0*rwf_randRand() - 1.0;
    r = v1*v1 + v2*v2;
   }
   need_newvars = 0;
   factor = sqrt(-2.0 * log(r) / r);
   result = v1*factor;
  } else {
   need_newvars = 1;
   result = v2*factor;
  }
  return result;
}
```

Other Properties of Normal Distributions

Besides occurring naturally in many problems, normal distributions have several other properties that make them applicable in several situations. As pointed out earlier, a normally distributed variable is characterized by two quantities: Its mean μ and its variance σ^2 (or equivalently, its standard deviation σ). The density function for a normally distributed variable is shown in Equation 4–8:

$$p(x) = \left(\frac{1}{\sigma\sqrt{2\pi}}\right) e^{-(x-\mu)^2/(2\sigma^2)} \qquad \textit{(Equation 4–8)}$$

One of the most important features of normally distributed random variables is that if x and y are independent, normally distributed random variables, then $z1 = x + y$ and $z2 = a*x$ are also normally distributed, where a is any nonzero number. The mean of $z1$ is the sum of the means of x and y, and the variance of $z1$ is the sum of the variances. So, if you can model any system as being composed of linear combinations of normally distributed random processes, then the resulting system will also be normally distributed. This can greatly simplify the analysis of complex systems. In most cases that you'll encounter in this book, you'll be using normally distributed random variables with zero mean, or at least all of them will have the same mean.

Generating normally distributed sequences with a particular mean and variance is easy. To generate sequences with a mean *mean* and standard deviation *stdev*, use Equation 4–9:

$$normal\_var = stdev * rwf\_randRandGaussian() + mean \qquad \textit{(Equation 4–9)}$$

Equation 4–9 applies for any distribution with a zero mean and a variance of 1.0, not just normal distributions.

Technically, *rwf_randRandGaussian()* can return any value from –*infinity* to +*infinity*. But the probability is amazingly small that it will return any value less than –10 or greater than +10. In some applications, however, it is important to limit the possible values to a certain range. This distribution is referred to as a *truncated normal distribution*. As long as the truncation limits are greater than about three standard deviations from the mean, there is virtually no difference between truncating the output and not truncating it because of the very small probabilities that the truncation will even make a difference. However, in more esoteric applications that use billions of random numbers, it can make a slight difference. So, it is something you should be aware of in case of those rare circumstances.

The fact that the sum of normally distributed variables is itself normally distributed is important when considering how to introduce random variations into a model, fractal, or another type of analysis. For instance, if the variable you are modeling, such as the lengths of branches in a tree or the height of a mountain, is normally distributed, then it is reasonable to assume, at least for a first guess, that the underlying processes are normally distributed as well. So, if you use normal variations of the generators in a fractal model, then the resulting figure will be normally distributed at all scales. This is quite a reasonable approximation for many natural processes.

To simplify the use of random variables in the various programs, you define the *RWFrand_RandomVariable* class as follows:

```
class RWFrand_RandomVariable {
private:
float mean, stdev;    // Mean and standard deviation
long seed;
protected:
public:

RWFrand_RandomVariable(void)
  {mean = 0.0; stdev = 1.0; seed = 1010101;};
// Constructor with mean and standard deviation
RWFrand_RandomVariable(float new_mean, float new_stdev)
  {mean = new_mean; stdev = ABS(new_stdev);
```

```
    seed = 1010101;};
  setSeed(long new_seed) {seed = new_seed;};
  setMean(float new_mean)      {mean = new_mean;};
  setDeviation(float new_stdev)
   {stdev = ABS(new_stdev);};
  float getMean(void) {return mean;};
  float getDeviation(void) {return stdev;};
  virtual float next(void);    // Get the next value
};
```

The *next()* member function returns the next value of the random variable. You may change any of the attributes using the corresponding *set()* member functions. This class lets you declare a variable directly as a random variable with the appropriate distribution, mean, and standard deviation. The classes *RWFrand_UniformRV* and *RWFrand_GaussianRV* are provided as examples of deriving classes from this base class. You can create random variables with more elaborate distributions as the need arises by adding whatever extra parameters and distribution functions you need.

A Normal Demonstration

In order to illustrate how normal distributions naturally arise, the software on the disk accompanying this book includes the program *pachinko.exe*. This program simulates a Japanese pachinko machine on your display, as shown in Figure 4–3. In the pachinko machine, a ball is dropped from the top of the machine down into the machine's center. Rows of pegs are aligned horizontally across the screen. The top row contains only one peg, so the ball can fall either to the left or right. The next row contains two pegs, lined up so that after the ball passes the top row, it lands on one of the pegs, and again falls either to the left or right. The next row contains three pegs, the next four, and so forth. At the bottom of the machine is a series of bins. After dropping several balls into the machine, you would probably like to know, on average, how many balls will end up in each bin on the bottom of the screen. You guessed it: The distribution is approximately normal, and will appear closer to normal as more balls are dropped into the machine.

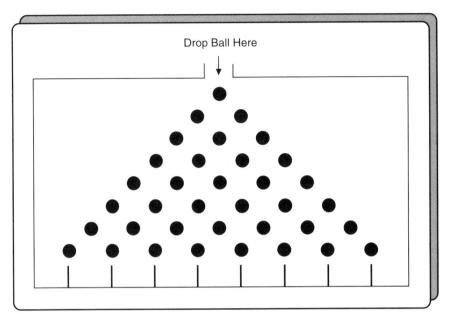

Figure 4–3. An idealized pachinko machine.

One nice feature of a computer-run simulation such as the pachinko machine is the ability to run the simulation with more balls or pegs than would be practical for a real pachinko machine. The program lets you vary both the number of rows and the number of balls that run through it. While a relatively simple example, the pachinko machine demonstrates how normal distributions occur in many types of natural systems.

Fractals and Randomness

You will see many examples in the later chapters of how to introduce random variations into a fractal model. In almost all fractal and procedural algorithms, random variations are introduced by varying some attribute of the fractal generators each time a generator replaces another piece of the object. In most cases, you will either use a normal, truncated normal, or uniform distribution. However, there are many cases where other distributions, such as Poisson, binomial, gamma, or others, are required to accurately model the underlying physical processes. None of the algorithms used in the fractal programs in this book depend on using any particular distribution. In fact, you'll see how using different distributions can produce strikingly different results in the final image. The only limits imposed by the programs in this book are truncation limits that keep random sequences from exceeding certain bounds, as any distribution with an infinite range occasionally will.

Next Up: Fractals

In this chapter, you have seen how to generate aperiodic sequences of random numbers with a uniform, exponential, or normal distribution. Other distributions may be generated using the methods presented here and by other techniques that go beyond the scope of this book. There are several references, including *Numerical Recipes in C* (Cambridge University Press, 1988) by William H. Press, Brian P. Flannery, Saul A. Teukolsky, and William T. Vetterling, listed in the bibliography that provide more detailed information about generating other distributions. A more general reference on probability and statistics is *Probability with Applications* (McGraw-Hill Book Company, 1975) by Michael Woodroofe.

The first four chapters of this book provide the technical foundation and tools you'll need to create fractal programs. Starting in the next chapter, you'll see how all these tools are combined to create powerful, flexible, and elegant fractal and procedural images and models. In Chapter 5, your patience will be rewarded with your first set of programs for generating some fantastic fractal imagery on your very own display; so read on!

Fractals of the First Kind: One-Dimensional Fractals

The real purpose of this book begins here: learning how to create and use fractal models. Using the tools of the previous chapters, you can display various types of graphical objects on your screen. In this chapter, you'll see how to add fractal-graphical objects to the list of display types. Our goal is to maintain the same type of object-oriented graphics structure presented in Chapter 3. A fractal object is just another type of graphical object with its own special set of drawing methods, just as the *RWFgraph_Circle* and *RWFgraph_Polygon* class objects are. You should be able to manipulate a fractal object the same way as any other object, including being able to translate, scale, rotate, change the rendering style, and so on using the same calls as other objects. By combining the flexibility provided by affine transformations with the encapsulation and inheritance properties of C++, you can create very elegant and efficient routines for drawing a tremendous variety of fractal objects.

117

A Question of Dimension

Before diving into the first fractal object, let's examine a portion of this chapter's title, *One-Dimensional Fractals*. When dealing with fractals, the notion of dimensionality can become quite confusing, as it became for many nineteenth- and twentieth-century mathematicians. The term *one-dimensional* fractals is not true for fractals if you consider standard Euclidean dimensions. First, all the plots in this chapter are actually made in two dimensions. However, a circle or polygon is still a one-dimensional object. For these types of "normal" curves, the points along the curve can be parameterized with a single parameter *t* and you plot *(x(t), y(t))*. You are probably most familiar with this from graphing functions. If you can write *y = f(x)*, then you plot the points *(x, f(x))* to create the graph. In this case, *x* is the single parameter. A figure such as a circle can be plotted by using a single angle parameter θ. The points on the circle are then located at *(r∗cos(θ), r∗sin(θ))*. In general, you can plot any one-dimensional curve in any integral number of dimensions by plotting the points *(x(t), y(t), z(t),...)*.

A one-dimensional curve is one in which the *(x, y)* coordinates are all, either explicitly or implicitly, functions of a single parameter. A two-dimensional curve (or surface) is one whose coordinates are functions of two parameters. This is the natural notion of Euclidean dimension; namely, that it requires an integral number of dimensions to completely describe any curve or shape. As was pointed out in Chapter 1, however, this simple way of classifying curves is not sufficient to cover all types. The problem comes about when you consider what happens if you have an infinite-length curve occupying a finite area.

Fractal curves, as Mandelbrot defined them, are those curves with a Hausdorff-Besicovitch dimension greater than its Euclidean dimension. Without getting into the technical implications of this definition, suffice to say that you cannot parameterize a fractal curve the same way as you can the one-dimensional curves you are used to. Mandelbrot therefore devised the notion of the *self-similarity dimension*, *D*, to help quantify the complexity of a fractal curve. As an example, the Peano Curve presented in

Chapter 1 has $D = 2$ to denote its plane-filling properties; that is, every point (x, y) can be shown to lie on the Peano Curve.

For most fractal curves, you cannot compute the self-similarity dimension, and usually it doesn't matter. It is sufficient simply to know that fractal curves have complex and intricate structures at all scales, which makes fractals very useful for modeling complex objects.

With this background on the dimensionality of fractals, let's return to why a portion of this chapter's title is *One-Dimensional Fractals*. The fractal objects described in this chapter are generated by following a recursive procedure of replacing a one-dimensional object, such as a line segment, with another set of one-dimensional objects, such as a collection of line segments, as shown in Figure 5–1. It is therefore natural to think of these types of fractal objects in the same way that you think of more traditional one-dimensional curves. At any finite stage of the recursion, the curve is actually composed of strictly one-dimensional pieces. Only in the infinite limit (applying the recursion generating rule an infinite number of times) does the curve become truly fractal, and not representable by a finite collection of one-dimensional pieces.

For all the applications in the book, you will use the fractal definition of a curve as a way to generate a finite approximation to the actual infinite fractal curve. When it comes to the practical matter of drawing these types of fractal objects on the screen, you must ultimately stop evaluating the recursive procedure at some point, and draw a point or line segment on the screen. Because you do not have infinite resolution display on your computer (and if you do, let us know where you acquired it), you stop drawing the fractal when the pieces being replaced are smaller than the display resolution of your screen. So, the image on the screen is ultimately only an approximation to the actual, infinite-resolution fractal object.

In the next chapter, you'll see how exactly the same methods and techniques are applied to generating fractals of greater dimensionality. Instead of using line segments, you will apply the same recursive procedures to transform two- (and higher-) dimensional shapes, creating even more complex fractal shapes.

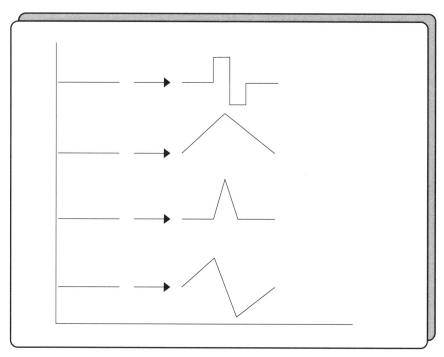

Figure 5–1. Some sample techniques of replacing a one-dimensional object with another collection of one-dimensional objects.

Now, let's look into how to create a general-purpose fractal object composed of one-dimensional pieces. Let's begin with the basic model, the Koch Curve, or snowflake curve, you first saw in Chapter 1.

Making Snow

The Koch Curve, or snowflake curve, is a member of a more general class of objects known as procedural objects. A *procedural object* is defined by an initial state (called the *initiator*) and a set of rules, known as *generators*, for converting the initiator into the final object. For fractal objects, the generators are defined recursively. A procedural object is created by starting with the initiator. Each component of the initiator is transformed by the generator(s). If the initiator is a square, for instance, then the generators are applied to each side of the square. The generators are then applied again to the new component created by the first step. At each step, the generators are scaled to match the size and orientation of the piece that each is to replace. Theoretically, the process continues indefinitely to create the final object. In practice, the recursion is continued until the pieces being processed are too small to make a difference, such as being too small to resolve on your display screen.

The snowflake curve and its many relatives are generated by following a recursive-replacement rule, as shown in Figure 5–2. For the basic snowflake, you start with a single line-segment initiator and replace it with the new generator shape as shown in the figure. The rule is then applied again to each line segment of the new figure. This process is implemented by the C++ code shown in Listing 5–1.

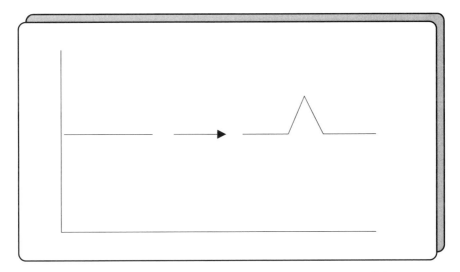

Figure 5–2. Recursive rule for generating the Koch Curve, or snowflake curve.

Listing 5–1. The member functions for drawing a Koch, or snowflake fractal

```
void
RWFvk_BasicObject::draw(void)
{
    // Start with unit line segment
    base_line.setFirst(0.0, 0.0);
    base_line.setEnd(1.0, 0.0);
    base_line.setColor(color);
```

```
    // Apply initial transformation for this object
    RWFgraph_Line passed_line = getMatrix() * base_line;
    generate(passed_line, 0);
}


void
RWFvk_BasicObject::generate(RWFgraph_Line &line_seg,
                            int level)
{
    // Reached max recursion level yet?
    if(level >= max_level) {
     line_seg.draw();
     return;
    }

    int next_level = level + 1;
    RWFgraph_Line temp_line;

    // Generate a matrix specifying the transformation
    // from the initiator to the current line segment

    RWFmat_Matrix tmatrix;
    tmatrix =
     rwf_graphLineToLineMatrix(base_line, line_seg);

    for(int i=0; i < numSegments(); i++) {
     // Must orient each piece of generator with this line
     // segment. Use the overloaded * operator between a
     // matrix and a line-segment type. This simply
     // applies the matrix to the line-generator segments
     temp_line = tmatrix * segments[i];
     generate(temp_line, next_level);
    }
}
```

The class *RWFvk_BasicObject* is the name of the fractal-graphics object class for the snowflake curves. It is derived from the basic *RWFgraphics_Object* described in Chapter 3, and therefore possesses all the same functions and attributes of that class, such as color, transformation matrix, drawing style, and so on.

If you have seen other C code for generating fractal curves, the code in Listing 5–1 probably seems either unfamiliar, odd, or both. Actually, it is fairly straightforward. The *draw()* member function takes the starting line segment and applies the object's transformation matrix to it to get the initial line segment in the correct position. After that, the *generate()* member function does all the work.

The *generate()* member function first checks to see if a preset maximum recursion level has been reached for the object. If not, then *generate()* uses the function *rwf_graphLineToLineMatrix()* to find the transformation matrix, mapping the initial line-segment (initiator) into the current line-segment orientation. This process is shown in Figure 5–3. This transformation is then applied to each segment of the generator. Each transformed line segment of the generator is then passed to a recursive call to *generate()* with the passed recursion level set to one higher than in the current call to *generate()*.

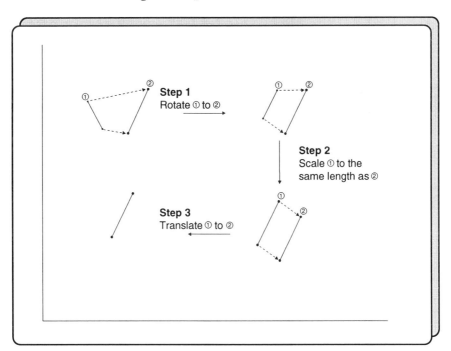

Figure 5–3. Finding the transformation to transform one line segment into another.

Several other member functions are invoked by *generate()* that also deserve mention. First, the generator is stored as a table of line segments, using the *RWFlist_SimpleTable* template class. By using this template class, you can easily alter the size (number of segments) and shape of the generator. The member function *numSegments()* returns the number of segments in the generator using the *size()* member function of the *RWFlist_SimpleTable* class. The member function *setGenerator()* lets you pass a new generator function to the *RWFvk_BasicObject* class. You may translate, scale, and rotate the Koch object just as you can any other graphics object, and use the same function names because it is derived from the base *RWFgraph_Object* class. (The complete source code and definition of the *RWFvk_BasicObject* class can be found on the disk that accompanies this book.)

It is important that the generator be constructed to replace the *base_line* line segment. In general, the endpoints of the generator must match the endpoints of the base line. The simplest way to do this is to always use the unit-length line segment from (0, 0) to (1, 0) and construct the generator accordingly. The Koch object will then be a unit size, which you can scale and position on the screen using the same calls as you would for any other graphics objects. You will learn more about how to ensure that the generator matches the initiator in the section on normalizing generators presented later in this chapter.

As an example of how to use the *RWFvk_BasicObject* class, the original generator for the snowflake curve is defined by the following code segment:

```
RWFgraph_LineSegmentTable ltable;
RWFvk_BasicObject        vk;

ltable[0].setFirst(0.0, 0.0);
ltable[0].setEnd(1/3.0, 0.0);
ltable[1].setFirst(1/3.0, 0.0);
// The generator forms two sides of an equilateral
// triangle with sides of 1/3
ltable[1].setEnd(1/2.0, (1/3.0)*sqrt(3.0/4.0));
ltable[2].setFirst(1/2.0, (1/3.0)*sqrt(3.0/4.0));
```

```
ltable[2].setEnd(2.0/3.0, 0.0);
ltable[3].setFirst(2.0/3.0, 0.0);
ltable[3].setEnd(1.0, 0.0);
vk.setGenerator(ltable);
vk.setColor(RWF_COLOR_WHITE);
// Now set an appropriate drawing scale
int xmax = RWFgraph_getMaxX();
int ymax = RWFgraph_getMaxY();
vk.scale(xmax / 3.0, ymax / 3.0);
// Center on the screen
vk.translate(xmax/2.0 - xmax/6.0, 100.0);
RWFgraph_Line unit_line(0.0, 0.0, 1.0, 0.0);
vk.setInitiator(unit_line);
vk.draw();
```

Purely Affine

The power of the method described in this section for generating Koch Curves is in its generality. A fractal generator may be thought of in two ways:

- ◆ as something that replaces one geometric shape with another composed of the original geometric shape; and

- ◆ as a sequence of transformations applied to a base or reference geometric shape.

The second view provides a clearer picture of where the fractal self-similarity arises. Each new piece is composed of affine copies of the original. The self-similarity scaling property is a direct result of the method of constructing the curve.

Strictly speaking, an object constructed in this manner is referred to as *self-affine*. In order to be strictly self-similar, the affine transformations must use the same scaling factors in all dimensions. Under most situations, you do not need strict self-similarity and no real distinction will be made between the two in the rest of this book.

By treating the Koch generator as a series of transformations, you can create an even more general C++ class for these types of objects. The generalized drawing routines are shown in Listing 5–2. Instead of defining the generator as a series of line segments, it is defined as a series of affine transformations stored as matrices. Because affine transformations can be applied to any of our graphical objects, you are not limited to using line segments as the reference geometrical object. Any class derived from the *RWFgraph_Object* base class may be used. This provides a tremendous amount of flexibility for creating unlimited types of Koch fractal objects.

Listing 5–2. Drawing a Koch fractal using a list of affine transformations to define the generator.

```
void
RWFvk_Object::draw(void)
{
 // base_object is an RWFgraph_Object pointer
 base_object->setColor(color);
 RWFmat_Matrix save_matrix = base_object->getMatrix();
 generate(getMatrix * save_matrix, 0);
 // Restore the object's original matrix
 base_object->setMatrix(save_matrix);
}


        void
RWFvk_Object::generate(RWFmat_Matrix &pmatrix,
            int level)
{
 // Reached max recursion level yet?
 if(level >= max_level) {
  base_object->setMatrix(pmatrix);
  base_object->draw();
  return;
 }

 int next_level = level + 1;
 for(int i=0; i < numSegments(); i++) {
  // Must orient each piece of generator with this line
  // segment. Use the overloaded * operator for
```

```
  // matrices.
  generate(pmatrix * transforms[i], next_level);
  }
 }
```

Note in Listing 5–2 that *generate()* is passed an affine transformation in the form of an *RWFmat_Matrix* object as discussed in Chapter 3, instead of a line-segment object. The passed matrix is then applied to each transformation matrix of the generator (using the overloaded ∗ operator for matrices) and passed as a new matrix for the next recursive call to *generate()*. The order for multiplying the matrices is important. For each recursive call to *generate()*, the current matrix must left multiply the generator transformation matrix. This ensures that the generator is placed in the same location as the object. The matrices defining the generator are stored in the matrix table *transforms*.

The steps in the *draw()* routine are straightforward. When the maximum recursion level is reached, the object is drawn by setting the transformation of the base object to the passed matrix and then calling the *draw()* member function for that object. Thanks to the inheritance property of C++ classes, the appropriate *draw()* function for the particular type of derived object is called. The *base_matrix* used in the initial call to *generate()* is simply the drawing matrix used by all graphical objects derived from the *RWFgraph_Object* class.

 The *setGenerator()* member function is overloaded so that you can pass either a table of line segments, as was done for *RWFvk_BasicObject*, or a table of matrices. For example, you can generate the same curve of Figure 5–4 with the following code segment:

```
RWFmat_MatrixTable mtable;
RWFvk_Object    vk;

// Define the generator by a series of transformations
// of a unit line segment
// First, scale by 1/3
mtable[0].scale(1/3.0, 1/3.0);
// Second segment, rotate and translate
mtable[1].scale(1/3.0, 1/3.0);
```

127

```
mtable[1].rotate(60.0);
mtable[1].translate(1/3.0, 1/3.0);
// Third segment, rotate and translate
mtable[2].scale(1/3.0, 1/3.0);
mtable[2].rotate(-60.0);
mtable[2].translate(1/2.0, 1/3.0 * sqrt(3.0 / 4.0));
// Final segment, translate
mtable[3].scale(1/3.0, 1/3.0);
mtable[3].translate(2/3.0, 0.0);

vk.setGenerator(mtable);
vk.setColor(RWF_COLOR_WHITE);
// Now set an appropriate drawing scale
int xmax = RWFgraph_getMaxX();
int ymax = RWFgraph_getMaxY();
vk.scale(xmax / 3.0, ymax / 3.0);
vk.translate(xmax/2.0 - xmax/6.0, 100.0);
// Finally, set the base object to draw
// In this example, use a line segment
RWFgraph_Line tline(0.0, 0.0, 1.0, 0.0);
vk.setInitiator(tline);
vk.draw();
```

Normalized Generators

If you pass a table of line segments to define a generator, the overloaded *setGenerator()* member function converts it into an equivalent table of affine transformations. One unresolved point, however, are the units of the generator. For instance, the snowflake generator is constructed such that the distance from the first point of the generator to the last is of unit length. In general, the endpoints of the generator should match the two endpoints of the line segment being replaced. This ensures that the fractal is a connected figure. It is therefore a good idea to normalize the generator to ensure that it properly scales the initiator object at each recursion level. *Normalization* of a generator forces the generator to match the objects within the initiator. It is analogous to normalizing a vector to unit length.

A line-segment table is not the most convenient way to specify a generator. A more common way is to use the *RWFgraph_Polyline* class to define a polyline. The *setGenerator()* member function is overloaded so you may use a polyline for the generator. This overloaded version of *setGenerator()* then creates a temporary table of line segments and calls the *setGenerator()* function with this temporary table.

For line-segment generators, normalization is fairly straightforward. The generator is always normalized with respect to a unit-length line segment from (–1/2, 0) to (1/2, 0). Using this unit vector keeps the generator centered, which is useful when using other types of objects besides line segments in the initiator. The normalization process is accomplished in three steps. First, the vector from the initial point of the generator to the last point is constructed. In the second step, you use *RWFgraph_LineToLineMatrix()* to find the transformation that changes this constructed line segment into the base-line segment. The final step is to apply the resulting transformation to all the line segments in the generator. The complete process is shown in Figure 5–4.

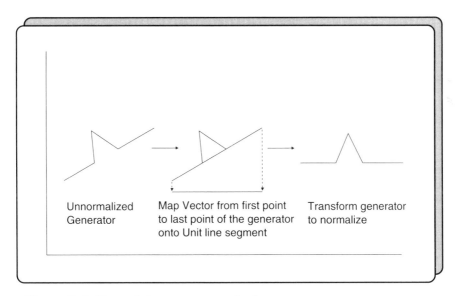

Figure 5–4. Normalizing a generator in three steps.

Following normalization, the resulting generator will then be correctly scaled, oriented, and translated for use in the *RWFvk_Object* class. The routine *RWFgraph_Normalize()* is provided to perform this normalization operation and is shown in Listing 5–3. There are two overloaded versions of this routine, one that takes a line-segment table as an argument, and one that takes a polyline as an argument. Both functions perform the identical operation.

Listing 5–3. The function *RWFgraph_Normalize()* ensures that the generator is properly scaled, translated, and oriented.

```
// Normalizing a generator line-segment table
void
RWFgraph_Normalize(RWFgraph_LineTable &lt)
{
 if(lt.size() <= 1)
  return;

 int last_seg = lt.size() - 1;
 RWFgraph_Point fpoint, lpoint;
 RWFvec_Vector coord1, coord2, delta_coord;
 RWFgraph_Line end_to_end;
 RWFgraph_Line unit(-0.5, 0.0, 0.5, 0.0);

 // Get the first and last points
 fpoint = lt[0].getFirst();
 lpoint = lt[last_seg].getEnd();

 // Set the normalization vector
 end_to_end.setFirst(fpoint);
 end_to_end.setEnd(lpoint);

 RWFmat_Matrix tmatrix;
 tmatrix =
  RWFgraph_LineToLineMatrix(end_to_end, unit);

 // Now scale everything with the overloaded * operator
 for(int i=0; i < lt.size(); i++)
  lt[i] = tmatrix * lt[i];
}
```

By using *RWFgraph_Normalize()*, you can acquire a generator by virtually any method, such as digitizing from the screen or generating one algorithmically. Any anomalies, such as a slight rotation or incorrect scale, will be corrected by the normalizing operation. The only requirement is that the endpoints of the generator must correspond to the endpoints of the line segment being replaced.

The same criteria for normalization applies to a generator specified as a sequence of affine transformations. An overloaded version of *RWFgraph_Normalize()* is available for normalizing a table of matrices using the same procedure as the version shown in Listing 5–3. In general, each transformation must scale down the object. Otherwise, the object will end up with many self-intersecting pieces. In the snowflake curve, for instance, each matrix is scaled by 1/3, thus, reducing the object size being processed by 1/3 at each recursion level. However, you will seldom want to specify a table of transformations directly when creating a fractal object. Instead, the transformations are constructed by specifying them geometrically, just as was done with the line-segment table. Affine transformations are used internally because of their generality; they are often not the most convenient way of specifying a generator. In the later chapters, you will see several other methods for specifying generators and generating their equivalent affine-transformation table.

Shapely Fractals

With the new *RWFvk_Object* class you can now create whole new types of fractal objects that are not necessarily composed of line segments. In the previous example, for instance, you can replace the line segment with a unit circle using the *RWFgraph_Circle* class. The resulting figure at various recursion levels is shown in Figure 5–5. As you might expect, the figure has the same basic appearance as the normal snowflake curve, especially as the recursion is continued to more and more levels. In the infinite limit, the curves would actually be the same, as the circles would collapse to points.

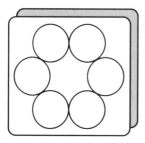 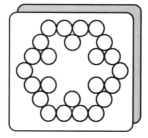 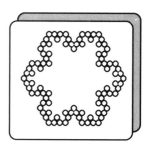

Figure 5–5. A Koch Curve, or snowflake curve, at various recursion levels using circles instead of line segments.

General Initiators

As it currently stands, the *RWFvk_Object* class only allows a single object as an initiator. The affine transformations of the generator are applied to the entire initiator. It is often convenient to have an initiator composed of more than one piece. For instance, generating the complete snowflake curve requires a starting hexagon to generate a six-sided figure. The hexagon is an initiator composed of six separate line-segment objects. Providing the additional capability of multiple object initiators is straightforward. The *RWFvk_Object* class is expanded to allow a table of objects to be defined as the initiator. Just as was done for the generator, you can view the initiator as composed of a sequence of affine transformations applied to a base object. For instance, each segment of a polyline or polygon may be thought of as an affine transformation applied to the unit line segment.

The *setInitiator()* member function is overloaded to allow for several types of object lists. An object list is simply an *RWFlist_SimpleTable* of pointers to *RWFgraph_Object* type objects. The initiator can therefore be composed of any series of objects, even mixing multiple types of objects, such as lines, circles, ellipses, and so forth. The most common type of initiator is an *RWFgraph_Polygon* or *RWFgraph_Polyline* object defining a sequence of line segments. The overloaded *setInitiator()* function then converts your passed initiator into an appropriate object list. For polylines and polygons, a list of transformed line segments is generated. The *generate()* function is then called for each object in the initiator. The modified *draw()* member function becomes:

Figure 5–6. Hexagonal Koch Curve, or snowflake curve.

```
RWFvk_Object::draw(void)
{
  RWFmat_Matrix save_matrix;
  // base_object is an RWFgraph_Object pointer
  for(int i=0; i < objectptrlist.size(); i++) {
    base_object = objectptrlist[i];
    base_object->setColor(color);
    // Use concatenated base matrix for the whole object
    // with matrix for the object itself
    save_matrix = base_object->getMatrix();
    generate(base_matrix * save_matrix, 0);
    // Restore the object's original matrix
    base_object->setMatrix(save_matrix);
  }
}
```

The revised *draw()* function assumes that the generator is appropriately normalized. If you use nonline segment objects such as circles, they must be "unit" objects, or objects with a size of 1 and centered at (0, 0). By sticking with these types of objects, the generator normalization used for line segments may be used to normalize the generators for other types of

objects. More commonly, you can use the same generators on different types of objects to create some amazing special effects.

In a sense, processing a polyline is a special case with *setInitiator()* because a polyline is defined by its vertex points rather than by a transformation of some "unit" polygon. *setInitiator()* uses the polyline to create an object-pointer table consisting simply of pointers to unit line segments. The only difference between each line segment is the transformation matrix used to put it in the right position on the polyline. In effect, the initiator is stored just like the generator, as a series of affine transformations applied to a single base object. In this case, it's stored as a unit line segment. Listing 5–4 shows how *setInitiator()* converts a polyline initiator into the appropriate table of objects and transformations.

Listing 5–4. The *setInitiator()* member function for a polyline argument.

```
void
RWFvk_Object::setInitiator(RWFgraph_Polyline &poly)
{
  if(poly.size() <= 1)
   return;

  objectptrlist.reset();        // Reset the object list

  RWFgraph_Line unit(-0.5, 0.0, 0.5, 0.0);
  RWFgraph_Line *new_line;
  RWFmat_Matrix matrix;

  // Loop through the points of the polyline
  for(int i=1; i < poly.size(); i++)
   new_line = new RWFgraph_Line;
   new_line->setFirst(poly[i]);
   new_line->setEnd(poly[i-1]);
   // Now find the transformation from the unit
   // vector to this one
   matrix = RWFgraph_LineToLineMatrix(unit, *new_line);
   // Now we can make new_line a unit vector
```

```
        // and set the matrix for it
        new_line = unit;
        new_line->setMatrix(matrix);
        new_line->setColor(color);
        objectptrlist[i-1] = new_line;
    }
}
```

While using tables of object pointers may initially seem like a lot of trouble (because it is), the processing is performed entirely behind the scenes. From your program's standpoint, you may simply define initiators as polygons or polylines and generators as polylines. The normalization process takes care of ensuring that the initiators and generators match up. You do not actually have to directly deal with the affine transformations at all. However, this approach is a very general one that you will see used throughout most of the fractal code in this book. In the next few chapters, these same methods are directly adapted for use with many different types of objects as both initiators and generators.

With this new capability for variable initiators in the *RWFvk_Object* class, you can now make most of the fractal drawings you have seen elsewhere. Figures 5–6 through 5–9 provide some examples, but the possibilities are truly limitless. The main trick is coming up with sets of initiators and generators that produce interesting patterns and do not have artifacts such as self-intersection (the generator is too large for the initiator). Furthermore, you may create any new graphical-object types derived from the *RWFgraph_BaseObject* type and use your objects to create other fractal figures. You do not have to create any new code; the new objects will simply plug into the *RWFvk_Object* class using the inheritance feature of C++. This not only provides extraordinary flexibility, it means you do not have to create new fractal functions for new object types, and you do not have to go through the process of debugging the new fractal-drawing routines.

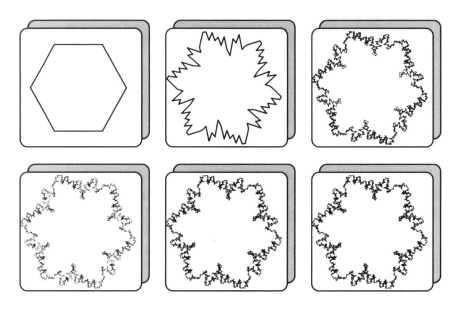

Figure 5–7. Sixteen-piece generator for the snowflake curve.

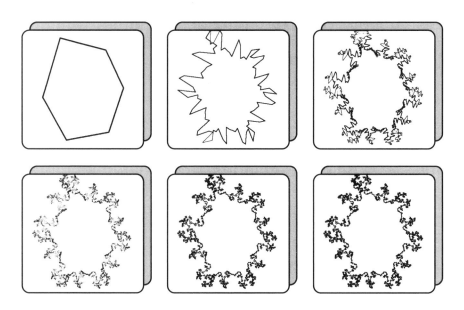

Figure 5–8. An irregular-shaped initiator and generator.

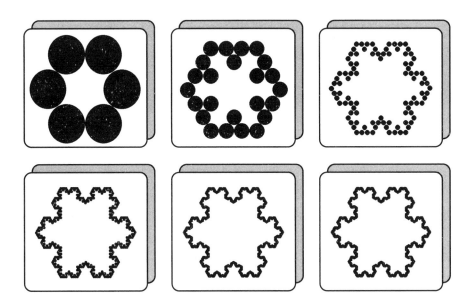

Figure 5–9. Fractal circles and ellipses.

Terminal Conditions

So far, the *generate()* member function has only one method for terminating the recursion: by reaching a predefined maximum recursion level. This is satisfactory in some cases, but you often have the problem of deciding how many recursion levels is enough. Furthermore, the number of recursion levels required is dependent upon the initial size and shape of both the initiator and the generator for a given fractal object. If the object is scaled down by 1/2, then it would be nice to reduce the number of recursion levels to avoid additional and unnecessary drawing computation. Generally, you would like to stop the recursion at the point where further recursions cannot be resolved on the display, that is, where the portion being drawn occupies only a few pixels on the display. Let's see how to implement this criteria with the *RWFvk_BasicObject* class.

Minimum distance

For the *RWFvk_BasicObject* class, the *generate()* member function is passed a current line segment to draw. Normally, you would like to terminate the recursion if the length of the line segment is less than a screen pixel. This criteria is easy to add by using the *length()* member function of the *RWFgraph_Line* type. The modifications for *generate()* are shown in the following code segment:

```
void
RWFvk_BasicObject::generate(RWFgraph_Line &line_seg,
                                int level)
{
 // Reached max recursion level yet?
 if(level >= max_level) {
  line_seg.draw();
  return;
 }

 // Is the line segment too small
 if(line_seg.length() <= min_line_size) {
  line_seg.draw();
  return;
 }

 // Continue with normal generation
 ...
}
```

The member function *setMinimumSize()* of the *RWFvk_BasicObject* class lets you set the size at which the recursion should terminate. By using this approach, the snowflake curve will only draw as much as it needs in order to match the resolution of the screen. So, if you magnify a snowflake object, the *draw()* function will automatically use more levels of recursion to draw greater detail. Conversely, if you shrink a snowflake object, fewer recursion levels are used. By default, the minimum size is set to one screen pixel.

Sizing up the snowflake

While the size criteria discussed in the previous section works well with line segments, what about the more general approach used by the

RWFvk_Object class? The same type of criteria can be used by providing one additional piece of information, the size of the base objects in the initiator. If the base objects are all line segments, such as when you use a polygon or polyline for the initiator, then the size is already known. The transformations stored in the generators are always applied to a unit line segment. If, however, you use an initiator composed of other types of objects, such as circles or ellipses then you must supply a size for these objects. In general, the size represents the maximum width of the object in any orientation.

Given the size of the base object, the only other task left to perform is to compute the effective object size after the object has been transformed by a matrix. You must account for the possibility that an affine transformation includes translation, rotation, and scaling. The only operation that affects the size of an object is scaling. You therefore need a means of extracting the overall scaling from a two-dimensional affine transformation. In most fractal generators, the transformations scale by the same amount in both x and y. However, in some cases you may want to use a stretched generator by using different x and y scale factors. One way to characterize the scaling properties of a transformation is by the determinant of the matrix representing the transformation. You can find the scaling factor for a two-dimensional matrix using the *RWFmat_getGlobalScalingFactor()* function shown in the following code segment:

```
float
RWFmat_getGlobalScalingFactor(RWFmat_Matrix &matrix)
{
  float det, scale;

  det = matrix.determinant();
  return (sqrt(ABS(det)));
}
```

Note that this function only works on a two-dimensional transformation, but you can easily generalize it to handle higher dimensions. In general, if the transformation is for n dimensions, then the scaling factor is the nth root of the determinant.

Once you have the matrix-scale factor, the effective size of the object is simply *scale* ∗ (object size). During the recursion, the base object is scaled down by $scale^{(level)}$ at each recursion level. As discussed earlier, if the scale factor for a generator is greater than or equal to 1.0, then you have a problem. This means that at least one of the generators does not reduce the size of the object. Thus, your drawing routine will not terminate until the maximum recursion level is reached. Furthermore, you will likely produce a very chaotic drawing rather than an interesting fractal shape.

To provide the capability for using differently sized objects, the *setInitiator()* member function has been overloaded in several different ways for passing an arbitrary set of objects defining the initiator:

```
// All objects in the table are a unit size
setInitiator(RWFlist_ObjectPtrTable &otable);

// All objects in the table have the size passed
// by size
setInitiator(RWFlist_ObjectPtrTable &otable, float size);

// An explicit table of sizes is passed
// Use the SimpleList template to define a size table
typedef RWFlist_SimpleTable<float>   RWFlist_SizeTable;
setInitiator(RWFlist_ObjectPtrTable &otable,
        RWFlist_SizeTable &size_table);
// Note: The object and size tables must have the same
// number of elements
```

The modifications to the *draw()* and *generate()* member functions are:

```
void
RWFvk_Object::draw(void)
{
 RWFmat_Matrix save_matrix;
 // base_object is an RWFgraph_Object pointer
 for(int i=0; i < objectptrlist.size(); i++) {
  base_object = objectptrlist[i];
  base_object->setColor(color);
  cur_object_size = objectsizelist[i];
```

```
  save_matrix = base_object->getMatrix();
  generate(base_matrix * save_matrix, 0);
  base_object->setMatrix(save_matrix);
 }
}


void
RWFvk_Object::generate(RWFmat_Matrix &pmatrix,
            int level)
{
 // Reached max recursion level yet?
 if(level >= max_level) {
  base_object->setMatrix(pmatrix);
  base_object->draw();
  return;
 }


 // Now, is the object too small?
 float scale = RWFmat_GetGlobalScalingFactor(pmatrix);
 if((scale * cur_object_size) <= min_line_size) {
  base_object->setMatrix(pmatrix);
  base_object->draw();
  return;
 }


 // Continue with normal generation
 ...
 }
```

Note that the *private* member *cur_object_size* has been added to the *RWFvk_Object* class to store the size of the object currently being processed. In addition, a table of object sizes is kept along with the list of pointers to the initiator objects. Under most circumstances, you should avoid using nonunit-sized objects in the initiator. This will ensure that the recursion terminates at an appropriate level for any particular screen resolution.

Using the effective screen size to determine when to stop the recursion is important in many applications. You only want to draw as much as you need. This will become especially important when rendering three-dimensional fractals, as discussed in Chapters 9 and 10. The fewer operations you have to perform, the faster the image will be created.

Interactive Snowflakes

As with most things, seeing is believing. The demonstration program *vonkoch.exe* provides an interactive means for you to see how the various combinations of generators and initiators can provide distinctly different shapes. The program lets you choose from a set of initiators and generators and then draws the selected combination. In addition, you may choose the random mode that will pick random combinations and draw them in random locations and orientations on the screen. This mode makes an interesting screen saver for your display.

Further Investigations

With the *RWFvk_Object* class, you have a very flexible means of generating many different types of fractal figures. Only a few of the myriad possibilities have been presented in this chapter. Despite the variety, however, all these figures are related by a common method of construction. They are all defined by recursive computations of affine transformations. The *RWFvk_Object* class separates a Koch-style fractal into two distinct pieces:

1. the affine transformations at each recursion level; and

2. the actual objects to draw when the recursion has proceeded far enough.

The graphical objects, whether they are lines, circles, or polygons, are not needed until the final recursion level where something must be drawn on the screen. The fractal structure is completely defined by the affine transformations. In fact, if the recursion is carried out to its infinite limit, it does not matter what type of object is used, the resulting image will be the same. There are, however, many cases where you do not want to carry the computation out to its final limit, as you will see in the next few chapters.

In this chapter, you have seen how to define fractal shapes as a recursive application of a procedure. For the Koch Curves in this chapter, the procedure is simply applying an affine transformation repeatedly. By creating the *RWFvk_Object* class, the fractal objects can be treated like any other graphical object. The main feature of interest in these objects is that they can be magnified ad infinitum and you will still see the similar structure in the shape. The fractal shapes never become smooth or uniform. As they are currently defined, however, the shapes are always the same and are not as interesting as they could be. In the next few chapters, you'll learn how to significantly improve their appearance and applicability to the real world by employing multiple generators and introducing controlled random variations.

In the next chapter, you will discover how to extend the use of affine transformations to drawing solid, two-dimensional figures, such as the Sierpinski Gasket and the Sierpinski Carpet. By generalizing the techniques shown in this chapter, you'll be able to create even more elaborately intricate, and, more importantly, useful figures. You will see how to unify all these types of procedural objects into a single base class, just as was shown for the Koch-type objects in this chapter. So, even as more types of figures are added to your repertoire, you need not add significantly more code to create them.

Fractals of the Second Kind: Two-Dimensional Fractals

In the previous chapter you saw how a very rich class of one-dimensional fractal curves can be defined by recursive applications of affine transformations. In this chapter, you will see how to define two-dimensional fractal shapes using the same basic method of specifying an initiator and a generator. For the two-dimensional case, the generators and initiators may define solid-filled objects rather than just collections of polylines and polygons. To implement this generalization of the Koch-type fractals, you further expand the definition of the *RWFvk_Object* base class to include arbitrary transformations with multidimensional initiators and generators. Using this new base class, you can then create an inexhaustible set of complex fractal objects that are very easy to use and combine. Because you will often want to manipulate these fractal objects in a variety of ways, a user-defined *action_func* function is provided that lets you draw, fill, and process a fractal object in a very general way, without having to define a whole new object class for each new drawing method. With the extra functionality available in this newly defined base class, you can incorporate procedural fractal objects as part of a more general-purpose graphics or analysis package. Thanks to the object-oriented benefits of C++, writing your own programs to explore the various fractal algorithms becomes much simpler with these new classes.

Two-Dimensions and Affine Transformations

In the same way that Chapter 5 dealt with one-dimensional curves, this chapter deals with generating fractal figures that lie in the two-dimensional plane. Instead of defining procedures for transforming one-dimensional curves and line-segment generators, you define very similar recursive methods for processing two-dimensional figures, such as triangles, rectangles, and circles. Generally, the generators and initiators define finite-area regions of the plane. You use polygonal generators and initiators most frequently because they are well behaved when mapped through an affine transformation. An affine transformation keeps straight lines straight; that is, a line segment always maps to another line segment. So, you can transform an entire polygon simply by transforming the vertices and reconnecting the transformed vertices. All the points inside the original polygon transform into points inside the transformed polygon boundary. Furthermore, the mapping is one-to-one and except for degenerate transformations (transformations that collapse the figure into a single point or a along a single line), you can get the original polygon back by using the inverse transformation. Every point in the original figure maps to a unique point in the transformed figure, and vice versa. This property is illustrated in Figure 6–1.

The one-to-one mapping property is true for any transformed, two-dimensional figure; it is just that finding the transformed boundary of an arbitrary two-dimensional shape is not as easy as it is for polygonal shapes. For instance, you can transform a circle into a rotated, translated ellipse with a suitable affine transformation. The boundary equation of the transformed circle is no longer simply the equation of a circle. The graphics package presented in Chapter 3 lets you transform any of the defined objects with an arbitrary affine transformation. All the member functions for manipulating the object, especially the *draw()* (draw the outline of the object) and *fill()* (make a solid-filled drawing) methods, can manipulate the transformed object. For instance, the *draw()* member function for a circle uses a polygonal approximation to draw a transformed circle. The ability to draw a transformed object is an important feature of the graphics package because it makes drawing all these fractal objects very straightforward to implement. Furthermore, you can create fractal objects out of different combinations of the primitive graphics objects, providing even more flexibility in the types and features of the fractals you can create, as you'll see in the examples found later in this and the next several chapters.

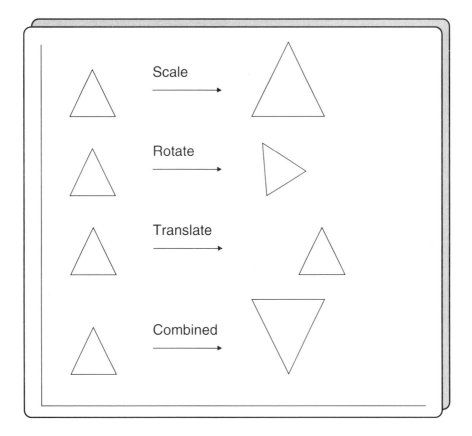

Figure 6–1. Affine transformations of polygons yield other polygons. For the nondegenerate transformations used for fractals, the transformation is uniquely invertible.

The Sierpinski Gasket

The Sierpinski Gasket is one of the most common examples of a fractal object. It is a strictly self-similar figure constructed in a very similar manner to the Koch Curves discussed in Chapter 5. Like the Koch curves, the gasket is defined by an initiator and a set of transformations for recursively generating the object. The initiator for the gasket is an equilateral triangle. The generator takes the triangle and creates a new triangle by connecting the midpoints of each side of the triangle. The new triangle is removed from the drawing, creating three new, half-sized, triangles. The process is then repeated on each of the newly created triangles. Figure 6–2 shows the initiator, generator, and resulting object.

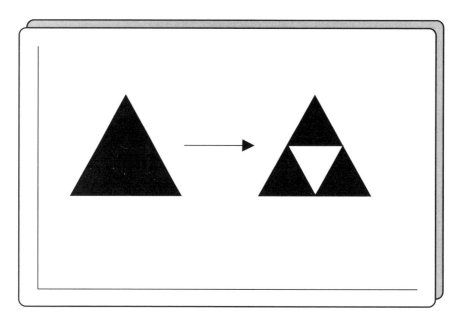

Figure 6–2. The initiator and generator for the Sierpinski Gasket and the resulting figure after one recursive step.

One interesting note about the Sierpinski Gasket is its similarity to the Cantor Set. You follow the same basic procedure of recursively removing portions, except now the procedure is performed in two dimensions using triangles. Just as with the Cantor Set, you remove the middle-third of each triangle and repeat the process ad infinitum. This type of procedural method is used for constructing many of the classic fractal images you have undoubtedly seen.

There are two different, but closely related ways to construct the Sierpinski Gasket. The first method follows the procedure discussed in Chapter 5 for Koch Curves. You start with an equilateral triangle, stored as a polygon. The polygon is then transformed three separate times, where each transformation scales the original by 0.5 in both x and y and then translates the copy to its appropriate corner. You then repeat the procedure for each new triangle.

The second approach takes a slightly different tack that directly implements the original construction method for the Cantor Set. Instead of using the recursion to determine which points are on the gasket, the recursion erases the portions of the triangle that are not part of the gasket. The drawing algorithm therefore begins by drawing the initiator triangle. The center triangle is then erased by filling in that triangle with the background color. The center triangle is also an affine transformation of the initiator. In this case, the transformation involves scaling by 0.5 in both x and y and then either rotating the triangle by 180 degrees or reflecting it about the x-axis. Either transformation yields the same result. The entire process is then repeated on the three remaining pieces.

The first method has the distinct advantage of being a direct extension of the procedure for constructing Koch Curves. As you will see, you can easily integrate this approach to generate both one- and two-dimensional fractals. The second method has the advantage of making a more interesting interactive demonstration. Using this approach, you can clearly see what happens at each recursion level, as the various portions are removed. Furthermore, you can stop this method at any given recursion level and then immediately restart it where you left off. In contrast, the first method must be restarted from scratch each time because it is only filling in the triangles at the final recursion level. Let's see how to implement both methods for drawing the Sierpinski Gasket.

Procedural Gaskets

The first procedure for drawing the Sierpinski Gasket is nearly identical to the Koch Curves of Chapter 5. In fact, the only difference occurs when the final recursion level is reached. When this level is reached, the object's (in this case, the triangle's) *fill()* method is called to draw a filled copy of the object, instead of the *draw()* member function to draw its outline. This commonality suggests a way of generalizing the *RWFvk_Object* class to draw objects such as the Sierpinski Gasket and snowflake curves. You need a base class that handles the processing of the transformations and then derives the various classes for specific types of objects from this base class.

To that end, the *RWFaf_Object* class (the *Affine Fractal* class) is defined as the base class for fractal objects defined by recursive applications of affine transformations. This class cannot be used to represent an actual fractal object. You use this class as a base class for deriving specific types. The member functions of *RWFaf_Object* handle all the processing of affine transformations.

In general, there are several action types you might like to invoke to draw an object. For Koch Curves, you invoke the *draw()* member function. For the Sierpinski Gasket, you invoke the *fill()* member function. It would be nice to provide a means of invoking any particular method you need for an object. To accomplish this, the *RWFaf_Object* class defines a generic *process()* member function to recursively generate the object. When *generate()* reaches the bottom recursion level, a user-defined function is called via a function pointer, *action_func*. The *action_func* function is passed two arguments: a pointer to the object to process and the current recursion level. You can easily create a generic object-drawing function as follows:

```
void rwf_afDraw(RWFgraph_Object *object, int level)
{
  if(object)
    object->draw();
}
```

Before diving into examples of how to define fractal objects with *RWFaf_Object*, let's see how it works. The *process()* member function uses a generalized initiator, just as shown in Chapter 5 for the *RWFvk_Object* class. Listing 6–1 shows the *process()* and *generate()* member functions for the *RWFaf_Object* class.

Listing 6–1. The *process()* and *generate()* member functions for the *RWFaf_Object* class.

```
void
RWFaf_Object::process(void)
{
  RWFmat_Matrix save_matrix;
  // base_object is an RWFgraph_Object pointer

  if(!action_func)
    return;    // No actions are defined!

  for(int i=0; i < objectptrlist.size(); i++) {
    base_object = objectptrlist[i];
    cur_object_size = objectsizelist[i];
    save_matrix = base_object->getMatrix();
    generate(base_matrix * save_matrix, 0);
    base_object->setMatrix(save_matrix);
  }
}


void
RWFaf_Object::generate(RWFmat_Matrix &pmatrix,
                       int level)
{
  // Reached max recursion level yet?
  if(level >= max_level) {
    base_object->setMatrix(pmatrix);
    (*action_func) (base_object, level);
    return;
  }

  // Now, is the object small enough?
  float scale = rwf_matGetGlobalScalingFactor(pmatrix);
```

```
    if((scale * cur_object_size) <= min_object_size) {
      base_object->setMatrix(pmatrix);
      (*action_func) (base_object, level);
      return;
    }

    int next_level = level + 1;
    for(int i=0; i < transforms.size(); i++) {
      // OK, go to the next recursion level
      generate(pmatrix * transforms[i], next_level);
    }
  }
```

You can set the action function to call with the *setAction()* member function. For instance, you can set the Koch drawing function with a call such as:

```
    object->setAction(&rwf_afDraw);
```

In general though, you will not need to do this explicitly in your program. Instead, you derive a new fractal object class from the *RWFaf_Object* class and make the *draw()* function for the class do the work for you. For instance, you can now define the *RWFvk_Object* class as a derived class of the *RWFaf_Object* class as follows:

```
class RWFvk_Object : public RWFaf_Object {
 private:
  protected:
  public:

  // The constructor defines the generator and initiator
  RWFvk_Object(void);

  // The drawing function also sets the action
  // and calls process()
  void draw(void)
    {if(!action_func)setAction(&rwf_afDraw); process();}
```

```
void fill(void)
   {if(!action_func)setAction(&rwf_afFill); process();};
};
```

Using this definition, an *RWFvk_Object* automatically sets the action function to the appropriate drawing function whenever the object is drawn by calling its *draw()* member function. This can, of course, be overridden later by another call to *setAction()* for the object. In most cases, however, you will want to simply use the default *draw()* and *fill()* functions *rwf_afDraw()* and *rwf_afFill()* because they perform the default drawing action you would normally want to use.

The *RWFaf_Object* class has the same *setGenerator()* and *setInitiator()* functions as *RWFvk_Object* does. Generators are always specified as a series of affine transformations. Unlike the *RWFvk_Object* class, generators do not have to form a connected sequence, nor do they have to be normalized in the same fashion as the Koch fractals. You may use any series of transformations. The transformations, however, must have a global-scaling factor less than 1.0, otherwise the fractal will expand at each recursion level, producing very undesirable results.

You can now understand at least part of the reason why the initiator is stored in the form that it is, namely, as a list of pointers to objects. This format is somewhat inconvenient for the Koch initiators, which are normally specified as polylines. However, this initiator format lets you generate fractal objects based on any graphics object, including solid-filled objects such as the triangles of the Sierpinski Gasket as well as the three-dimensional objects you will see in later chapters.

Similarly, the *RWFaf_Object* class has no explicit references to the dimensionality of the affine transformations used. You can therefore use the *RWFaf_Object* to generate multidimensional objects with the same ease as the Koch objects. Using the generalized action function, you can perform any desired processing at the bottom recursion level, such as drawing, filling, three-dimensional projection, or analysis.

Classical Gasket

Defining the Sierpinski Gasket, as well as most other procedural fractal objects, using the *RWFaf_Object* class is straightforward. You derive a new class for your fractal object from *RWFaf_Object*, and then define its constructor to supply the appropriate initiator and generator for the object. The definition for a Sierpinski Gasket object is shown in Listing 6–2.

Listing 6–2. Definition of the Sierpinski Gasket as a derived class from RWFaf_Object.

```
class RWFsg_Gasket : public RWFaf_Object {
  private:
  protected:
  public:

  RWFsg_Gasket(void);
  // both draw() and fill() fill the bottom-level
  // triangles
  void draw(void)  {if(!action_func)setaction(&rwf_afFill);process();};
  void fill(void)  {if(!action_func)setaction(&rwf_afFill);process();};
}


// Void constructor for the Sierpinski Gasket
// This set's both the generator and the initiator
RWFsg_Gasket::RWFsg_Gasket(void)
{
  RWFmat_MatrixTable mtable;
  float height = sqrt(0.75);

  // Define the generator by a series of transformations
  // operating on a centered triangle
  // First, scale by 1/2
   mtable[0].scale(1/2.0, 1/2.0);
  // Now translate to the lower corner
   mtable[0].translate(-0.25, -height/4.0);
  // Second triangle, scale and translate to other corner
```

```
 mtable[1].scale(1/2.0, 1/4.0);
 mtable[1].translate(0.25, -height/4.0);
 // Third triangle, scale and translate vertically
 mtable[2].scale(1/2.0, 1/2.0);
 mtable[2].translate(0.0, height/4.0);

 setGenerator(mtable);

 // Now set the initiator, a simple, unit-sided triangle
 RWFlist_ObjectPtrTable otable;
 RWFgraph_Polygon *triangle = new RWFgraph_Polygon;

 // Note that the initiator must be allocated by new
 // so that the object-pointer table can be appropriately
 // destroyed when the object is destroyed

  (*triangle)[0].setCoord(-0.5, -height/2.0);
  (*triangle)[1].setCoord( 0.5, -height/2.0);
  (*triangle)[2].setCoord( 0.0,  height/2.0);
 otable[0] = triangle;
 setInitiator(otable);
}
```

Now you may use the *RWFsg_Gasket* object just as any other graphical object because *RWFsg_Gasket* is derived from *RWFaf_Object*, which in turn is derived from the *RWFgraph_Object* base class. So, a *RWFsg_Gasket* object may be rotated, scaled, translated, drawn in different colors, and used in the same way as are any of the other graphics objects, such as circles and lines. In general, you may create a class for any procedurally defined fractal object by deriving it from the *RWFaf_Object* class. You simply define any special actions, such as drawing, filling, setting the color based on the recursion level, or any other action you would like to perform on the object at the bottom recursion level. The only significant code you must add is in the object's constructor, which is done by defining the initiator and the generator. In the Sierpinski Gasket, for instance, the constructor defines the initiator as an equilateral triangle and the generator as the three transformations to apply to the triangle. You can easily create a new type of Sierpinski object that uses, for example, circles instead of triangles or five transformations instead of three. The

RWFaf_Object handles all the work of implementing the recursion; you need only specify the specific shapes and transformations you would like to use. This gives you an incredible amount of flexibility to create new fractal objects of your own design.

In accordance with good object-oriented programming techniques, there are many things that the *RWFaf_Object* class takes care of behind the scenes. For instance, an object must make sure to delete all the data that it used whenever it is deleted. For the *RWFaf_Object*, this includes destroying the data associated with the initiator and the generator. Whenever you use *setInitiator()*, *RWFaf_Object* makes a copy of the object table you pass. However, only the actual table and the pointers in the table are copied; the structures addressed by the individual pointers are not copied. When an *RWFaf_Object* is deleted, the table is deleted and the destructor for each object that the pointers in the table reference are deleted. Similarly, the matrices defining the generators are deleted as well.

However, things get a little more complicated when using derived classes and tables of pointers, such as when you are storing the initiator. When you use *setInitiator()*, in the constructor for the Sierpinski Gasket, you must use *new* to allocate the base initiator, in this case, a triangle. You could simply declare the triangle locally in the constructor, and the triangle would be deleted when the constructor returns. This, however, would mean that the pointer in the table passed to *setInitiator()* would no longer be valid. The triangle is automatically deleted when the constructor returns. You must therefore allocate the triangle from the heap, so that it is not prematurely deleted after the constructor is finished.

The situation is not the same for the *setGenerator()* member function. For this function, you pass a table of matrices, in which each element of the table is itself a matrix. When you call *setGenerator()*, it copies each of the matrices in the table. You can therefore use a local matrix table, as was done in the constructor for *RWFsg_Gasket*. The local table is copied by *setGenerator()*, so the original table does not need to be kept around. In general, whenever you pass a table of objects to a class, the class makes a copy of the table and all its elements for its own use. If you use a table of pointers, only the pointers are copied (as they are the actual elements of the table), not the objects the pointers reference.

The point to all this is that the issue of how these tables are stored and manipulated is internal to the *RWFaf_Object* class. As long as you properly allocate the initiator objects in the object's constructor, everything will be properly handled when the object is deleted, or otherwise manipulated. From your application program's standpoint, you do not have to worry about the internal structure used by the class, you only have to pass data in the format that the class' member functions requires. This is the essence of object-oriented programming: to define classes that deal with all the subtle implementation issues for you and require little or, preferably, no knowledge of how the details are sorted by the class. You may then derive new classes from this base class and gain all the functionality of the class with almost no effort. The fractal classes of this chapter are just one example of how C++ can greatly simplify your code and let you concentrate on your specific application.

Sierpinski Variations

You can now create many different types of fractal curves using the *RWFaf_Object* class. A number of other examples are provided on the disk that accompanies this book. The *Sierpinski Carpet* is based on using squares instead of the triangles of the gasket, but the procedure for constructing the figure is very similar. You begin with a square and divide it into nine smaller squares, as shown in Figure 6–3. Then, you remove the middle square and repeat the process on the eight remaining squares. Just as with the gasket, this procedure is a two-dimensional analog of constructing the Cantor Set. The generator for the carpet consists of eight transformations. Each transformation simply scales the square by a third in both x and y, and then translates it to one of the eight positions for the remaining squares. The *RWFsg_Carpet* class is provided on the disk that accompanies this book to generate this figure. The resulting figure is shown in Figure 6–3.

Figure 6–3. The Sierpinski Carpet.

Another variation on the same approach is shown in the next object, which is based on hexagons. Here, you start with an initiator hexagon that is not centered. You then apply a generator that rotates and shrinks the hexagon. The final figure shows a hexagon spiraling toward the center of the object. You must be careful to choose the rotation angles and scale factors appropriately to prevent the objects from overlapping. The resulting figure is shown in Figure 6–4.

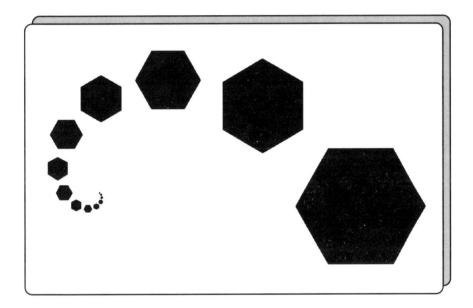

Figure 6–4. A spiraling hexagon.

There are so many possibilities with these types of objects that it is impossible to even remotely present them. However, the fact that each fractal object may be treated as a graphics object in its own right lets you combine them in intriguing ways. For instance, Figure 6–5 shows a Sierpinski Carpet in which instead of using squares, uses a gasket as the initiator. You should try experimenting with various combinations of initiators and generators to see the rich set of fractal figures you can produce.

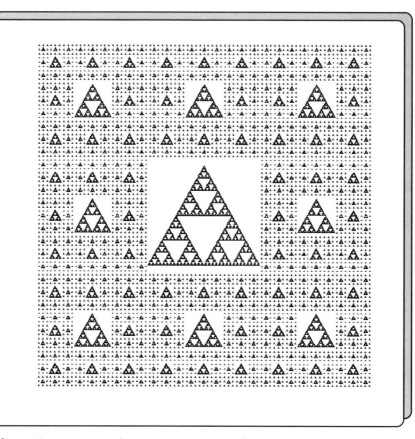

Figure 6–5. A Sierpinski Carpet composed of Sierpinski Gaskets.

A *Second Drawing Method*

As previously mentioned, there is another approach that can be taken to draw the gasket. Basically, you draw the filled initiator and then start erasing the portions of it that do not belong to the gasket. Despite the differences in this drawing approach from the one described for the *RWFaf_Object* classes, you can modify the *generate()* function to draw the object in this manner. Two new member functions, *process_reverse()* and *generate_reverse()*, are used to invoke this modified drawing method. The only difference in *process_reverse()* is that it calls *generate_reverse()* instead of *generate()*, and it draws the initiator before starting the recursive calls to *generate_reverse()*. The only difference in *generate_reverse()* is that it "erases" the regions that do not belong to the object at each recursion level, rather than waiting to reach the bottom recursion level before drawing anything.

To use this drawing method, you must provide two sets of initiators. The first initiator is the same as the one used in the normal drawing method. The second initiator, called the erase initiator, specifies the region to "erase" at each recursion level. The erase initiator is specified relative to the first initiator; that is, it is properly scaled to specify the regions to erase in the main initiator. The simplest way to do this is to copy the first initiator and then set the transformation matrix for the erase initiator appropriately. For example, the erase initiator for the Sierpinski Gasket may be constructed from the equilateral triangle used for the main initiator with the following code segment:

```
// Use the same triangle as the initiator
RWFgraph_Polygon *copy_tri = new RWFgraphPolygon;
RWFlist_ObjectPtrTable etable;
(*copy_tri) = (*triangle);
copy_tri->rotate(180.0);      // Rotate by 180 degrees
copy_tri->scale(0.5, 0.5);    // Scale by 1/2
copy_tri->translate(0.0, -height/4.0);
copy_tri->setColor(RWFGRAPH_COLOR_BLACK);
etable[0] = copy_tri;
setEraseInitiator(etable);
```

To simplify the creation of erase initiators, the *setEraseInitiator()* member function is provided in several overloaded forms. The first is the same as *setInitiator()*, where you provide a table of pointers to objects to be drawn. The second overloaded form takes a table of matrices as an argument. This version of *setEraseInitiator()* applies the matrices to the main initiator, creating a new object-pointer table for the erase initiator. Using this form of *setEraseInitiator()* is easiest because you only have to specify the series of transformations to apply to the base initiator.

While the default action for the erase initiator is to erase the region not belonging to the fractal object, it may also be used in other ways. For instance, you can fill in the region by drawing another object. Figure 6–6 shows one example in which each removed region of a gasket is filled with an inverted gasket. The *process_reverse()* and *generate_reverse()* routines are shown in Listing 6–3.

Figure 6–6. A Sierpinski Gasket filled with other gaskets.

Listing 6–3. The *process_reverse()* and *generate_reverse()* member functions for the *RWFaf_Object* class.

```
void

RWFaf_Object::process_reverse(void)

{

 RWFmat_Matrix save_matrix;
 // base_object is an RWFgraph_Object pointer

 if(!action_func)
    return;    // No actions are defined!
```

```
   for(int i=0; i < objectptrlist.size(); i++) {
     base_object = objectptrlist[i];
     cur_object_size = objectsizelist[i];
     save_matrix = base_object->getMatrix();
     // Draw the initiator
     base_object->setMatrix(base_matrix * save_matrix);
     (*action_func)(base_object, 0);
     generate_reverse(base_matrix * save_matrix, 0);
     base_object->setMatrix(save_matrix);
   }
}


void
RWFaf_Object::generate_reverse(RWFmat_Matrix &pmatrix,
                                 int level)
{
  // Reached max recursion level yet?
  if(level >= max_level)
    return;

  // Now, is the object small enough?
  float scale = rwf_matGetGlobalScalingFactor(pmatrix);
  if((scale * cur_object_size) <= min_object_size)
    return;

  int next_level = level + 1;
  // OK, now erase the appropriate regions
  for(int i=0; i < erase_object.size(); i++) {
    RWFmat_Matrix save_matrix;
    save_matrix = erase_object[i]->getMatrix();
    erase_object[i]->setMatrix(pmatrix * save_matrix);
    (*action_func) (erase_object[i], next_level);
    erase_object[i]->setMatrix(save_matrix);
  }

  for(i=0; i < numTransforms(); i++) {
    // OK, go to the next recursion level
      generate_reverse(pmatrix * transforms[i], next_level);
  }
}
```

The action function is used to draw both the main initiator and the erase initiator. It is therefore important to set the colors of the objects in each initiator appropriately. If they are set to the same colors, you will not see anything drawn on the screen, except the main initiator. The erase initiator is stored in the private *erase_object* object-pointer table, in exactly the same way as the main initiator.

For each of the Sierpinski classes, *RWFsg_Gasket* and *RWFsg_Carpet*, there are equivalently defined reverse classes, *RWFsg_ReverseGasket* and *RWFsg_ReverseCarpet*. They are virtually identical to the original classes, except that they draw their respective objects using the *process_reverse()* function. If you simply create one of these objects and then draw it, you will create the same resulting image using either type. The differences show up when you start to provide new drawing functions for *setAction()*. The reverse drawing method provides considerably more flexibility in making a more colorful and instructive image because you can pause as each recursion level is drawn.

Adding a Little Color

By using this second drawing method, you now have considerably more flexibility in adding color to the drawing. For instance, you can use a different color for the regions erased at each recursion level. The following drawing function cycles through the various colors:

```
void
rwf_afDrawColorCycle(RWFgraph_Object *object, int level)
{
 if(!object)
 return;
object->setColor((level % 15) + 1);
object->draw();
}
```

Assuming you use no more than 15 levels of recursion, each pixel in the resulting image is assigned a color value that indicates the recursion level at which it was erased. The initiator is first filled with the color value of 1 pixel. Using this drawing function, succeeding regions are erased by filling with pixel values of 2, 3, and continuing until 15, depending on the recursion level. When the drawing is completed, any pixels storing the value of 1 belong to the final fractal figure, all the other pixels were removed at some point during the recursion.

The reverse drawing method is also better for interactively creating the image. The demonstration program presented at the end of this chapter illustrates this by showing images created by both means. With the reverse method, you are erasing areas of the screen, which means that you can pick up an image wherever it leaves off with a suitable modification to the drawing function. To facilitate this, the global functions *RWFaf_setLastLevel()* and *RWFaf_getLastLevel()* are provided to let your drawing function track the last processed level. The modified drawing function to track levels is:

```
rwf_afDrawLastLevel(RWFgraph_Object *object, int level)
{
  int old_level = RWF_afGetLastLevel
  if(!object || level <= old_level)
    return;

  object->draw();
}
```

Initially, you would set the last level to -1, indicating that all levels should be processed. If the Sierpinski Gasket were drawn to recursion level three, and you wanted to now draw it to level five, you would set the maximum level to five for the gasket, and then call *rwf_afSetLastLevel(3)*. Only levels four and five will actually be processed, usually resulting in a considerable improvement in drawing speed. This is how the demonstration program steps through recursion levels relatively quickly without having to blank the screen and start over each time.

Interesting Combinations

As mentioned earlier, you can combine the various procedural fractal objects to produce some interesting figures. By properly structuring your base classes, the actual code to produce the figures is remarkably short. For instance, the code to produce the image in Figure 6–6 is simply:

```
RWFsg_ReverseGasket main_gasket;
RWFsg_Gasket erase_gasket;
RWFlist_ObjectPtrTable etable;

// Set up the appropriately transformed gasket
erase_gasket.rotate(180.0);
erase_gasket.scale(0.5, 0.5);
erase_gasket.translate(0.0, -sqrt(0.75)/4.0);
erase_gasket.setColor(RWFGRAPH_COLOR_WHITE);
etable[0] = &erase_gasket;

// Remove default erase initiator and replace with
// the gasket
main_gasket.setEraseInitiator(etable);


main_gasket.setColor(RWFGRAPH_COLOR_GREEN);
main_gasket.fill();
main_gasket.setColor(RWF_COLOR_GREEN);
main_gasket.draw();
```

The only real work is in specifying the transformation of the erase initiator. Everything else is the same as what you would need to draw any other graphics object. Notice that you can also easily use other types of objects, not just triangles in the gasket. For instance, you can use a circle for the erase initiator to create a close relative of the gasket as shown in Figure 6–7. Furthermore, by skewing the generators and initiators, figures such as the one in Figure 6–8 can be produced. You should start with the various demonstration programs provided on the disk that accompanies this book and try your own variations to see what the effects of altering the initiators and generators are.

Color plates one, two, and three show some of the more colorful combinations of objects you can create with these classes. The programs for generating each of these screen images may be found in the modules *plate1.cpp*, *plate2.cpp*, and *plate3.cpp*. You will see that even though the images are quite elaborate, the actual code is fairly short and easy to read. As with most object-oriented programming, all the effort goes into developing a strong set of base classes that encapsulate the essential parts of the algorithm. All these fractal objects are related by one fundamental algorithm: recursively iterating through a series of affine transformations on a set of base objects, regardless of the type of base objects used (even other fractal objects may be used).

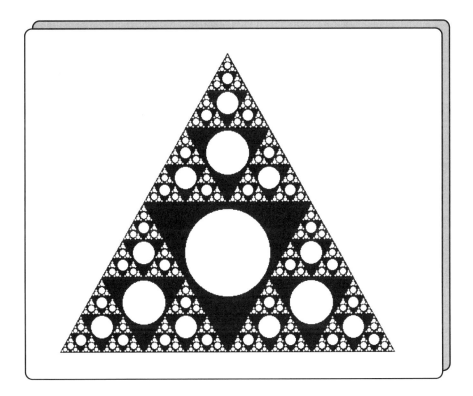

Figure 6–7. Using a circle as the erase initiator in the Sierpinski Gasket.

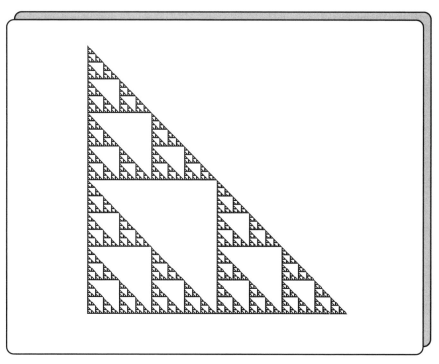

Figure 6–8. By skewing the initiator triangle, the generators produce some interesting effects on the basic gasket.

A Procedural Demonstration

To illustrate the flexibility of the drawing methods for procedural objects, the program *gaskets.exe* is provided on the disk accompanying this book. Just as with the *vonkoch.exe* demonstration program from the previous chapter, *gaskets.exe* lets you select the initiators from several different objects and then erase the initiators of the various gasket-type fractals. Additionally, the objects are drawn in a variety of colors, letting you observe how the recursion progresses. When your selected object is completed, the color palette is cycled to create a very colorful fractal display. The program will also run in an unattended mode, randomly selecting the initiator and generator combinations. Even with these limited sets, the program has a very long cycle before repeating any given combination.

Closer to the Real World

In this chapter, you have seen how to unify all the self-affine fractal objects into one consistent base class, the *RWFaf_Object* class. These objects include the Koch Curves, the Sierpinski Gasket and Carpet and their innumerable relatives, along with the three-dimensional fractals presented in Chapter 9. The C++ programming language provides a direct means of expressing the underlying structure of this type of fractal object. Specific fractal objects, such as the Sierpinski Gasket, are then easily derived from the *RWFaf_Object* class and may then be drawn or processed in a variety of ways. By providing a general *action* function through the *setAction()* member function, you can use these fractal objects in other ways besides simply drawing them on the screen. This flexibility lets you create many of the classic fractal images and many that you have probably never seen by mixing and matching initiators and generators.

In the next chapter, you'll see how these procedural models may be extended even further to incorporate random variations characteristic of natural phenomena. Perfect self-similarity, like the perfect line, is not found in nature. Instead, self-similarity occurs in a statistical sense, namely that the self-similar components are approximately, rather than precisely, the same. As Mandelbrot observed, self-similar structures can be found in many natural objects, from the plants in your garden to the stars in the galaxies. The techniques presented in Chapter 7 provide a way to merge the idealized self-similar models of this chapter with realistic models of natural objects. So it's back to nature in the next chapter!

Natural Fractals

I n the previous chapter, you learned how to generalize the procedural modeling techniques introduced in Chapter 5 to create a variety of procedural-based fractal objects in any number of dimensions. These fractal objects, however, do not correspond directly to any real objects you might find in nature. Fractals such as the Koch Curve and the Sierpinski Gasket are purely mathematical constructs, just as Euclidean lines, circles, and curves are. Such mathematical objects are really abstractions of what you find in nature.

These mathematical shapes are useful because they closely, though not exactly, approximate the geometry of nature. Any real object will not have a mathematically ideal shape. An object like a soap bubble may resemble a sphere, but it will not be a perfect sphere. There are always random variations that perturb the bubble from its idealized shape. In this chapter, you'll learn how to turn the ideal mathematical fractals from the previous chapter into more realistic objects by introducing random variations. By matching the random variations in our fractal model to those found in real objects, you can create excellent approximations of many complex objects found in nature.

The appeal of these fractal models extends beyond their properties that let you accurately recreate the structure and appearance of natural objects, of course. Fractal models of real objects provide the very important capability of letting you magnify an object to see new detail. Just as you can magnify the Koch Curve ad infinitum and still see fine detail, you can also magnify any of the fractal shapes described in the previous chapters. A traditional polygonal model of a tree, for instance, requires that you digitize and store every leaf and branch of the tree. This can become quite an extensive data base, requiring massive amounts of storage. And regardless of how much data you store, you will ultimately reach a maximum resolution of data.

A fractal model solves this problem of reaching a maximum resolution by providing a simple computational means of generating greater detail only as you need it. You can zoom into the Sierpinski Gasket (by scaling it) as much as you like, and the drawing algorithm will always generate portions of the gasket at finer resolution, for instance. Similarly, if you have a fractal model of a tree, you can zoom in on a particular branch and see its details. A fractal model of a tree requires far less storage than a traditional purely geometric description of a tree, and it provides far greater detail.

By introducing random variations to your fractal models, you can make them appear far more realistic. However, you must introduce these variations in a controlled way so you always get the same tree each time you draw a particular fractal object. This is why the structure of the random-number generators described in Chapter 4 are so important. By always starting with the same random seed, the fractal will always be the same, regardless of how you manipulate it. This feature is especially vital in three-dimensional drawing applications, as you will see in Chapters 9 and 10.

Statistical Self-Similarity

As an example of introducing randomness to a fractal shape, let's consider the problem of making a more realistic snowflake out of the Koch

Curve. One approach to introducing randomness is to alter the generator randomly at each recursion level. Instead of using the same generator, you randomly modify the generator and use this modified transformation for the next recursion level. The question then becomes: Exactly how do you vary the generator?

The answer, of course, depends on what effect you are trying to introduce. A simple way to modify the Koch Curve generator is to vary its height, as shown in Figure 7–1. At each level of recursion, a new height is generated using the following expression:

$$height = mean\_height + sigma * rwf\_randGaussian(seed)$$

(Equation 7–1)

Equation 7–1 is the general expression used to generate a random variable with a known mean (represented by the variable *mean_height*) and standard deviation (represented by the variable *sigma*). In this example, normally distributed heights are generated, but you can use any other random-number generator in place of *rwf_randGaussian()*. The particular random-number generator used is not important in this example, but it is quite important when you are trying to match a particular real-world object. You will see a number of examples of the effects of using different distributions throughout this and the following chapters.

As shown in Figure 7–1, the mean height of the Koch Curve generator is *(1/3 * sqrt(3/4))*. The value for the standard deviation, *sigma*, may be chosen arbitrarily. In general, though, you would probably not want to use a value greater than the mean height because such large deviations tend to produce quite unusual and not always desirable effects.

To use this randomized generator, you must modify the *generate()* member function to do the following:

1. compute the new height of the generator for this iteration of *generate()*;

2. turn the polyline definition of the generator into its corresponding matrix definition; and

3. apply the randomized generator to the next recursive call to *generate()*.

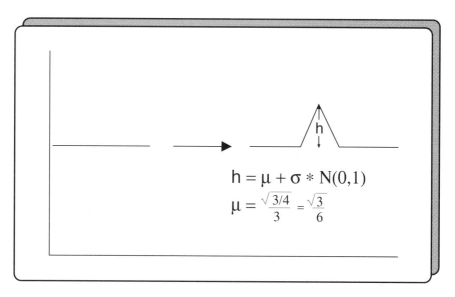

$$h = \mu + \sigma * N(0,1)$$
$$\mu = \frac{\sqrt{3/4}}{3} = \frac{\sqrt{3}}{6}$$

Figure 7–1. Randomly varying the height of the Koch Curve generator.

For the first step, use Equation 7–1 to compute the new generator height. Recall that the *setGenerator()* member function of the *RWFvk_Object* class has an overloaded version that takes a polyline and converts it into its corresponding matrix representation. This overloaded version uses the function *RWFmat_PolylineToMatrixTable()* to perform the conversion, and then calls *setGenerator()* with the resulting matrix table. One way to implement the randomized generator for the Koch Curve is to use *RWFmat_PolylineToMatrixTable()* in a modified *generate()* function to compute the new generators based on randomized polyline definitions of the generators. This accomplishes the second step of the randomizing procedure. The third step is accomplished the same way it usually is, except that now the randomized generator is used instead of the normal Koch Curve generator. The randomizing process is shown in Figure 7–2.

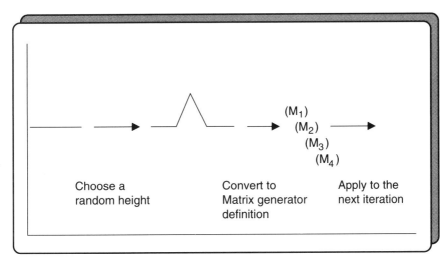

Figure 7–2. Randomizing the Koch Curve consists of three steps.

Figure 7–3 shows several randomized Koch Curves at various recursion levels. There are three basic curves with different values of *sigma* across the figure horizontally. Each Koch Curve uses the same mean height. As you can see, simply varying *sigma* can have a significant effect on the appearance of the curve. However, each curve still appears quite similar to the original, non-randomized Koch Curve. Because these curves have different random variations at each recursion level, they are not truly self-similar. Rather, they possess a property known as statistical self-similarity.

Statistical self-similarity simply means that the curve possesses the self-similarity property in an average statistical sense. For the Koch Curve, you can magnify a section of the curve by a factor of three, and the resulting figure will have the same general structure as the original curve. This is not surprising from the method of construction. The generator is still the same basic shape, only the height changes at each recursion level. The resulting curves are very similar, just not identical. This corresponds to what you see in the real-world objects around you. The leaves of a tree are not precisely identical, but they all possess the same basic shape and structure. By introducing randomness into these fractal models, you can create more realistic models of naturally occurring objects and phenomenon.

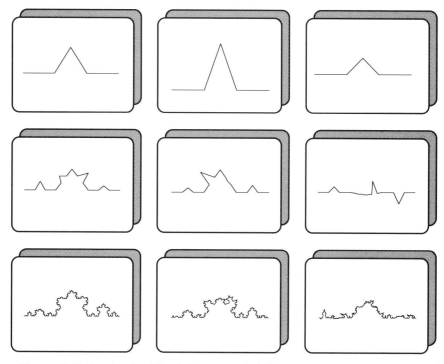

Figure 7–3. Randomized Koch Curves with different values of sigma going across and different recursion levels going down the figure.

General Randomness

You can vary the Koch Curve generator in ways other than the one just presented. For instance, you could randomly vary the point at which the first segment ends and the second one begins. Similarly, you could adjust the peak point of the generator (endpoint of the second segment) both vertically (adjusts the height) and horizontally (moves it side to side). In general, you can modify a generator in a variety of ways, depending on the particular application you have in mind. For polyline-based generators, these variations are characterized simply by changing the points along the polyline, with the exception of the first and last point. As pointed out in Chapter 5, the first and last point must remain fixed to retain a connected figure. (You could, however, vary the positions of the first and last points as long as the generator is renormalized at each step. This isn't usually done because of the extra computational expense). This leads to a general method of randomizing Koch Curves: taking the unmodified generator and producing a new generator by randomly moving the points along the polyline. Then you use *RWFmat_PolylineToMatrixTable()* to generate the matrix form of the generator.

To implement this method, you modify the *RWFvk_Object* class to include a provision for a randomizing function that's similar to the action function described in Chapter 6. Your user-supplied function performs any desired modification to the polyline generator. The function is passed the normal polyline generator as a reference for randomizing. Whenever you call the *setGenerator()* member function for an *RWFvk_Object* object, it creates both the matrix representation and the polyline representation of the generator. Your randomizing function is passed the polyline description of the generator as one of its arguments. The revised version of *generate()* is shown in Listing 7–1.

Listing 7–1. Version of generate() with support for a randomized generator.

```
void
RWFvk_Object::generate(void)
{
  // Initialization and checks for reaching the final
  // recursion level

  ...

  // The only difference in this version of generate()
  // is in the call to randomize the generator
  if(random_func) {
    (*random_func)(basepoly_generator, level, rand_data,
            ranpoly_generator);
    // Now find matrix transformations
    RWFmat_PolylineToMatrixTable(ranpoly_generator,
                  transforms);
  }

  int next_level = level + 1;
  for(int i=0; i < numTransforms(); i++) {
```

```
        // OK, go to the next recursion level
        generate(pmatrix * transforms[i], next_level);
    }
}
```

The function pointer *random_func* points to the randomizing function you provide. This function is passed the polyline version of the generator, the current recursion level, another pointer for user-supplied data, and an output polyline in which to store the result. In general, the output polyline should have the same number of points as the input polyline. When your function returns the randomized polyline, *generate()* converts it into the equivalent matrix-table representation and uses the new polyline in place of the base generator.

In addition to the base polyline generator, your randomizing function is also passed the current recursion level and a pointer to user-supplied data. The recursion level may be used by your randomizing function to vary the randomizing characteristics. If you are using normally distributed random numbers, for instance, you might want to change the standard deviation of the distribution at the finer recursion levels. You can even incorporate changes such as using different distributions at different recursion levels. You will see several examples that exploit this capability in the succeeding chapters on simulating Brownian movement (random fluctuations in the motion of microscopic objects in a fluid that are caused by the constant bombardment by the surrounding molecules) and terrain modeling.

The user-supplied data pointer provides the mechanism for passing a pointer to any type of structure you like. You can, for instance, define a structure (or a class) that specifies the mean and standard deviation to use in the random-number generation, as in the following:

```
class my_random_data {
  public:
    float mean, stdev;
};
```

In general, you will also want to include a random-number seed in the passed data. By passing an explicit seed, you can recreate a particular "random" curve exactly by using the same seed.

The user-defined data pointer provides considerable flexibility in the type of information you can pass to generate a randomized fractal object. Let's implement the function for randomizing the height of the Koch Curve generator, for instance. You must create a randomizing function and a data structure to specify the mean height and standard deviation. You then call the *setRandomFunction()* member function of the *RWFvk_Object* class to specify that the Koch Curve is to be randomized.

```
// A sample class to specify the data for the curve

class RWFvk_HeightData {
  public:
  long initial_seed;  // Random-number seed
  float mean, stdev;
};

// Now define the randomizing function

void
rwf_vkRandomizeHeight(RWFgraph_Polyline &basepoly,
  int level, void *rand_data, RWFgraph_Polyline &outpoly)
{
  float new_height;
  RWFvk_HeightData *hdata = (RWFvk_HeightData *)rand_data;
  long seed;

  // Temporary coordinate to hold the (x, y) position
  // of the center of the generator
  // Note the use of the constructor with an integer
  // argument to create a two-element vector
  RWFvec_Vector temp_coord(2);

  // Copy the base polyline to the output polyline
  outpoly = basepoly;
  // If no data, then don't randomize
```

```
    if(!hdata)
      return;

    // Use the starting seed if we are at the first level
    if(level == 1)
      seed = hdata->initial_seed;

    new_height = hdata->mean +
      rwf_randGaussian(seed)*hdata->stdev;

    // Now replace the y coordinate with the new height
    temp_coord = outpoly[2].getCoord();
    temp_coord[1] = new_height;  // Set the y coordinate
    outpoly[2].setCoord(temp_coord);

    return;
}


RWFvk_Object snowflake;
RWFvk_HeightData hdata;

// Initialize the snowflake object as in Chapter 5
...

// Now setup the data and randomize
hdata.mean = (1.0/3.0) * sqrt(3.0 / 4.0);
hdata.stdev = hdata.mean / 2.0;
hdata.initial_seed = 1010101;
snowflake.setRandomFunction(&rwf_vkRandomizeHeight,
                  &hdata);
snowflake.draw();
```

In this particular example, the *level* parameter is used to set the initial seed. Whenever *generate()* processes the first level, the seed is reset to the initial seed passed in the user-defined data structure. By including the random-number seed in this structure, you ensure that the same figure is generated for a particular object by using the same seed. The ability to exactly reproduce a randomized fractal will be very important later when you create the terrain models of Chapter 10.

One nice feature of this approach to randomizing a polyline generator is that you do not have to worry about the scale or orientation of the object. Your randomizing function always works on the generator at the same scale and orientation, regardless of how the fractal object is scaled, rotated, or translated. Similarly, you do not have to worry about the current recursion level whenever your randomizing routine is called. Because of affine-transformations usage, the generator is automatically scaled by the proper amount as the recursion proceeds, just as in the non-randomized case. The *RWFvk_Object* class completely separates the problem of randomizing the generator from putting it in the proper position on the object. This greatly simplifies the implementation of the randomizing function, as the Koch Curve demonstrates.

You should note that we added the randomizing capability to the *RWFvk_Object* class in a completely transparent way, that is, without changing the syntax or calling sequence of any other member functions. Although the *generate()* member function was modified to support the randomizing capability, it is still completely compatible with the deterministic fractals of Chapters 5 and 6. If a randomizing function has not been set by a call to *setRandomFunction()*, then *generate()* behaves exactly as it did before. Providing new object capabilities without obsoleting other object attributes or features is an important aspect of good object-oriented design and one you should remember when adding new features, though it's not *always* possible to do. However, C++ makes it much easier to maintain compatibility in this manner because you can overload the same function names with different arguments (for instance, to pass additional parameters to support new features) and freely add new member functions to the same class.

There are many other ways in which the polyline can be varied, including shifting points both vertically and horizontally or performing such actions as flipping the generator so it points up or down, based on a random selection. Furthermore, you can pass as much data as you need to the randomizing routine by putting whatever data is required into the passed structure. The randomizing capabilities of the *RWFvk_Object* class provide you with the means for exploring the effects of introducing random variations into Koch Curves. This approach, however, does not solve the problem of the more general case in which the generator is purely a sequence of affine transformations that are not derived from a polyline generator. Let's see how to add the randomizing capability to the more general *RWFaf_Object* class.

Plants and Trees

Instead of diving right into the mechanics of randomizing the *RWFaf_Object* class, let's consider the more practical problem of creating realistic models of naturally occurring objects such as plants and trees. A tree can be thought of as a self-similar object in that—within a reasonable range of scales—each branch of a tree has a number of branches connected to it. For many types of trees, each branch resembles the branch to which it is attached, but only smaller. To keep things simple, let's start with a two-dimensional model of a tree. As you'll see, you can easily extend this model to produce a realistic three-dimensional model of the tree.

Figure 7–4 shows the basic approach to creating a model of a tree. You begin with the trunk of the tree and attach several branches along the trunk. The same procedure is applied to each new branch in a hopefully now familiar recursive manner. The process is then carried out until a final branching stage is reached. This corresponds to reaching a prespecified maximum recursion level. In this simple model, each branch is drawn as a straight line. At each recursion step, the branch is scaled, rotated, and translated to a new position on the parent branch. For each branch, the generator defines the number of child branches to attach to the parent.

Just as with the Sierpinski Gasket, you want to draw each branch as it is generated. You therefore use the *process_reverse()* method to draw the tree. Unlike the gasket, you do not need to erase portions of the tree with an initiator. For the tree, you set the initiator and the erase initiator to be exactly the same object, a unit line segment. The *process_reverse()* member function then draws the branches at every recursion level you desire. In order to orient the tree properly on the screen, the line segment is oriented vertically with one end at (0, 0) and the other end at (0, 1).

Listing 7–2 shows how to derive a class, the *RWFaf_SimpleTree* class, to generate the tree shown in Figure 7–4. You will notice that the class is very similar to the *RWFsg_ReverseGasket* class in Chapter 6.

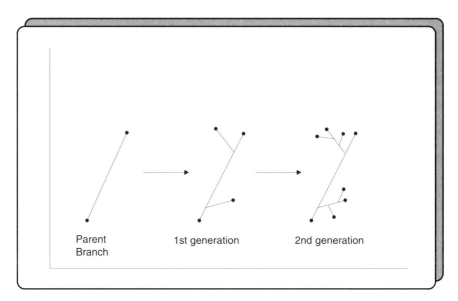

Figure 7–4. Creating a tree by creating a branch as a self-similar copy of the parent branch.

Listing 7–2. Definition of a simple tree object class derived from *RWFaf_Object.*

```
class RWFaf_SimpleTree : public RWFaf_Object {
  private:
  protected:
  public:

  RWFaf_SimpleTree(void);
  // both draw() and fill() just draw lines
  // process_reverse is used because
  // you want to draw at every level
  void draw(void)
    {setaction(&RWFaf_Draw);process_reverse();};
  void fill(void)
    {setaction(&RWFaf_Draw);process_reverse();};
```

```
}

RWFaf_SimpleTree::RWFaf_SimpleTree(void)
{
  RWFmat_MatrixTable mtable;
  // First branch, 1/2 length, rotate 30.0
   mtable[0].setIdentity();
   mtable[0].scale(0.5, 0.5);
   mtable[0].rotate(30.0);
   mtable[0].translate(0.0, 0.3);

  // Second branch, 1/3 length, rotate -45.0
   mtable[1].setIdentity();
   mtable[1].scale(1.0/3.0, 1.0/3.0);
   mtable[1].rotate(-45.0);
   mtable[1].translate(0.0, 0.6);

  // Add as many branches as you like by adding more
  // elements to the matrix table

  // Finally, set the table generator table
  setGenerator(mtable);

  // Now set the initiator, a unit line segment
  RWFlist_ObjectPtrTable otable;
  RWFgraph_Polyline *unit_line = new RWFgraph_Polyline(2);

  unit_line[0].setCoord(0.0, 0.0);
  unit_line[1].setCoord(0.0, 1.0);

  otable[0] = unit_line;
  setInitiator(otable);

  // Now use the same one for the erase initiator
  RWFgraph_Polyline *unit2 = new RWFgraph_Polyline(2);
  *unit2 = *unit_line;
  otable[0] = unit2;
  setEraseInitiator(otable);
}
```

You can create a number of different tree types by varying the number of branches as well as their sizes, orientations, and locations on the parent branches. The *RWFaf_SimpleTree* class creates a default tree type, but you may override it by calling *setGenerator()* with your own set of branch definitions. Several different types of trees are shown in Figure 7–5.

Figure 7–5. By changing the branching pattern, you create a variety of tree types.

You can create slightly more realistic drawings of trees by using something other than a simple line segment for the initiator. Figure 7–6 illustrates how to use a simple polyline definition for a branch. The only changes required for the *RWFaf_SimpleTree* class is replacing the unit-line-segment initiator with a more elaborate polyline outlining an elongated trapezoid. Furthermore, you can now have the *fill()* member function fill the trapezoid to give the tree a more solid appearance. By using variations of the *RWFaf_DrawColorCycle()* function, you can make the branches different colors at each recursion level. You can also create your own drawing function that draws a leaf at the end of the current branch upon reaching the final recursion level, instead of returning. A simple way of creating a leaf is an elongated ellipse. The final image in Figure 7–6 illustrates how the leaves can improve the overall look of a fractal tree.

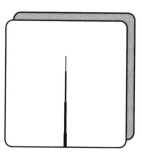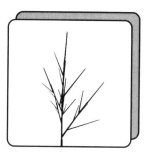

Figure 7–6. Using a polyline definition for a branch instead of a single line segment. The final image shows how adding leaves improves the appearance of a plant or tree.

Random Trees

The main problem with the tree model is that it appears too strictly geometric. Unlike real trees, these trees have a rigid structure imposed on them. You need to add randomness to the model so that it can vary the orientations, sizes, shapes, and locations of the branches as they are added. In addition, you may want to structure the new class in such a way that it can be generalized for randomizing other types of fractal objects.

Ideally, you'd randomize the generator matrices in a simple, well-controlled fashion. The randomized polyline generators work in this way. However, you do not want to directly randomize the elements of the generator matrix. For the tree model, you characterize each new branch by the following attributes:

◆   its size relative to the parent branch, which corresponds to scaling the initiator;

◆   its orientation relative to the parent branch, which corresponds to a rotation of the initiator;

◆ whether the branch appears on the left or right of the parent, which corresponds to a reflection about the parent branch; and

◆ its location on the parent branch, which corresponds to a translation of the initiator.

Each of these corresponds to a distinct attribute that you change, depending on the type of tree you were modeling. The simplest statistical model would be to vary each of these parameters independently, in effect, treating each parameter as an independent random variable. The choice of the statistics to select for each one is, of course, dependent on what you are trying to model. For the moment, you'll use normally distributed random variables.

Just as you did for the polyline generators, you can create a structure to define all the characteristics of a new branch. Each statistical parameter is defined as a random variable, using the *RWFrand_UniformRV* and *RWFrand_GaussianRV* classes described in Chapter 4.

```
class RWFtree_BranchData {
  public:
  int id;
  RWFrand_GaussianRV length, angle;
  RWFrand_UniformRV  offset, side;

  RWFtree_BranchData(void);
};

// Declare the default constructor
RWFtree_BranchData::RWFtree_BranchData(void)
{
  id = 0;
  length.setMean(0.5);
  length.setDeviation(0.25);
  angle.setMean(30.0);
  angle.setDeviation(10.0);
  offset.setMean(0.75);
  offset.setDeviation(0.25);
  side.setMean(0.0);
  side.setDeviation(1.0);
};
```

Notice that an *id* parameter has been added to the *RWFtree_BranchData* class. This variable may be used to identify which branch is being processed. Given the four parameters in the *RWFtree_BranchData* class, you can construct the matrix specifying the transformation of the parent branch to the sibling branch as follows:

```
int
rwf_treeFindBranchMatrix(void *data,
                         int level,
                             RWFmat_Matrix &bmatrix)
{
  RWFtree_BranchData *branch = (RWFtree_BranchData *)data;
  float factor, factor2;

  bmatrix.setIdentity();
  factor = branch->length.next();
  bmatrix.scale(factor, factor);
  factor = branch->angle.next();
  // Use the side parameter to decide whether
  // angle is positive (right side) or
  // negative (left side)
  factor2 = branch->side.next();
  if(factor2 > 0.0)
    factor = -factor;
  bmatrix.rotate(factor);
  // Finally, translate the branch
  factor = MAX(MIN(branch->offset.next(), 1.0), 0.0);
  bmatrix.translate(0.0, factor);

  return 1;
}
```

For efficiency, the matrix to set is passed as an argument to this routine. The matrix set by *rwf_treeFindBranchMatrix()* is the generator matrix needed for an individual branch. The branch data structure is passed as a *void* pointer for the same reason that the user data was passed as a *void* pointer for the polyline routines—to generalize this function type to other data-structure types. The final problem to solve is incorporating this routine into the *generate()* and *generate_reverse()* member functions of the *RWFaf_Object* class. You may then use this class to construct tree-type fractals, as well as many other types of randomized fractal shapes.

Generating the Generator

Recall that the generator is stored as a table of matrices. By using the branch data stored in the *RWFtree_BranchData* class, you can construct the matrix you need for each branch. So, instead of storing individual matrices for the generator, you should store the branch data and use the *rwf_treeFindBranchMatrix()* function to create the matrix whenever it is needed. The simplest way to do this is to add yet another function pointer, *matrix_func*, to the *RWFaf_Object* class to indicate whether a matrix-generating function is provided. The *setGenerator()* function is then overloaded with a version to allow the passing of a table of pointers to user-defined data, just as shown earlier for the random polyline generators. The modification to the *generate()* member function is then:

```
void
RWFaf_Object::generate(RWFmat_Matrix &pmatrix,
            int level)
{
   int valid = 1;
   // Perform the same checks for reaching the maximum
   // recursion level of minimum size

   ...

   // Now go to the next level
   int next_level = level + 1;
   for(int i=0; i < numTransforms(); i++) {
     if(matrix_func)
       valid = (*matrix_func)(user_data[i], level,
                    transforms[i]);
```

```
    if(valid)
        generate(pmatrix * transforms[i], next_level);
    }
}
```

A similar modification to the *generate_reverse()* member function provides the same functionality for randomizing it. You define a matrix
function with a call to the *setMatrixFunction()* member function. To
provide the user data, you must make a call to *setGenerate()* with a table
of pointers to user-defined structures, such as the *RWFtree_BranchData*
structures. You define a class for this type of table with the following
declaration:

```
typedef RWFtable_SimpleTable<void *>      RWFaf_UserDataTable;
```

In the example of the tree fractal, we created a table that has as many
elements as branches. The table of pointers is then passed with a call
to *setGenerate()*. Also, note that the current recursion level is passed as
an argument to the matrix-generating function so that it may be used
to alter the statistics or characteristics as a recursion-level function.

As you can see from the code segment, the matrix-generating function
returns an integer result, either one (indicating that the matrix is valid)
or zero (indicating that the transformation should be skipped). This
feature provides the capability for varying the number of branches generated at any one time. You set the generator to the maximum number of branches possible to generate for any branch. The matrix-generating function can then decide how many branches or elements to
generate based on the current recursion level or other criteria passed
in the user data. One simple way to do this is to include a probability
of branch generation as one of the arguments to the matrix-generating
function.

A Class of Trees

Just as was done for the Sierpinski Gasket, you can derive a new class, *RWFtree_Object*, from the *RWFaf_Object* class. The constructor for this tree class defines the unit line segment as the initiator and erase initiator. As an example of how to use this class, the following code is all that is needed to generate the fractal tree of Figure 7–7:

```
RWFtree_Object tree;
RWFaf_UserDataTable udtable(3);
RWFtree_BranchData btable[3];

// Use the default for the first branch
// Now make a short branch near the base
btable[1].length.setMean(0.3);
btable[1].length.setDeviation(0.1);
btable[1].offset.setMean(0.1);
btable[1].offset.setDeviation(0.05);

// Now make a longer branch near the top
btable[2].length.setMean(0.4);
btable[2].length.setDeviation(0.2);
btable[2].offset.setMean(0.8);
btable[2].offset.setDeviation(0.05);

udtable[0] = &(btable[0]);
udtable[1] = &(btable[1]);
udtable[2] = &(btable[2]);

tree.setGenerator(udtable);
tree.setMatrixFunction(&rwf_treeFindBranchMatrix);
// Set the appropriate scale and color of the tree
...
// Now draw the tree
tree.draw();
```

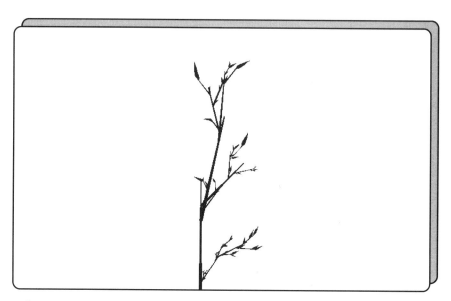

Figure 7–7. Fractal tree with randomized branching.

You can now create whole forests with trees of different species and attributes. In 1984, Dr. Alvy Ray Smith, former president of Pixar Inc., introduced some formal definitions for describing plants and trees using fractals. He coined the term *graftal* to describe a language for classifying plants and trees by the recursive rules used to generate them, just as done here.

The *RWFtree_Object* class can produce all these types of objects. The trick is in specifying the branching rules and other characteristics for the tree. While most of the examples presented so far have used a simple line segment as a generator, you are certainly not limited to that. As with all the other fractal objects, you may use any type of object for the initiator. You should experiment with the effects of different shapes on the tree models, as well as varying the statistics and shapes of the branches. Color plate 4 provides an example of the wide variety of plants and trees you can generate with this approach. The code for generating the color plate is found in the file *plate4.cpp*.

Plate 1. Colorful combinations of Sierpinski Gaskets.

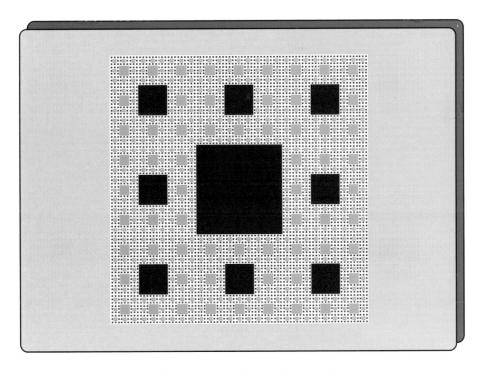

Plate 2. The Sierpinski Carpet.

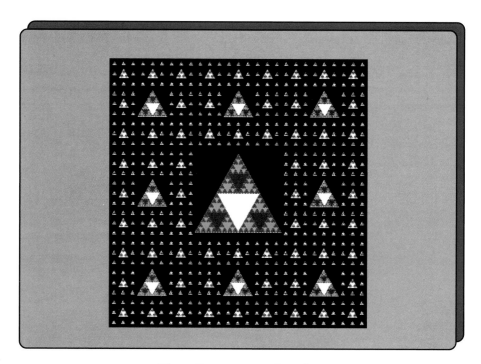

Plate 3. A carpet of gaskets.

Plate 4. Fractal botany.

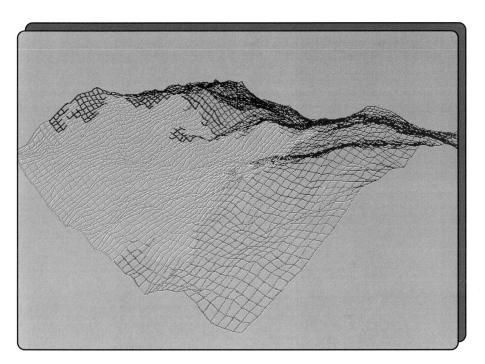

Plate 5. Combining discrete and continuous fractional Brownian Motion for mapping.

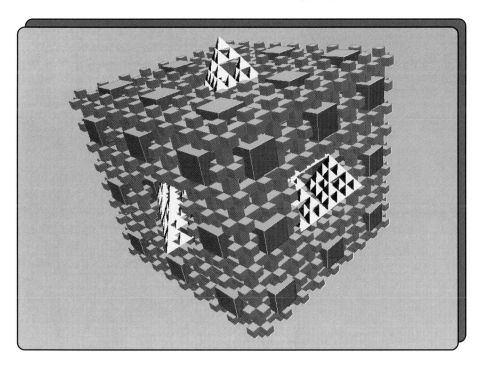

Plate 6. An inverted Menger Sponge with three-dimensional gaskets.

Plate 7. Fractal clouds.

Plate 8. A fractal forest on a partly cloudy day.

Plate 9. Encirclements of the Julia set for the transformation $z \rightarrow z^2 + c$.

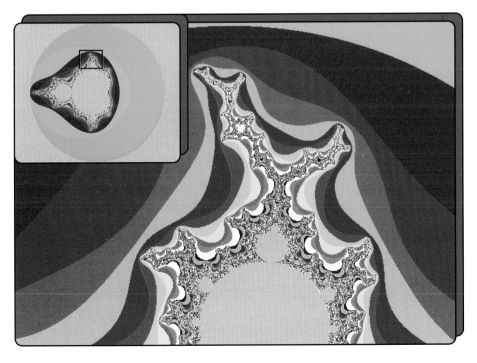

Plate 10. A colorful Mandelbrot set for the transformation $z \rightarrow z^2 + c$.

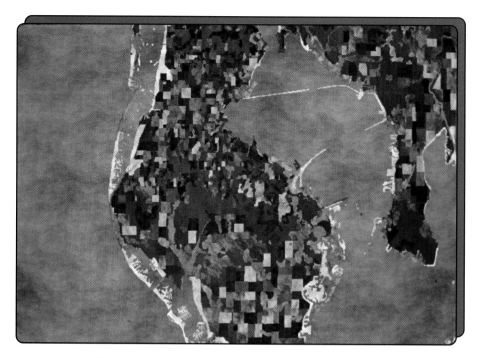

Plate 11. A color-coded digital terrain map of
St. Petersburg, Fl. *(Source: IVEX Corporation)*

Plate 12. Fractal terrain as seen from an IVEX visual system.
(Source: IVEX Corporation)

Plate 13. Another out-the-window view of
IVEX visuals. *(Source: IVEX Corporation)*

Plate 14. Three-dimensional fractal terrain.
(Source: IVEX Corporation)

Plate 15. Original image and the result of fractal compression/decompression. *(Source: Iterated Systems, Inc.)*

Plate 16. Another example of fractal compression.
(Source: Iterated Systems, Inc.)

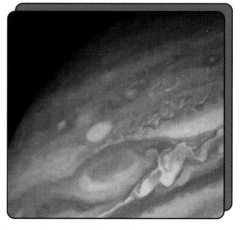

Plate 17. Fractal compression of the red spot of the planet Jupiter.
(Source: Iterated Systems, Inc.)

Pockets of Fractals

While plants and trees provide an appealing variety of self-similar objects found in nature, they are not the only ones. Let's consider something on a slightly larger scale such as a planetary body like the moon, which has been struck by many meteors. The meteor impacts produce craters of different sizes and distributions. In general, you see more small craters than large ones; this is because small meteors occur more frequently than large ones. This effect is partially because large meteors break up before striking the surface, while the smaller meteors tend to cluster together. The distribution of craters can be considered a fractal process, in which large craters are covered with smaller and smaller craters of varying shapes and sizes. All craters look similar, just at different scales. The distribution of craters appears very similar to the tree-modeling problem, in which each branch resembles the parent. Like different types of trees, craters tend to cluster into a variety of shapes. For simplicity, let's consider clusters that form elliptical shapes.

Our model of the moon begins with a single, pristine lunar surface consisting of a single screen-filling circle. The crater generators take the circle and map it into a smaller elliptical cluster by scaling, rotating, and translating the parent circle to a new location within the parent cluster. Each succeeding cluster element tends to move toward the center of its parent cluster, which is modeled as Gaussian Distribution at the center of the child cluster relative to its parent. Similarly, the size and orientation of the child cluster is chosen at random. The process is continued for each cluster, until microscopic craters are reached, which—in this case—correspond to filling individual dots on the screen.

Figure 7–8 shows the basic construction method of these craters. Like the tree fractals, the craters are drawn using the *process_reverse()* and *generate_reverse()* functions; meaning, you draw the craters at each recursive step. Listing 7–3 shows the matrix-generating function for the crater clusters.

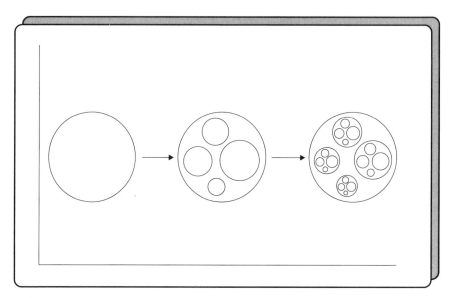

Figure 7–8. Generating lunar craters. You start with a circle and then transform it into smaller clusters. New clusters tend to stay close to the center of the parent cluster.

Listing 7–3. The crater data class and associated matrix-generating function.

```
class RWFtree_CraterData {

  public:
  int id;
  // Probability of generating this star
  RWFrand_UniformRV prob_occurring;
  //
  RWFrand_GaussianRV distance;
  RWFrand_GaussianRV xscale, yscale;
  RWFrand_UniformRV  angle, orientation;

  RWFtree_CraterData(void);
};


int
rwf_treeFindCraterMatrix(void *data,
          int level,
             RWFmat_Matrix &bmatrix)
{
```

```
RWFtree_CraterData *cluster =
                (RWFtree_CraterData *)data;
float dist, angle;

if(cluster->prob_occurring.next() < 0.2)
  return 0;

bmatrix.setIdentity();
// Gaussian-distributed stars within an ellipse
bmatrix.setScale(cluster->xscale.next(),
            cluster->yscale.next());
bmatrix.rotate(cluster->orientation.next());
// Finally, position it relative to the current center
// The angle is uniformly distributed, but the distance
// from the center is normally distributed
angle = cluster->angle.next();
dist = ABS(cluster->distance.next());
xtrans = cosD(angle)*dist;
ytrans = sinD(angle)*dist;
bmatrix.translate(xtrans, ytrans);

return 1;
}
```

The only step left is to produce the generators. However, because of the construction of the *RWFtree_CraterData* class, the simplest method is simply to generate as many as you like (20 is a reasonable number) all with the same statistics, but each with a different starting seed for every random variable. An example of this technique is shown in the source code to the demonstration program night.exe, which is on the disk that accompanies this book.

You can create many interesting combinations by varying the number of generators and their relative statistics. Figure 7–9 shows an example crater distribution of a nonexistent (at least as far as we know) moon. There are many other types of phenomenon that are constructed in this manner. For instance, many types of pebbled sidewalks are made up of collections of different-sized pebbles and stones similar to the lunar-crater distribution. Similarly, many types of porous material, such as Styrofoam, exhibit this type of randomly distributed holes in an otherwise uniform material. The derived-class *RWFtree_CraterObject* provides a suitable class for modeling craters on the moon, pebbles on the ground, and other similarly constructed objects.

Other phenomenon may be modeled with a variation of the *RWFtree_Crater-Object* class as well. For instance, you can create a reasonable model of star clustering by using the normal *process()* and *generate()* methods with the *RWFtree_CraterObject* class. In this case, you do not draw the "craters" at every recursion level, but rather at the final recursion level so as to draw individual stars. By using a fractal distribution, you create a more realistic pattern of stars, instead of simply randomly distributing stars in a sky.

Figure 7–9. A heavily cratered moon

The Evening Sky

The demonstration program for this chapter creates a scene of trees silhouetted by stars in the night sky with a rising moon in the background. The program night.exe first generates a suitably starry background with a hunter's moon (large and bright, suitable for tracking down small furry animals). A small forest of trees is then drawn in the foreground. Different species of trees are demonstrated by randomly selecting the various branching parameters. You may create new scenes simply by pressing the Enter key after a scene is complete. Because of the random variations in the both the trees and fractals, it is extremely unlikely you'll ever generate the same scene twice, so catch the images you prefer while you can!

Other Random Fractals

The tree and crater fractals provide a means of producing fairly realistic models of many natural objects. They are, like our other fractal objects, straightforward to use. Constructing a program to draw images with them is easy; the biggest effort is in defining the branching and scaling attributes. You can create a tremendous variety of fractal shapes from just the two classes *RWFtree_Object* and *RWFtree_CraterObject*. Virtually, any object composed of self-similar copies of itself (or a collection of base objects) can be drawn using one of these two classes.

Despite their flexibility, these classes do not encompass many other types of fractals. In the next part of the book, you'll learn how to construct fractals using some alternative techniques, including Brownian movement, fractional Brownian movement, Mandelbrot and Julia sets, and discrete fractals that let you effectively interpolate from discrete data sets. You'll also see how easily the classes described in this and the previous chapters can be adapted to produce three-dimensional fractal models. These model types can be adapted to many types of applications, including flight simulation and medical imaging.

Complex Fractals

The fractals you saw in the previous chapters belong to the same class of procedurally constructed fractals. Each of these fractal objects is defined by a recursive procedure for replicating a basic shape, know as the initiator, at smaller and smaller scales using affine transformations. The self-similarity for these types of fractal objects is a direct product of their method of construction. The self-similarity of objects such as the Koch Curve and Sierpinski Gasket is built in from the way they are defined, for instance.

An affine transformation of an object produces a copy of the original object, just at a different scale, orientation, and location. Affine transformations, however, represent only a small class of the many transformation types you can apply to a figure. In this chapter, you'll see how you can construct fractal objects using several types of nonlinear transformations, rather than just affine transformations. Fractals that have a nonlinear self-similarity transformation are referred to as simply *nonlinear* fractals. These fractals have the same self-similarity property as the fractals of the previous chapters: The figure is constructed by repeated application of a common transformation operation. As you'll see, it is generally more difficult to predict what type of fractal shape a nonlinear transformation will produce.

One of the principle uses for nonlinear fractals is to provide a way of visualizing the structure contained within a system of equations. This chapter shows you how to take a set of equations from physics, mathematics, engineering, biology, or any other discipline and examine the intricacies of them in a new way. The chapter also provides a means for analyzing those equations to study such properties as the stability and periodicity inherent within the equations.

Nonlinear Fractals

Drawing nonlinear fractals requires a different approach from the methods of the previous chapters because of the innate complexity of nonlinear transformations. For many types of transformations, the resulting transformed figure may bare little or no resemblance to the original figure. It was relatively easy to use affine transformations on the initiators of the Koch Curve, Sierpinski Gasket, and their related objects because all the graphic objects that make up the initiator, such as line segments and polygons, are easily altered by such transformations.

To transform a polygon, for example, you simply apply the affine transformation to each of the polygon vertices and reconnect the transformed vertices, as shown in the top half of Figure 8–1. You cannot do this with a nonlinear transformation because, in general, such a transformation typically does not transform straight lines in the input figure to straight lines in the output figure. You therefore cannot simply apply the nonlinear transformation to the vertices of a polygon and reconnect the resulting vertices. A more complicated procedure must be followed in which you divide the polygon edges into smaller line segments and transform each small line segment, as shown in the bottom half of Figure 8–1. This procedure requires more computations to transform even the simplest figure, and it can be quite difficult to implement for arbitrary shapes, such as circles or ellipses.

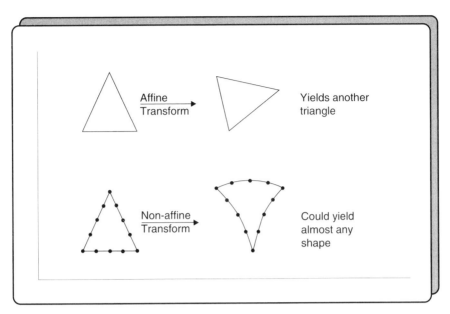

Figure 8–1. Applying an affine transformation is easy when compared to most nonlinear transformations.

The situation is even more difficult when transforming two-dimensional filled figures, such as the triangle used in the Sierpinski Gasket. When drawing the Sierpinski Gasket, you implicitly assume that you can merely transform the triangle vertices and fill in the resulting figure. Once again, you cannot make the same assumption for a nonlinear transformation of the triangle. You must use other ways to find the result of applying a nonlinear transformation to an object.

When you first try to generate nonlinear fractals, take the same initiator / generator approach used to generate the fractals of the previous chapter. For example, a typical nonlinear transformation is: $(x,y) \rightarrow (x^2, y^2)$. You can construct a nonlinear Sierpinski Gasket using this transformation, which employs the method shown in Figure 8–2. The starting generator triangle for the Sierpinski Gasket is depicted in the left half of Figure 8–3. One method for generating the transformed triangle is to simply scan the triangle and for each pixel within the triangle, compute the transformed coordinate, and plot that point in the output image. The result of this operation is shown in the right half of Figure 8–3. Note that there are quite a few holes in the resulting transformed figure. These so-called holes are where output pixels were erroneously skipped. You will almost always miss filling some pixels in the output figure if you use this type of *forward* transformation because the transformation is computed for each pixel inside the starting figure and the points plotted at the transformed coordinates.

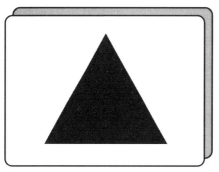 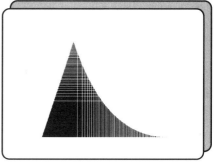

Figure 8–2. Generating a transformed figure by a forward transformation. This method always leaves unfilled holes in the resulting figure.

A better approach for finding the resulting transformed figure is to use the *inverse* transformation. Instead of scanning the original image of the initiator, you scan the output raster and compute the inverse transformation for each pixel. For our example transformation, the inverse function is $(\sqrt{x}, \sqrt{y})$. If the resulting value is within the original triangle, then the output pixel is filled in; otherwise, the output pixel is left unprocessed. There are two possible values for each square root, the positive and negative square roots, and both values must be checked. The result of this operation for the same triangle used in Figure 8–2 is shown in Figure 8–3.

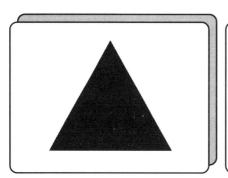 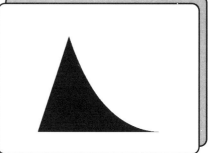

Figure 8–3. The inverse transformation method. Now you get a better approximation of the transformed shape without leaving unwanted holes.

Now that you have a method for finding the result of a transformation applied to a figure, you can proceed with adapting this method to drawing a nonlinear fractal. Recall that the basic approach used in the previous chapters was to repeatedly apply the generator transformations to the initiator shape. The same approach may be used to create nonlinear fractals. You apply the transformation repeatedly to the initiator until some predefined criterion, such as maximum recursion level or minimum desired size, is reached. However, as you just saw, it is a little trickier with nonlinear fractals because you really want to use the inverse transformation from the output image of the initiator to determine which points belong to the fractal and which do not.

Figure 8–3 represents one iteration of the inverse transformation. An output pixel is part of the transformed object if the inverse transformation of the output pixel maps to a pixel within the original input image. Suppose you apply the transformation again to the transformed object in Figure 8–3. You can determine which pixels are in the now doubly transformed object by computing the inverse transformation twice and seeing if the resulting coordinate is within the original input image. To find the image of the nth transformation of the object, you perform the inverse transformation n times. A fractal object is essentially the limit of applying one or several transformations an infinite number of times. This observation provides another method for constructing a two-dimensional fractal, called the *inverse mapping* method, as shown in the following procedure:

```
Loop over all y-coordinates {
  Loop over all x-coordinates {
    For n iterations {
      Compute the inverse function;
    }
    if((x,y) is in the initiator)
      turn the pixel on
    else
      leave the pixel alone
  } // End of x-loop
} // End of y-loop
```

The number of iterations of computing the inverse function corresponds to the maximum recursion level setting for the affine fractals in Chapters 5 and 6. Note that this inverse-drawing method provides yet another means for drawing fractals like the Sierpinski Gasket. For affine fractals, you use the inverse of the generator matrix to compute the inverse coordinates. If there is more than one generator, there is also more than one transformation that must be used; that is, there are multiple inverse functions that must be tried. In fact, you must compute all possible combinations of the inverse generators to get the final object. Clearly this can become quite impractical if you have more than one or two generator matrices. Another drawback to this method is that it does not lend itself well to adopting other types of stopping criteria, such as the minimum-object-size criteria in Chapter 6.

The inverse mapping method is not the preferred method for rendering most nonlinear fractals because of the computational complexity and other limitations it possesses. So, you will develop another method for creating nonlinear fractals that leads to some very beautiful and interesting figures. The first step in developing this drawing method is to provide a more consistent means of expressing a nonlinear transformation of objects in the plane.

Complex Variables

Many of the equations you are likely to encounter in engineering, physics, and mathematics are expressed in terms of complex numbers. One reason for this is that complex numbers provide an easy way to express a two-dimensional transformation. We assume you have at least some familiarity with complex variables, but let's review some of the basics you will need for the fractals in this chapter.

The easiest way to think of a complex number z is to think of it as a point (x,y) in the plane, as shown in Figure 8–1. You can write z as:

$$z = x + iy = r * e^{(i * \theta)} \qquad\qquad \textit{(Equation 8–1)}$$

As you can see, the coordinates (x, y) are just the familiar Cartesian coordinates with the x-axis corresponding to the real portion of the complex number and the y-axis corresponding to the imaginary portion. The number i is equal to the $\sqrt{-1}$. The second way to express a complex number uses *polar* coordinates, specified by the quantities r and θ. r is the distance of the point from the origin and is referred to as the *magnitude* of the complex number, defined as $|z| = sqrt(x^2 + y^2)$. θ represents the angle the vector makes (from the origin to the point) with the positive x-axis, as shown in Figure 8–4. Note that the positive angles are counterclockwise. All the familiar rules of arithmetic work for complex numbers. For instance, you multiply two complex numbers by multiplying the components, keeping in mind that $i*i = -1$, as follows:

$$(x1 + iy1) * (x2 + iy2) = (x1*x2 - y1*y2) + i(y1*x2 + x1*y2)$$

The quantity $e^{i\theta}$ in the polar representation is defined by the equation:

$$e^{i\theta} = cos\theta + i*sin\theta$$

The polar form is quite useful for multiplying and dividing complex numbers. Multiplying the same two complex numbers in polar coordinates becomes:

$$(r1 * e^{(i*\theta_1)}) * (r2 * e^{(i*\theta_2)}) = (r1 * r2) * e^{(i*(\theta_1 + \theta_2))}$$

The result of multiplying two complex numbers in polar form is simply to multiply the magnitudes and add the angles. So, complex multiplication corresponds to scaling (multiplying the magnitudes) and rotation (adding the angles). Similarly, dividing two complex numbers divides the respective magnitudes and subtracts the angles. The effect of multiplying two complex numbers is shown in Figure 8–5.

While the theory of complex variables is a very rich area of study, you will only need these basics to construct the nonlinear fractals in this chapter. To further assist you, the Borland C++ package (and almost all other compilers) comes with the predefined class *complex*, which lets you declare and manipulate complex variables just as any other data type. All the standard arithmetic operators have been overloaded for the *complex* class, so you may use complex variables just as you use *float* variables. You will find this very convenient not only for the fractal programs of this chapter, but for writing many different types of engineering and scientific programs.

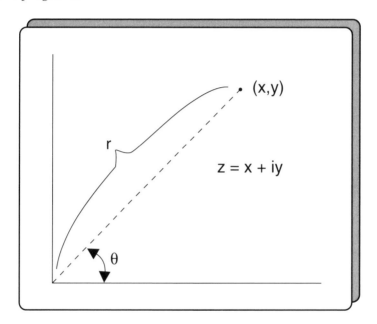

Figure 8–4. Representing a complex number as a point in the (*x*, *y*) plane.

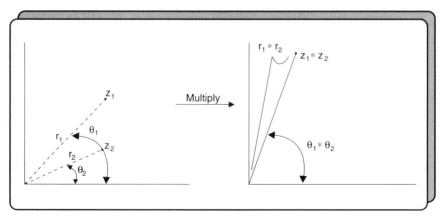

Figure 8–5. Multiplying a complex number by another complex number corresponds to rotation and scaling.

Complex Graphics

There is a one-to-one correspondence between the complex numbers and points in the (*x*, *y*) plane. You can think of the graphics display as a representation of the complex plane, in which each (*x*, *y*) screen coordinate corresponds to the complex value *x* + *iy*. In effect, you can think of complex numbers as a convenient way of representing a two-dimensional coordinate. A transformation function, such as one of the affine transformations you have already used, tells you how to take any (*x*, *y*) and transform it into a new (*x*, *y*) location. All the graphics operations you have already seen, such as rotation, translation, and scaling, can be represented as equivalent operations on complex numbers. Because you can represent a coordinate by a single complex number, you can express an arbitrary two-dimensional transformation as:

$$z \rightarrow f(z) \hspace{4cm} \textit{(Equation 8–2)}$$

We can, for instance, express a transformation that rotates its input by an angle θ about the origin by letting *f(z)* = *z*∗*e*$^{i\theta}$. Similarly, you can easily construct corresponding affine-transformation functions to perform translation (add a complex offset), scaling, and reflection. Equation 8–2 specifies a rule for taking each point in the complex plane and mapping it to another point in the plane. Our primary interest is in what happens when you apply the transformation repeatedly, just as was done with the affine transformations for the fractal objects of the previous chapters.

The fractal figures in this chapter are generated by scanning the screen pixel by pixel and then applying Equation 8–2 to the complex coordinate of each screen pixel. To simplify this process, you need a convenient way to generate the *complex* coordinate for a given screen pixel. Furthermore, as with any of the other graphics objects like circles and polygons, you need to be able to map the screen coordinates into a specific range of the complex plane, so you can examine different parts of the object. For instance, sometimes you'll want the screen to represent the portion of the complex plane from -1 to +1 in both *x* and *y*, and sometimes you'll want the range to be -10 to +10 or -100 to +100, or some other suitable range.

The *RWFgraph_ComplexObject* provides a base-class object for defining objects in the complex plane. The *RWFgraph_ComplexObject* class is a derived class from the *RWFgraph_Object* class. It acts as a rectangular window in the complex plane. You specify an area of the screen that you want to use (by default, it is the whole screen) and the corresponding complex coordinates of the window boundary. The default window boundaries range from -1 to +1 in both *x* and *y*. A *RWFgraph_ComplexObject* is not intended to be used directly, rather you use it as a base class for objects specified in the complex plane. *RWFgraph_ComplexObject* has several useful member functions that greatly simplify your programming tasks for several types of nonlinear fractals. Using this class is straight-forward: You derive a new object from this base class and construct a *draw()* member function to actually draw the object as follows:

```
class RWFgraph_MyObject:
  public RWFgraph_ComplexObject
{
  private:
  protected:
  public:

  void draw(void);
}


void
RWFgraph_MyObject::draw(void)
{
  Complex z;
  RWFcolor color;
  // Do whatever setup is needed

  // Main drawing loop
  int xmin = getMinX(), xmax = getMaxX();
  int ymin = getMinY(), ymax = getMaxY();
  for(int j=ymin; j < ymax; j++) {
    for(int i=xmin; i < xmax; i++) {
      z = getComplex(i, j); // Get complex coordinate
      // Now do whatever you need with the complex value
      ...
```

```
         // Finally, draw the pixel
         rwf_graphPlot(i,j, color);
      }
    }
  }
```

The member functions *getMinX()* and *getMaxX()* return the minimum and maximum *x*-screen coordinates respectively for the object. Similarly, *getMinY()* and *getMaxY()* return the minimum and maximum *y*-screen coordinates. By default, the object is mapped to the entire screen, but this may be overridden by a call to the member function *setScreenWindow()*. The screen window is the portion of the screen on which your complex object is drawn. The mapping of screen-pixel coordinates to complex values is determined by the current setting of the mapping window. The mapping window is initially set for the *x*- and *y*-coordinates of the complex numbers to range from -1 to +1. The scale and location of the mapping window may be changed with a call to the member function *setWindow()*. The relationship between the screen window and the complex coordinates is shown in Figure 8–6.

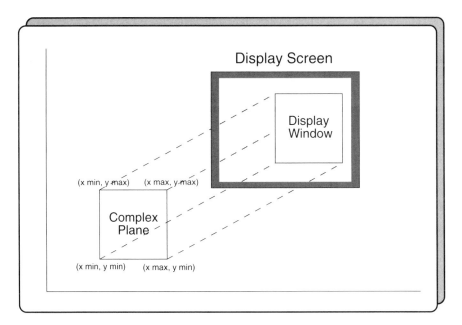

Figure 8–6. The *RWFgraph_ComplexObject* class defines a window on the screen and a corresponding range of complex values inside of the window.

The member function *getComplex()* returns the complex value corresponding to the passed screen coordinates. You move a complex object around the screen by calling *setScreenWindow()*. You can change the scale and orientation of the window with a call to *setWindow()*, but the function *zoomWindow()* provides a more convenient way to do this. *zoomWindow()* takes three arguments: The first two specify the (x, y) coordinate at the center of the object and the third argument specifies a scale factor that multiplies the current range of the window. If the scale factor is greater than 1.0, then the range is reduced, effectively magnifying the object. If, for instance, you specify a scale factor of 2.0 for an object with the default range of -1 to +1, the new range will be -0.5 to +0.5. Similarly, if the scale factor is less than 1.0, the range is correspondingly increased. *zoomWindow()* is very useful for moving around an image and zooming in to see fine detail. The demonstration program at the end of this chapter makes extensive use of this function to allow interactive viewing of nonlinear fractals. Table 8–1 provides a list of all the member functions for the *RWFgraph_ComplexObject* class for quick reference.

Table 8–1. Member functions for the *RWFgraph_ComplexObject* class.

Member Function	Description
int getMinX(void)	Returns the minimum *x*-screen coordinate for the current setting of the screen window.
int getMaxX(void)	Returns the maximum *x*-screen coordinate for the current setting of the screen window.
int getMinY(void)	Returns the minimum *y*-screen coordinate for the current setting of the screen window.
int getMaxY(void)	Returns the maximum *y*-screen coordinate for the current setting of the screen window.

Table 8–1. *continued*

Member Function	Description
void setScreenWindow(int xmin, int ymin, int xmax, int ymax)	Sets the screen window for the complex object. By default, the screen window is set to the entire screen.
void getScreenWindow(int &xmin, int &ymin, int &xmax, int &ymax)	Gets the screen window for the object.
void setWindow(float xmin, float ymin, float xmax, float ymax)	Sets the range of complex values for the object.
void getWindow(float &xmin, float &ymin, float &xmax, float &ymax)	Gets the current range of complex values for the object
void zoomWindow(float x, float y, double scale)	The point (*x, y*) becomes the center of the window. The current window scale is multiplied by *scale.*

With the *RWFgraph_ComplexObject* class, you now have a simple means for scanning a window into the complex plane. Our next task is to see how to construct nonlinear fractals based on a specified transformation within the complex plane.

Julia Sets

The behavior of nonlinear equations has been studied for centuries. But only now, with the aid of computers and computer graphics, has it become possible to visualize many of the rich intricacies contained within seemingly simple sets of equations. The French mathematician Gaston Julia, who lived from 1893 to 1978, developed much of the theory of dynamical systems for the case of rational polynomials (systems whose state can be expressed as the ratio of two polynomials with rational coefficients, such as $f(z) = z^2$). Dynamical systems are those that evolve in time.

The next state of the system can be computed from the previous state using a transformation function, just as we did for transforming the two-dimensional figures shown earlier. For many systems, a discrete time approximation is made so that the transformation is applied at regular time intervals. You simulate the behavior of such a system by specifying an initial state for all the variables and successively running these values through the system equations. One of the main questions of interest with a dynamical system is this: Given a particular starting condition, is the system:

◆ stable (the output settles down to a single value);

◆ periodic (the output oscillates between a set of values in a regular fashion); or

◆ unstable (the output is neither stable nor periodic)?

If you are analyzing such a system, you would probably like to be able to construct a map that tells you which starting values are unstable and which are stable or periodic. To create such a map, think of the complex plane as representing all the possible starting input values for the system. For each point in the plane, start applying the transformation to the point. Continue running the resulting values through the transformation until you can determine that the value does not stabilize (unstable), settle down (stable), or oscillate periodically (periodic). In effect, you continue the iteration until a stopping criterion is satisfied, similar to the minimum-sized criteria used in Chapter 6. By following this process, you can create a map in the complex plane in which each point is classified as one of the following three values:

◆ The system output tends to infinity for the given input. The set of points which do this is called the *escape set*.

◆ The system output tends toward a single fixed-output value, known as a fixed point. A *fixed point* satisfies the equation $z = f(z)$. Once a system reaches this state, it will remain at this value.

◆ The system tends to oscillate between a set of values periodically. This set of points along with the fixed points is called the *prisoner set*.

The *Julia Set* is defined as the boundary between the escape set and the prisoner set. Consider $f(z) = z^2$, for example. You can easily see that points outside of the unit circle will always increase in magnitude with each iteration of the transformation because $|z^2| = |z|^2$. Similarly, points with a magnitude less than one (inside the unit circle) tend to zero, and points on the unit circle will always map to other points on the unit circle. In this example, the Julia Set is the unit circle, a simple geometric figure. However, by introducing one addition to the transformation function $f(z)$, namely $f(z) = z^2 + c$, things become considerably more complicated.

The Julia Set has several interesting mathematical properties, the main one being that it is *invariant* under the transformation operation. The invariance property means that if you transform a point in the Julia Set, you get another point in the Julia Set. More formally, if z is a member of the Julia Set, then so is $f(z)$. The fractal nature of the Julia Set is a direct result of the invariance property. Given a set of points within the Julia Set, you can repeatedly transform these points to find other members of the Julia Set. This is the equivalent of the forward-transform method (the initiator/generator approach) for defining a fractal object. Depending on which initial set of points you use, you probably will not find all the points of the Julia Set for the same reason that the forward transformation when applied to the triangle initiator left holes in the resulting output image. To avoid these problems, you use a modified procedure to find the Julia Set boundary for a given transformation $f(z)$.

Closing In on the Julia Set

The most common method for plotting the Julia Set is to identify the points that are members of the escape set for $f(z)$. For the function $f(z) = z^2 + c$, it can be shown that z is a member of the escape set if the magnitude of z is greater than either two or the magnitude of c, that is:

$$z \text{ is in the escape set of } f(z) = z^2 + c \text{ if } |z| > max(2, |c|) \quad \textit{(Equation 8–3)}$$

So, you can find the Julia Set by following a relatively simple iterative process. Treating the screen as a map of the complex plane, you scan the

213

image pixel by pixel and compute *f(z)* for each pixel. If the magnitude of the result is greater than *max(2, |c|)*, then the point is a member of the escape set, and you no longer need to consider that pixel. If the magnitude is less than *max(2, |c|)*, then proceed with the next iteration. This repetitive process is similar to the recursion used to draw the fractals of the previous chapters. Just as with the reverse method for drawing those fractals, the transformation is successively applied to identify and remove those points that do not belong to the prisoner set. The basic drawing method is shown in the following pseudocode:

```
complex z;
int level, max_level;

complex c(0.5, 0.5);
// Set c to whatever value you wish. In this case,
// it is 0.5 + 0.5i

int xmin = getMinX(), xmax = getMaxX();
int ymin = getMinY(), ymax = getMaxY();
for(int j=ymin; j < ymax; j++) {
  for(int i=xmin; i < xmax; i++) {
    z = getComplex(i, j); // Get complex coordinate
    level = 0;
    while(z.magnitude() < MAX(2.0, c.magnitude() &&
          level < max_level) {
      z = z*z + c;
      level++;
    }
    // Finally, draw the pixel
    if(level < max_level)
      rwf_graphPlot(i,j, level);
    else
      rwf_graphPlot(i,j, 0);

  } // End of x-loop
} // End of y-loop
```

The *max_level* parameter determines the maximum number of iterations to process before giving up. In this example, the escape set is color coded, so the color indicates at which iteration level the point was identified as belonging to the escape set. Only the members of the escape set are color coded, the prisoner set and fixed points are left as the background color.

Using this drawing process, you can now create some interesting pictures of fractal Julia Sets. Figure 8–7 shows how the Julia Set for $c = 0.5 + 0.5i$ is constructed by removing points within the escape set at each step of the iteration. Each figure results from terminating the process after a fixed number of iterations; the number of iterations is indicated beneath each figure. The top-left figure represents one iteration, leaving a circle of radius two. Each successive iteration refines the image of the Julia Set. Each iteration is said to *encircle* the prisoner set with more iterations, producing a tighter approximation to the actual prisoner set. The Julia Set is the boundary of the enclosed figure. Note that this process does not guarantee to find all the members of the escape set because, in general, there is no upper boundary for the number of iterations required to determine if a point is a member of the escape set or not. So, you can only hope to produce a reasonable approximation to the members of the Julia Set.

Figure 8–7. Encirclements of the prisoner set for $f(z) = z^2 + c$ with $c = 0.5 + 0.5i$. The image of the Julia Set becomes more detailed as more iterations are processed.

The Julia Set Class

By using the *RWFgraph_ComplexObject* class, you can easily define a suitable class for rendering Julia Sets. The *RWFJulia_Object* class is derived from the *RWFgraph_ComplexObject* class, and thus inherits all the functions of that class, as well as all the member functions for the graphics object-base class *RWFgraph_Object*. In most respects, you can use the *RWFJulia_Object* class the same way you use the affine-fractal base-class *RWFaf_Object*. You define the maximum iteration level with the *setMaximumLevel()* function, just as you would for the *RWFaf_Object* class. The *process()* member function implements the pseudocode you saw earlier for drawing the Julia Set. Because the drawing method is not recursive, there is no separate *generate()* member function for *RWFJulia_Object*. Listing 8–1 shows how *process()* is defined for the *RWFJulia_Object* class.

Listing 8–1. Illustrates how *process()* is defined for the *RWFJulia_Object* class.

```
void
RWFJulia_Object::process(void)
{
complex z;
int level;

int xmin = getMinX(), xmax = getMaxX();
int ymin = getMinY(), ymax = getMaxY();
for(int j=ymin; j < ymax; j++) {
  for(int i=xmin; i < xmax; i++) {
    z = getComplex(i, j); // Get complex coordinate
    level = 0;
    while(!(*escape_func)(z, level, escape_data) &&
          level < max_level) {
      z = (*transform_func)(z, level, transform_data);
      level++;
    }
    // Finally, draw the pixel
    (*action_func)(i, j, level, max_level, action_data);
  } // End of x-loop
```

```
} // End of y-loop

} // End of process()
```

Because of the different drawing method used for Julia Sets, there are several significant differences from the affine-fractal classes. The function pointer *transform_func* points to a transformation function that you provide. You may also provide a pointer to user data that is passed to your transformation function. This optional data is analogous to the user data provided for the randomizing functions of Chapter 7. The following transformation function, for instance, computes the expression $f(z) = z^{power} + c$, where *power* is any positive integer exponent:

```
struct RWFJulia_zpowerdata
{
  int power;
  complex c;
  float cutoff;
};


Complex
rwf_juliaZPowerTransform(complex &z, int level,
          void *data)
{
  RWFJulia_zpowerdata *zdata = data;
  complex result(0.0, 0.0);

  if(!zdata || zdata->power < 1)
    return result;

  result = z;
  for(int i=1; i < zdata->power; i++)
    result *= z;

  return (result + zdata->c);
}
```

The data structure *RWFJulia_zpowerdata* provides the constants *power* to define the exponent, and *c* to define the offset. The *cutoff* variable is the magnitude that determines whether or not a complex value is a member of the escape set. You set the transformation for a *RWFJulia_Object* with a call to the member function *setTransformation()*. The transformation function performs the same task that the generator matrices do in the affine fractals of the previous chapters.

The function pointer *escape_func* points to a function you provide to determine whether or not the passed complex value is a member of the escape set. This function returns 1 if the passed z is a member of the escape set and 0 otherwise. The escape function is passed the current value of z, the current iteration level, and a pointer to an optional data structure containing other information the function might need. You set the escape function with a call to *setEscapeFunction()*, which is passed the address of the function, and a call to the pointer of the optional data structure for the escape function. In most cases, you should simply pass the pointer to the same data used by the transformation function. An example of a limit function for the transformation $f(z) = z^{power} + c$ is:

```
int
rwf_juliaZPowerEscape(complex &z, int level,
        void *escape_data)
{
  RWFJulia_zpowerdata *zdata = escape_data;

  if(!zdata)
    threshold = 2.0;
  else
    threshold = zdata->cutoff;

  if(z.magnitude() < threshold)
    return 0; // Indeterminate
  else
    return 1; // It's in the escape set

}
```

Just like *RWFaf_Object*, you use an action function to define what action to take once the threshold has been reached or the maximum iteration has been performed. Unlike the action function for *RWFaf_Object*, the *RWFJulia_Object* action function is passed the following arguments:

- *int i* and *int j*, specifies the screen-pixel coordinate being processed;

- *int level*, the iteration level that was reached;

- *int max_level*, the maximum iteration level allowed (you can determine whether the point is a member of the escape set by checking to see if *level < max_level*); and

- *void *action_data*, an optional pointer to additional data for use by the action function (normally, this is the same data that is passed to the transformation function).

A typical action function that simply sets the pixel to a color corresponding to the iteration level is:

```
void
rwf_juliaDrawColor(int i, int j,
                   int level, int max_level,
                   void *action_data)
{
  RWFJulia_zpowerdata *zdata = action_data;

  // Scales the colors so that encirclements are
  // always colored from 1 to max colors
  float color_level = (float) level / (float) max_level;

  if(level < max_level)
    rwf_graphPlot(i,j,
      (int)(color_level * RWFgraph_MaxColor()));
  else
    rwf_graphPlot(i,j, 0);
}
```

The actual color displayed for each iteration level depends on the particular look-up table you set for the screen.

Now you have all the pieces for the program to create the Julia plots of Figure 8–7. The program is shown in Listing 8–2. Note that just as with the other fractal programs discussed, the program is very short and succinct thanks to all the built-in capabilities of the *RWFJulia_Object* and *RWFgraph_ComplexObject* classes.

Listing 8–2. Program to draw the prisoner set for the function $f(z) = z^2 + c$, where $c = 0.5 + 0.5i$.

```
RWFJulia_Object jobject;
RWFJulia_zpowerdata zdata;

// Create the data for the transformation
zdata.power = 2;
zdata.c = Complex(0.5, 0.5);
// Compute the cutoff threshold
zdata.cutoff = MAX(2.0, zdata.c.magnitude());

jobject.setTransformation(&rwf_juliaZPowerTransform,
                &zdata);
jobject.setEscapeFunction(&rwf_juliaZPowerEscape,
                &zdata);
jobject.setActionFunction(&rwf_juliaDrawColor,
                &zdata);
// Zoom out by a factor of 2 to get whole figure
jobject.zoomWindow(0.0, 0.0, 0.5);
// Set the maximum recursion level
jobject.setMaximumLevel(10);

// OK, now clear the screen and draw it
rwf_graphClearScreen();
jobject.process();
```

The successive plots of Figure 8–7 are created simply by changing the value of the maximum number of iterations with a call to *setMaximum-Level()*. You can easily zoom to any portion of the set to examine its details with a call to *zoomWindow()*, as well as select new sets by changing the elements of *zdata*, such as the offset *c* or the power. To redraw the object, just set your program to change the parameters and then call the *process()* member function again. The demonstration program at the end of this chapter illustrates the flexibility of this approach to drawing Julia Sets.

The only function examined so far has been $f(z) = z^2 + c$. With the *RWFJulia_Object* class, you can create and study virtually any function you like. You must create an appropriate transformation function and decide on a suitable test condition for termination of the iteration. The termination condition is almost always a variation of the threshold test used by the *rwf_juliaZPowerEscape()* function. Other types of termination conditions you can use include:

```
ABS(z.real()) > threshold
ABS(z.real()) + ABS(z.imag()) > threshold
ABS(z.real()) > threshold || ABS(z.imag()) > threshold
```

There are, of course, many other possible alternative termination conditions, but the options shown here produce some interesting plots. In addition, many other types of transformations produce some amazingly intricate results. Figures 8–8, 8–9, and 8–10 show results using various other transformation functions. With the demonstration program at the end of the chapter as a guide, you now have a powerful set of tools for studying the structure of many types of complex transformation functions.

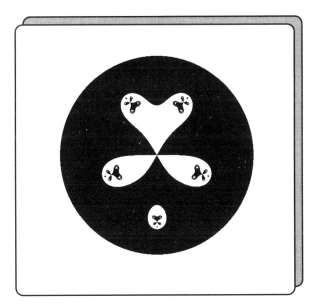

Figure 8–8. Julia Set for $f(z) = z^5 + z^3 + c$, with $c = 2.0i$.

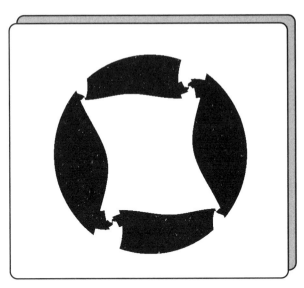

Figure 8–9. Julia Set for *f(z) = cosh(z) + c*, with *c = 0.5 + 0.5i*. The function *cosh(z)* is defined as *cosh(z) = (e^z + e^{-z}) / 2.0*.

Figure 8–10. Zooming to a region of Figure 8–8. Figure 8–8 is replicated in the small region of the upper-left corner, with a small box drawn around the magnified area. By using the *setScreenWindow()* function, it is easy to create multiple sequence views like this one using multiple *RWFJulia_Object* objects.

The Mandelbrot Set

As explained earlier, Julia Sets exhibit several interesting mathematical properties, including fractal self-similarity and invariance under the transformation operation. Another unusual property is that prisoner sets (and their corresponding Julia Sets) can be classified in two distinct categories: They either form a single connected set or a two-dimensional Cantor Set. A *connected* set is one with the property that for any two points in the set, there exists a continuous curve connecting the points that is entirely contained within the set. For instance, the Julia Set for $f(z) = z^2$ is the unit circle (a connected set). However, as you have already seen, the Julia Set is radically different for a different value of c, such as $c = 0.5 + 0.5i$.

Recall that a two-dimensional Cantor Set is a totally disconnected set that is dense in the plane (essentially meaning that any finite region of the plane always contains some points in the Cantor Set). Because the prisoner set is dense and disconnected, all the points in the prisoner set are, in effect, isolated, but they can be arbitrarily close to one another. The mathematical reasons for this dichotomy are beyond the scope of this book, but this observation led Mandelbrot to study a variation of the Julia Set algorithm, which leads us to one of the most famous fractal subjects, the Mandelbrot Set.

You can determine if the Julia Set for $z^2 + c$ is connected or not by examining the behavior of $z = 0$ in the transformation. If the sequence is unstable and zooms off to infinity, then the corresponding Julia Set for that value of c is a Cantor Set. If the sequence is stable, then the corresponding Julia Set is connected. Mandelbrot observed that you can construct a map similar to the Julia Set map that shows which values of c are connected to the Julia Set. Instead of considering the screen as an image of starting values for a fixed transformation function, you can instead think of it as a map of different values of c. For each pixel, you begin with the value zero (or equivalently the value c because $z^2 + c = c$, when $z = 0$) and perform the same iteration as you did for the Julia Sets, looking for values that exceed the threshold magnitude.

223

You can easily adapt the *RWFJulia_Object* drawing method to create an image of the Mandelbrot Set. The following transformation function performs the work for you:

```
Complex
rwf_juliaMandelbrotTransform(Complex &z, int level,
                              void *data)
{
  RWFJulia_zpowerdata *zdata = data;
  complex result(0.0, 0.0);

  if(!zdata || zdata->power < 1)
    return result;

  // First iteration of this point?
  if(level == 0) {
    // Save the initial value to be used as the offset
    zdata->c = z;
    // Set the cutoff threshold correspondingly
    zdata->cutoff = MAX(2.0, z.magnitude());
    return z;
  }

  result = z;
  for(int i=0; i < zdata->power; i++)
    result *= z;

  return (result + zdata->c);
}
```

The key difference between this function and the *rwf_juliaZPower-Transform()* function is in the detection of the first iteration. At this point, *rwf_juliaMandelbrotTransform()* saves the passed *z* value as the offset *c* and sets the cutoff value to the appropriate magnitude. In all other respects, the Mandelbrot Set is drawn by the same method as the Julia Set objects. Figure 8–11 is an image of the entire Mandelbrot Set while Figure 8–12 zooms into a portion of it to show details of an offshoot of the set.

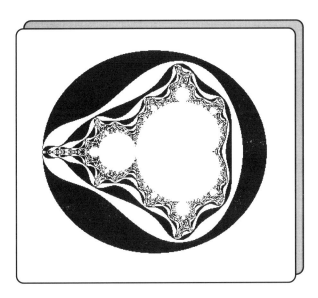

Figure 8–11. The Mandelbrot Set generated using the *rwf_juliaMandelbrotTransform()* function.

Figure 8–12. Zooming into a portion of the Mandelbrot Set.

The Mandelbrot Set is a fantastically intricate structure that many scientists continue to avidly study. Besides being a map of the connectivity of Julia Sets, it also acts as a sort of dictionary for the Julia Sets. As you zoom into various portions of the Mandelbrot Set, especially along the "islands" around the main heart-shaped boundary, the map of the Mandelbrot Set looks almost exactly like the corresponding Julia Sets about these points, except that they are scaled differently (you must scale up the Mandelbrot Set to see the correspondence).

So, the Mandelbrot Set seems (we say seems because it has yet to be rigorously proven) to contain all of the Julia Sets within it. Given the complexities of the Julia Sets, this means that the Mandelbrot Set is indeed a remarkably complex and intricate map. There will undoubtedly be much more study of the Mandelbrot Set before its mathematical properties are completely understood.

Julia Set Mania

The Julia and Mandelbrot Sets of this chapter must be seen to be truly appreciated. To that end, the program *julia.exe* gives you an interactive means of viewing some of the possible transformation functions for both the Julia and Mandelbrot Sets. *julia.exe* lets you interactively roam about any of the Julia Sets for the transformation $f(z) = z^{power} + c$, where you can specify the exponent and the *offSet c*. Once the image is displayed, a cross hair appears that lets you select a new region to center the view about. In addition, you may use the + and - keys to zoom in by factors of two, or press the letter z to enter another zoom factor. The letter p lets you select a new exponent, and the letter m lets you select a maximum recursion level. You may also view the Julia Set or Mandelbrot Set centered at the same location of the complex plane. As an added bonus, you may create a colorful interactive display by having *julia.exe* cycle through the color palette after the image is completed, providing a moving depiction of the number of iterations for each encirclement of both the Mandelbrot and Julia Sets. Finally, by pressing the r key, you can have the program wander around the Julia Set randomly, which makes for an interesting screen saver.

Nonlinear Conclusions

Part of the fascination with Julia and Mandelbrot Sets is the complex structure that arises from the relatively simple transformations involved. This complexity should not actually be that surprising. Consider the iterative process involved: After one iteration, you have generated *f(z)*, at the next iteration, you have computed *f(f(z))*, at the third *f(f(f(z)))*, and so forth. For the transformation $f(z) = z^2 + c$, this means that by the tenth iteration, you have actually evaluated a 20th-degree polynomial with the starting value of *z*; by the 100th iteration, you are evaluating a 200th-degree polynomial. The encirclement at each iteration tells you which values have a magnitude that exceed a specified limit. You might expect that the map of such a high-degree polynomial would be quite complicated. But the surprising part is the amount of order and beauty contained within these polynomials. Before the advent of computer graphics, it simply was not possible to predict or demonstrate the behavior of such complex mathematical entities.

Nonlinear transformations provide an extremely rich source for generating interesting fractals. Even with what appear to be the simplest transformations, you find structures whose intricacies are still not well understood. With the classes and functions in this chapter, you now have the tools to explore both the classic nonlinear fractals and many others that have yet to be tried. In fact, you can easily take the demonstration program *julia.exe* and modify it to use other combinations of transformation functions.

Unlike research into Julia Sets, very little work has been performed in studying the Mandelbrot Sets for other types of transformations to answer questions such as do the Mandelbrot Sets always act as Julia Set dictionaries or is $z^2 + c$ a special case? As an example of what you might try, you can use *julia.exe* to examine the Mandelbrot Sets of different exponents or, with a simple addition, study the Mandelbrot Set for the *cosh(z)* transformation of Figure 8–9. The flexibility of the *RWFJulia_Object* class makes it easy to try any combination of transformation, escape criteria, and coloring scheme you like.

In most cases, nonlinear fractals require considerably more computer time and analysis (for instance, determining an appropriate stopping criteria) to generate than their affine counterparts. Because of the strange effects of nonlinear transformations on objects, you can not simply take the initiator/generator approach to create nonlinear fractals. There are, in fact, two ways to solve this problem. The first uses the *inverse transform* approach to work backward from the figure to the initiator. This method, however, is limited because you must have an explicit function for the inverse transformation and you must deal with the fact that there can be more than one value output from the inverse function (such as having both the positive and negative square root). The second method uses an iterative approach that determines if a given initial value exceeds some predetermined escape condition. This second method provides a means not only for drawing nonlinear fractals, but also for studying the structures and properties of dynamical systems by creating a map of all the stable input values. With the aid of this map, you can determine which initial values should be avoided to keep a real system stable. This type of systems analysis is only now possible thanks to the low-cost and widespread availability of powerful personal computers and their associated graphic displays.

Just as engineering and physics professionals try to approximate nonlinear systems with linear models, you will often use affine fractals to simulate real-world phenomenon because they are generally easier to analyze, manipulate, and generate. In the next chapter, you'll see how the randomizing techniques of Chapter 7 are extended to solve a universal problem in graphics, engineering, and physics: providing a realistic model of an object with a very limited amount of data. These models will then be extended to create realistic three-dimensional models of objects with which you are quite familiar, including hills, mountains, and clouds.

Fractal Interpolation

O ne of the more appealing aspects of fractal models is their ability to provide complex, natural-looking structures defined by a small number of parameters. The fractals of Chapters 5 and 6 demonstrate how you can combine just a few simple rules to create shapes of enormous detail and complexity. In Chapter 7, you saw how to introduce random variations into a fractal model to produce more lifelike models of natural phenomenon. In this chapter, you'll learn how to combine the techniques of the previous chapters to generate a different type of fractal curve.

Your goal in this chapter is to find a fractal method for solving a common problem in science and engineering, namely, interpolating data points from a set of known measured points. This type of fractal modeling lets you compute intermediate data points based on the measured characteristics of a signal without having to take an inordinate number of samples of the signal. Fractals provide a method of encoding the complex structure of a real signal with just a few parameters. So, a complex signal can easily be recreated from a very small set of parameters. Furthermore, these fractal algorithms are quite computationally efficient.

One of the principal applications for fractal interpolation is to model variations in the height of measured terrain data, which produces very realistic images of mountains, hills, oceans, and lakes. However, you can easily adapt fractal interpolation for use with many other types of problems, including image compression and decompression and general curve-matching problems.

Brownian Movement

You will frequently encounter the problem of interpolating new data points from a set of known data points. The known points may have either been calculated directly from the equation of some curve, generated from a mathematical model, or acquired experimentally. Figure 9–1 shows the most common methods of interpolation, which use a technique known as curve fitting. The simplest approach is just to connect adjacent points with straight lines. However, the resulting curve is not very smooth, especially at the known data points. To make a more appealing curve, you generally use higher-order polynomials and attempt to find the polynomial coefficients that most closely match the known points. This approach is useful in many engineering applications where the curves and surfaces you are attempting to model are known to be smooth and continuous. However, this approach is not very good when you want to model intrinsically rough surfaces, such as a mountain range, craters, or the serrated edges of a leaf. To create useful models of these types of curves requires a technique that more closely matches the random variations found in nature, such as the one used to create the fractals in the previous chapters. Our model for fractal interpolation is derived from a physical phenomena known as Brownian motion.

Brownian motion is named after botanist Robert Brown, who first observed the phenomena in 1827. Brownian motion is the motion of small particles caused by continual bombardment by other neighboring particles. You can see Brownian motion for yourself by observing a drop of water through a microscope. Small particles of dust and dirt in the water droplet always appear to be in constant random motion. The dust particles are constantly bombarded by millions of surrounding water molecules.

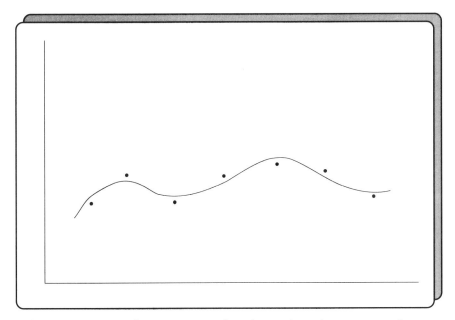

Figure 9–1. Curve fitting to interpolate data points along a curve. Curve fitting works well when the curve is smooth but is not very useful for modeling rough or irregularly shaped curves.

The water molecules are always moving because of the thermal agitation caused by the water being room temperature. Due to the huge numbers of molecules in the water drop that are moving in virtually all directions, the average position of the dust particles remains the same: The dust particles are simply agitated back and forth as they are struck repeatedly.

The Mathematics of Brownian Movement

To analyze the structure of Brownian motion, let's consider what happens if you restrict the motion to one dimension. In other words, the particle can only move along the x-axis and can only be struck from the left or right. As a further simplification, assume that each impact moves the particle a fixed distance, known as l, to the left or right (each water molecule transfers the same momentum to the particle) and that only one

impact occurs at a time. The particles starts at position 0 on the x-axis. Because the particle can be struck from the left or right with equal **probability**, you would expect the particle to remain at 0 generally.

You'll probably find the average deviation of the particle position from the origin of greater interest. The most common way to measure **the deviation** is to measure the square of the distance of the particle position from its initial position. In probabilistic terms, the square of this distance is the *variance* of the particle position. You can easily show that the **variance** of particle position is simply nl^2, where n is the number of times the particle is struck while it is being observed.

Assuming that the particle is bombarded at a constant rate (meaning n is proportional to the length of time you observe the particle), **then the** variance of the particle from its initial position is proportional to tl^2, where t is the observation time. So, the longer you observe **the particle**, the more likely the particle moves away from its initial **position**. Because the variance is a measure of the square of the particle-position change, the absolute value of the change in particle position is **the square** root of the variance. In this case, the standard deviation of the particle position is $\sqrt{t} * l$.

More formally, you can represent the position of the particle as a random variable X. A water molecule striking the particle can be considered as a sample of a random variable L, where L can take on only one of two possible values, either $+l$ (struck from the left) or $-l$ (struck from the right). So, you can write X as the sum of L, where the L_i are summed **over all** instances of the particle being struck. This results in Equation 9–1.

$$X(n) = \sum_{i=1}^{n} L_i \qquad\qquad \textit{(Equation 9–1)}$$

Each L_i is independent and identically distributed; they will take **on the** value $+l$ or $-l$ with equal probability. From Equation 9–1, you can see that the mean value for $X(n)$ is 0 because the mean value of **each L_i is** 0. Furthermore, the variance of each L_i is l^2. So, the variance **of X is** nl^2, as explained earlier. Finally, for n large, the central-limit **theorem** of probability states that the distribution of X will be Gaussian because X is the sum of independent, identically distributed random variables. The assumption of large n is quite valid for any reasonable length of time such as one second because even in such a short time interval the particle will, on average, be struck thousands of times.

Perhaps the most interesting feature of Brownian motion is the property that the variance in particle position increases linearly over the time of observation. Furthermore, this property holds, no matter when you start the observation. It is therefore independent of any particular starting time for the measurement. The distribution of particle position is always Gaussian, with a variance dependent solely on the length of time of your observation. A process with this property is an example of a *stationary Markov* process. The general study of Markov processes is quite interesting. The references in the bibliography at the end of the book provide more information about this topic.

But for our purposes, you only need to know the one basic property: Given an initial measurement of the variable X at a particular starting time, the position at any subsequent time is a random variable whose mean is the initial position, and whose variance is proportional to the difference in time from the initial position. Mathematically, this property reduces to the condition specified by Equation 9–2, where *Var(X)* is the variance of the random variable X.

$$Var(X(t_2) - X(t_1)) = k * |t_2 - t_1| * l^2 = |t_2 - t_1| * \sigma^2 \qquad \textbf{\textit{(Equation 9–2)}}$$

In Equation 9–2, the number of particle strikes (n from Equation 9–1) has been replaced by the observation time t because n is assumed to be proportional to t. The proportionality constant k simply provides the proper scaling between time measurements and particle strikes. In general, the factor k is simply absorbed into the l^2 factor and denoted by a single constant σ^2. You can easily verify Equation 9–2 by substituting in the definition for $X(t_2)$ and $X(t_1)$ from Equation 9–1, making the appropriate substitutions of time t for particle strikes n.

Fractal Motion

The fractal nature of Brownian motion becomes evident when you consider Equation 9–2 and what happens as you examine shorter time intervals. No matter what time interval you examine, the curve still has the same basic structure in which subsequent positions are based on a Gaussian distribution of the previous position. The standard deviation of the position *changes* is proportional to the square root of the length of time under consideration (because the variance, the square of the standard position *changes*, is directly proportional to the time interval). To better understand this, let's plot the position of the particle as a function of time.

For our plot of the particle position, the horizontal axis will represent the time of observation, and the vertical axis will represent the position of the particle along the *x*-axis. An initial position of the particle (call it *x(0)*) is specified. For convenience, consider the plot from time *t=0* to the time *t=1* and the variance of the Gaussian distribution to simply be proportional to the elapsed time ($\sigma^2 = 1$). You can construct the position of the particle at *t=1* by sampling a Gaussian random variable with the mean of 0 and standard deviation of 1. You can also construct this position by adding this value to the initial position *x(0)*. So, *x(1) = x(0) + N(0,1)*, where *N(0,1)* is a sample of a Gaussian random variable. The problem now is to construct intermediate points for times between 0 and 1 and *x(t)*, where the position behaves according to Equation 9–2.

Consider the position at time *t = 1/2*, *x(1/2)*. Because the first and last endpoints are already known, *x(1/2)* must satisfy Equation 9–2 for both endpoints at *x(0)* and *x(1)*. You can ensure this by letting *x(1/2) = (x(0) + x(1))/2 + N(0, 1/sqrt(2))*, where *N(0,1/sqrt(2))* is a sample of a Gaussian random variable with the mean 0 and variance 1/2 (standard deviation is *1/sqrt(2)*). So, the mean position at *x(1/2)* is just the average of the two endpoint positions, as you might expect. In accordance with Equation 9–2, the variance is 1/2, which is used to generate *x(1)*.

Now you can generate other points along the curve using a simple recursion. Take the two halves from *[0,1/2]* and *[1/2, 1]* and repeat the identical operation on them: Find the midpoint of the interval, compute the mean as the average of the two endpoints, and take a sample from a Gaussian random variable with the mean 0 that has a variance scaled by 1/2 for each recursion step. This method for generating intermediate points for particle position is called *random-midpoint displacement*. Figure 9–2 shows how a particle-position plot is generated by recursively subdividing time intervals until a desired resolution is reached, in exact analogy to the size criteria used in the recursive subdivision methods of Chapters 5 and 6.

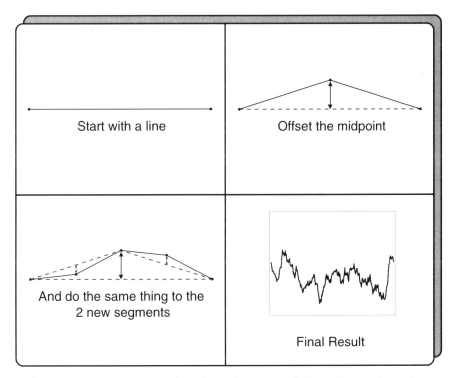

Start with a line

Offset the midpoint

And do the same thing to the 2 new segments

Final Result

Figure 9–2. Generating a plot of one-dimensional Brownian motion using random-midpoint displacement.

You can see that the random midpoint displacement method is very similar to the randomizing procedure for the affine fractals of Chapter 7. For the Brownian-motion plot, the initiator is simply the line segment connecting *x(0)* to *x(1)*. The recursion simply divides the line segment in half, displaces the midpoint, and then repeats the operation on the two new segments. The subdivision is very similar to applying two generator matrices to the initial line segment to transform it into two separate pieces, as was done for the Koch Curve generator. It is not, however, quite the same process because you always displace the midpoint in the vertical direction, regardless of the orientation of the line segment. For the affine fractals of Chapters 6 and 7, each new segment is transformed perpendicular to its current orientation. The difference between these two processes is shown in Figure 9–3.

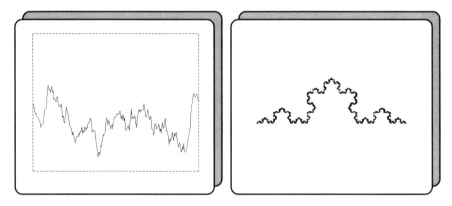

Figure 9–3. Random-midpoint displacement (shown on the left) only displaces the *y*-coordinate and is therefore suitable for interpolation. An affine fractal (shown on the right) transforms the rotated segments and is not useful for interpolating points.

There are distinctly different uses for the fractals of the previous chapters and the Brownian motion fractal. The randomized affine fractals of Chapter 7 are useful for defining natural shapes. The Brownian motion fractal is useful for interpolating between known data points. In the plot of the Brownian motion, the position at *x(1)* was generated from the initial position at *x(0)*. But this is not usually necessary. The point at *x(1)* can also be a measured point. You can then interpolate intermediate points using the recursive subdivision until the desired intermediate points are generated.

Fractional Brownian Movement

Now that you have seen the theoretical basis for modeling Brownian motion, you can step back and see how to use it and, more importantly, how flexible this model can be. First of all, Brownian motion provides a way of interpolating between pairs of known data points. The resulting curve is continuous, but nowhere differentiable. As currently shown, however, the model is not very flexible. You can greatly expand the types of curves you generate with this approach by examining the interpolation procedure via algorithms. Each recursion level involves three distinct steps:

1. Take the current interval and divide it into two halves.

2. Compute the plot value at the midpoint of the interval with an expression of the form: *y = (y1 + y2)/2 + N(0,stdev)*, where *y1* and *y2* are the plot values at the endpoints. Note that you can compute *N(0, stdev) = stdev*N(0,1)*.

3. Repeat the procedure on the two new intervals, scaling down the standard deviation for the new intervals by *1/√2*.

There are several ways to generalize this method by specifying a few more parameters. First, you must specify an initial scale factor, corresponding to σ^2 from Equation 9–2. This parameter sets the vertical scale for the curve. Next, the standard deviation is scaled by *1/√2* each time the interval is subdivided. Suppose you use a different scale factor, so the variance is not exactly halved according to Equation 9–2. This change results in a new class of curves referred to as *fractional Brownian motion*, or *fBM*. Figure 9–4 shows the result of using several different scaling factors. Rather than specifying the scale factors directly, they are usually parameterized by a quantity designated as *H* in the expression shown in Equation 9–3.

scale = 1.0 / (2.0^H)   *(Equation 9–3)*

For pure Brownian motion, $H = 0.5$. H is a measure of the fractal dimension of the resulting curve. You can, in fact, show that the fractal dimension is equal to $(2-H)$. When H is larger than 0.5, the curve generally becomes smoother than normal Brownian motion because the scale factor becomes smaller, reducing the variations at each subdivision. As H approaches 0, the curve becomes rougher because the scale factor gets closer to 1. When H is 0, the curve reduces to a type of extremely noisy curve known as *white noise*. The scale factor corresponds precisely to the global scaling factor introduced in Chapter 5. For fBM, the scale factor determines both the fractal dimension and the relative roughness of the resulting curve.

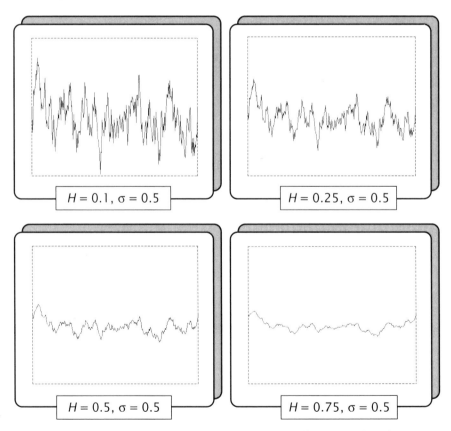

$H = 0.1, \sigma = 0.5$

$H = 0.25, \sigma = 0.5$

$H = 0.5, \sigma = 0.5$

$H = 0.75, \sigma = 0.5$

Figure 9–4. Fractional Brownian motion using different scaling factors that correspond to different values of the parameter H. When H is less than 0.5, the resulting curve is rougher than normal Brownian motion; when H is greater than 0.5, the curve becomes substantially smoother.

One final method of altering the fBM curves is to use something other than a Gaussian distribution for the random variables, that is, for $N()$. While the resulting curve will not correspond to any type of physical distribution, you can create slightly different effects. Figure 9–5 shows the result of using both a uniform distribution and a symmetric exponential. The uniform distribution is especially useful because you can guarantee that the random variable will never exceed a specified range. If you decide to use a different distribution, you should use one that is symmetric about 0 and has a standard deviation of 1, so it can be easily incorporated into the fBM functions described in the next section.

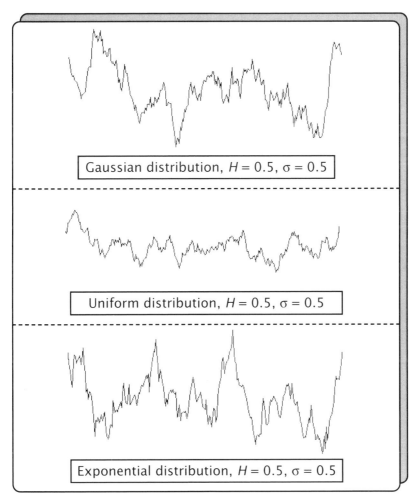

Figure 9–5. Using different types of non-Gaussian distributions to generate an fBM-like curve.

Generating fBM Curves

The main reason for developing the fBM fractal algorithms is to provide a method for fractal interpolation between known data points. You can easily define an fBM graphics-object class the same way you did for the affine fractals of the previous chapters. However, the most common way to use fBM fractals is as follows. Given the starting and ending values *y1* and *y2* of the quantity to interpolate over an interval, generate the interpolated data values at regularly spaced points along the interval. The function *rwf_fbm1DGenerate()* shown in Listing 9–1 performs this operation. You pass the *y*-data values (*y1* and *y2*) to interpolate, a pointer to the random-number generator you wish to use, the initial standard deviation for the random-number generators (*initial_stdev*), the scaling factor for the standard deviation (*level_scale*), and the number of recursion levels (*nlevels*) to process. *rwf_fbm1DGenerate()* then fills an array with the interpolated data values. The array must be large enough to hold $2^{nlevels} + 1$ total data points. The first and last elements of the array will always be set equal to the endpoint values *y1* and *y2*.

Listing 9–1. The function *rwf_fbm1DGenerate()* generates an array of interpolated data for the fixed endpoints of fractals.

```
void
rwf_fbm1DGenerate(float y1, float y2,
                  float (*random_func)(void),
                  float stdev, float level_scale,
                  int nlevels, float *values)
{
  if(nlevels == 0) {
    // Only the endpoints are set
    values[0] = y1;
    values[1] = y2;
    return;
  }

  // OK, compute the midpoint
  float ymid = (y1 + y2) / 2.0;
  if(random_func) {
```

```
    ymid += stdev * (*random_func)();
  } else {
    ymid += stdev * rwf_randGaussian();
  }

  if(nlevels == 1) {
    // In this case, we can finish directly because
    // there are only three points to process
    values[0] = y1;
    values[1] = ymid;
    values[2] = y2;
    return;
  }

  float new_stdev = stdev * level_scale;
  // Number of points is 2**nlevels + 1
  int npoints = (1 << nlevels) + 1;
  // values[nhalf] starts the second half of the array
  int nhalf = npoints/2;

  // OK, now process the first half
  rwf_fbm1DGenerate(y1, ymid, random_func,
                    new_stdev, level_scale,
                    nlevels-1, &(values[0]));

  // Now do the second half
  // The trick is to pass the address of the second
  // half of the data array
  rwf_fbm1DGenerate(ymid, y2, random_func,
                    new_stdev, level_scale,
                    nlevels-1, &(values[nhalf]));

  return;
}
```

The random-number generator pointed to by *random_func* returns a *float* value with the mean of 0 and standard deviation of 1. You may use any of the random-number generators described in Chapter 4, or you may use one of your own creation. If you pass a *NULL* pointer, then the Gaussian random-number generator is used by default.

241

If *nlevels* is either 0 or 1, then the array can be directly filled, and the function returns immediately. If *nlevels* is greater than or equal to 1, then the interval is divided in half, and the midpoint value is generated using the random-displacement algorithm. The function is then called recursively to fill each half of the data array. In this implementation, you take advantage of being able to pass the starting address of the data array for both halves, using the *&* operator to get the starting address of each half of the data array as shown.

When you call *rwf_fbm1DGenerate()*, the argument *stdev* sets the initial standard deviation for the curve. This effectively sets the scale of the curve. For each recursive call, the standard deviation is multiplied by the argument *level_scale*. For a pure Brownian motion curve, *level_scale* is set to *1.0 / sqrt(2.0)*. Listing 9–2 shows an example of how to use *rwf_fbm1DGenerate* to plot the graph shown in Figure 9–2.

Listing 9–2. Sample program to generate the Brownian motion graph shown in Figure 9–2. Note that the fBM curves of Figure 9–4 can be generated simply by using a different scale factor.

```
float stdev = 0.5;
float scale = 1.0 / sqrt(2.0);
int nlevels = 8;
float values[257];

// Set an initial random-number seed
rwf_randSrand(1010101);
rwf_fbm1DGenerate(0.0, 0.0, &rwf_randGaussian,
                  stdev, scale, nlevels, values);

// Now plot the results
int npoints = 1 << nlevels;

RWFgraph_LineSegment seg;
float x = -1.0;
float xinc = (1.0 - -1.0) / (float)npoints;
for(int i=0; i < npoints; i++) {
    seg.setFirst(x, values[i]);
    seg.setEnd(x+xinc, values[i+1]);
```

```
        seg.draw();
    x += xinc;
}
```

Note that the random-number seed is set prior to calling *rwf_fbm1DGenerate()*. Recall from Chapter 4 that if you initialize the random-number generator with the same seed, you will always generate the same sequence of random numbers. Although not important in this example, this feature is quite important later. To ensure that the same curve is generated, you should always initialize the random-number generator.

Another important feature of random-midpoint displacement is that as long as you use the same random-number seed, you can generate the curve with different numbers of points (different maximum recursion levels), and the curves will still match up at their common points. For instance, generate the points along the curve using three recursion levels (resulting in five data points) and compare the result to generating the curve using four recursion levels (nine data points). The five data points from the third recursion level will contain the same values as the even indexed elements of the fourth recursion level.

So, you can independently generate the same curve with any desired resolution and be assured that the curves will properly align. This feature results from the definition of the algorithm by the order in which the midpoints are generated. The randomized affine fractals of Chapter 7 possess the same property by virtue of their recursive definition. The inherent reproducibility of fractal models at different resolutions is one of the primary reasons fractals are used to generate three-dimensional computer images, as will become evident in the next chapter.

Multidimensional fBM

While the one-dimensional fBM is interesting, our primary interest in this method of random-fractal dimension is in the multidimensional case. Instead of interpolating points along a line, you can now interpolate points on an entire surface (two dimensional) or within a volume (three dimensional). Multidimensional Brownian motion can be generated by many

243

methods, but for now, we'll only consider the two most common. This discussion will only cover the two-dimensional extension. The three-dimensional extensions are presented in the next chapter.

The first method, known as the *grid fBM* method, starts with four points arranged in a square, as shown in the first step of Figure 9–6. These points lie in the *x*-*y* plane. A *z*-value (the quantity you wish to interpolate) is specified for each of the points. Your problem now is approximating an fBM surface inside the square. Following the basic methodology for one dimension, you divide the square into four new squares. The *z*-value at the center point is computed as a random variable whose mean is the average of the four *z*-values at the corners, and whose variance is half that of the corner points, just as in the one-dimensional case. To complete the definition of the four squares, you must generate *z*-values for the midpoints of each edge. This is done by applying the one-dimensional fBM method of the previous section to each edge. You have now divided the original square into four new squares as shown as the second step of Figure 9–6. You can apply the same operation to each of the four squares, subdividing them to generate a finer and finer grid.

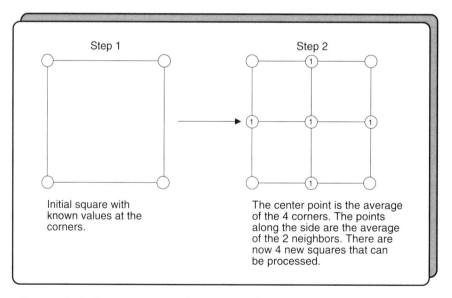

Step 1

Initial square with known values at the corners.

Step 2

The center point is the average of the 4 corners. The points along the side are the average of the 2 neighbors. There are now 4 new squares that can be processed.

Figure 9–6. Generating two-dimensional fBM to approximate a surface. Starting with four points, the initial square is recursively subdivided until the desired resolution is reached.

There is, however, a slightly more subtle consideration in the two-dimensional case that does not occur in the one-dimensional fBM. As shown in the initial step of Figure 9–7, you must generate the values at the points marked with *x*'s that lie along the internal edges of the four new squares. You could use the one-dimensional fBM approach along the two internal edges (the two edges connecting the midpoints of each side) to generate these points. This, however, would introduce some undesirable artifacts along those edges. You will learn more about why these artifacts occur in Chapter 10. You only need one slight modification to avoid this problem. The mean position of the midpoints is determined by averaging together the four surrounding points, as shown in the second step of Figure 9–7. The only exceptions to this rule are the points along the outside edges. For these cases, you are basically stuck using a one-dimensional fBM procedure to complete the computation.

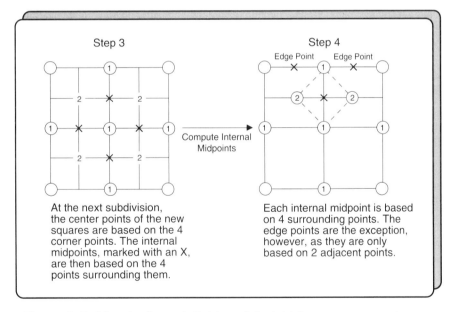

Figure 9–7. After the first subdivision of the initial square, you must generate values at the midpoints of the internal edges, marked with an *x* as in the first step. You use the generated midpoint of each new square to compute these points, as shown in the second step.

You'll see in Chapter 10 how this method of generating fBM can be used to make realistic models of digital terrain, complete with mountains, hills, and valleys. Figure 9–8 shows a three-dimensional perspective view of the two-dimensional fBM surface generated using the grid fBM approach.

A second method for generating terrain uses a method similar to the construction of the Sierpinski Gasket. This method is known as the *triangle fBM* method. You start with three points at the corners of an equilateral triangle, as shown in Figure 9–9. The midpoints of the three edges are generated using one-dimensional fBM along each edge. This breaks the original triangle into four new equilateral triangles. Each new triangle is then recursively subdivided further. Again, you must be careful with this approach and compute the position of the internal edges' midpoints by averaging together all the neighboring points. In general, we'll stick with the grid fBM method for rendering surfaces because it is easily adapted to regularly spaced terrain data. This application for fBM fractals is covered in more detail in Chapters 10 and 11.

Two-Dimensional fBM Classes

Implementing the two-dimensional grid fBM class is not a simple extension of the one-dimensional case. The reason for this is twofold: First, you must handle the outside edges as a special case, and second, you must compute the midpoints of the internal edges based on the midpoints of the other subdivided squares. In fact, it is easier to implement two-dimensional fBM as an iterative, rather than a recursive algorithm. As was done for the one-dimensional fBM, Listing 9–3 shows the *rwf_fbm2DGenerate()* function, which fills a two-dimensional array of interpolated data values.

Listing 9–3. The function *rwf_fbm2DGenerate()* generates a two-dimensional array of fractally interpolated data using four data points at the corners of a square.

```
void
rwf_fbm2DGenerate(float corners[],
```

```
                    float (*random_func)(void),
                    float stdev, float level_scale,
                    int nlevels, float **z)
{
  int i, npoints;

  if(nlevels == 0) {
    // OK, fill in the corners
    z[0][0] = corners[0];
    z[1][0] = corners[1];
    z[0][1] = corners[2];
    z[1][1] = corners[3];
    return;
  }

  npoints = (1 << nlevels);
  float *temp_z = new float [npoints+1];
  // First, take care of the outside edges

  // Columns are easiest
  // First column
  rwf_fbm1DGenerate(corners[0], corners[2], random_func,
                    stdev, level_scale, nlevels,
                    &(z[0][0]));
  // Last column
  rwf_fbm1DGenerate(corners[1], corners[3], random_func,
                    stdev, level_scale, nlevels,
                    &(z[npoints][0]));

  // Filling the top and bottom edges requires using
  // the temporary array
  // Bottom edge
  rwf_fbm1DGenerate(corners[0], corners[1], random_func,
                    stdev, level_scale, nlevels,
                    temp_z);
  for(i=1; i < npoints; i++)
    z[i][0] = temp_z[i];

  // Top edge
  rwf_fbm1DGenerate(corners[2], corners[3], random_func,
                    stdev, level_scale, nlevels,
```

```
                        temp_z);
    for(i=1; i < npoints; i++)
      z[i][npoints] = temp_z[i];

    delete temp_z;

    // Now fill in the rest of the array

    // Loop over recursion levels
    int nhalf = npoints;
    float cur_stdev = stdev;
    int x,y;
    for(int level=0; level < nlevels; level++) {
      nacross = nhalf;
      nhalf = nhalf / 2;
      // Compute all the midpoints for this level
      // These are the points at the centers of the
      // new square
      for(x=nhalf; x < npoints; x += nacross) {
        for(y=nhalf; y < npoints; y += nacross) {
          z[x][y] = (z[x-nhalf][y-nhalf] +
                     z[x-nhalf][y+nhalf] +
                     z[x+nhalf][y-nhalf] +
                     z[x+nhalf][y+nhalf]) / 4.0;
          z[x][y] += cur_stdev * (*random_func)();
        }
      }
      // Ok, now compute midpoints of subdivided edges
      // These points correspond to the circled points
      // of Figure 9-7.
      if(level < 0) {
        // Must do points along x and y separately
        int xs = nhalf;
        int ys = nacross;
        for(x = xs; x < npoints; x += nhalf) {
          for(y = ys; y < npoints; y += nhalf) {
            z[x][y] = (z[x][y-xs] +
                       z[x][y+xs] +
                       z[x-xs][y] +
                       z[x+xs][y]) / 4.0;
            z[x][y] += cur_stdev * (*random_func)();
```

```
        }
      }

    xs = nacross;
    ys = nhalf;
    for(x = xs; x < npoints; x += nhalf) {
      for(y = ys; y < npoints; y += nhalf) {
        z[x][y] = (z[x][y-ys] +
                   z[x][y+ys] +
                   z[x-ys][y] +
                   z[x+ys][y]) / 4.0;
        z[x][y] += cur_stdev * (*random_func)();
      }
    }
  } // Ok, finished with the other midpoints

  // Update the standard deviation
  cur_stdev *= level_scale;
  } // Finished looping over all recursions


  return;
}
```

rwf_fbm2DGenerate() is passed a four-element array defining the values at the four corners of the grid. The corner elements are numbered as shown in Figure 9–6. The passed two-dimensional array must have enough space to hold $(2^{nlevels} + 1) * (2^{nlevels} + 1)$ elements. All the other arguments are exactly the same as for *rwf_fbm1DGenerate()*.

Figure 9–8 shows a perspective view of the result of successive iterations of generating two-dimensional fBM data. You'll see in Chapter 10 how to create these perspective views, as well as learn other extensive uses for two-dimensional fBM in terrain modeling.

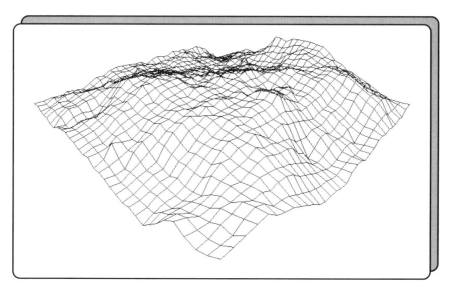

Figure 9–8. Perspective view of the data generated from several iterations of *rwf_fbm2DGenerate()*.

Discrete fBM

Both the fBM fractals of this chapter and the affine fractals of the previous chapters dealt with creating continuous curves and surfaces. Even if the resulting fractal is quite rough, it will still be a continuous curve. There is, however, another important type of modeling problem that you can solve using fractal algorithms. Instead of interpolating from a continuous variable, suppose that the system you are modeling can only take on one of finitely many discrete values or states of the system. The job of the interpolation algorithm is then to choose what the output of the system is during the transition from one state to another, given the states at the starting and ending times or the positions in space.

Let's consider the one-dimensional case first and think of the system as evolving in time. At time *t1*, the system is in state *A*, and at time *t2*, the system is in state *B*. The simplest interpolation is just to say that the system remains in state *A* until the time *(t1 + t2)/2*, at which point it switches to state *B*. You can add some random characteristics with a modified version of the *rwf_fbm1DGenerate()* algorithm as follows:

1. Take the current interval and divide it into two halves.

2. Determine which state the system is in at the midpoint by evaluating $N(0,1)$. (If the result is positive, the system is in state *A* at the midpoint. Otherwise, the system is in state *B*.)

3. Repeat the procedure on the two new intervals. If both endpoints of a subinterval are in the same state, then all intermediate times are in that state.

In one dimension, this algorithm does not produce very interesting results. The result of the calculation is to keep the system in state *A* for a random amount of time and then switch to state *B*. You can get the same effect by simply choosing a random time between *t1* and *t2* and changing the state of the system at this transition time. However, the algorithm produces more interesting results in multiple dimensions.

In two dimensions, you basically follow the same approach. Starting with an initial square with four states at the corners, you subdivide the square and select the state at the midpoint by randomly choosing the state at one of the corners. Continue the process, always choosing a midpoint state as one of the nearby states. Several stages of this process are shown in Figure 9–9. The result of this process is a set of well-defined and randomized boundaries between the four states.

As with the continuous fBM functions, the functions *rwf_fbm1DDiscreteGenerate()* and *rwf_fbm2DDiscreteGenerate()* compute discrete fBM fractals for the one- and two-dimensional cases respectively. Instead of arrays of *float* variables, these functions use arrays of *int* variables because the output represents discrete states.

As the discrete fBM algorithm is currently defined, you have no real control over how states are chosen. The procedure always picks one of the four corner values with equal probability. You can provide more structure to the resulting boundaries by assigning weights to the various classes, indicating the preference of one class over another. In Chapter 11, you'll see how to apply discrete fBM fractals to help solve the complex problem of defining natural-looking boundaries between regions of a coarsely digitized map.

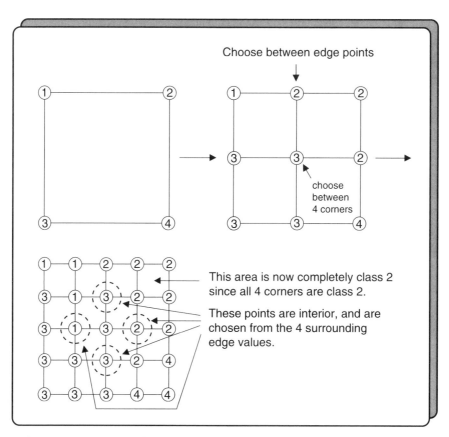

Figure 9–9. Discrete fBM algorithm in two dimensions. The process creates a randomized boundary between disparate classes.

Demonstrating fBM

The demonstration program *fbmdemo.exe* illustrates some of the properties of both one- and two-dimensional fBM. The program begins by performing successive plots of one-dimensional fBM, up to the screen resolution of your display. Plots with different values of *H* and different random-number generators are shown for comparison. Two-dimensional fBM is demonstrated for both the continuous and discrete cases. For the continuous case, the black and white intensity is modulated, producing a textured surface. Once again, different values of *H* are used to demonstrate their relative effects. Discrete fBM is demonstrated using four different colors at the boundary. As each recursion level is processed, the subdivided squares are colored according to the color at the upper-left corner of each square. Finally, both the continuous and the discrete fBM are combined to produce a single image by modulating the color from the discrete fBM with the intensity from the continuous fBM. As you can see, this produces interesting effects. Color plate 5 shows some of the output from *fbmdemo*.

Beyond Two Dimensions

All the fractals presented to this point have either been one- or two-dimensional entities. However, all the algorithms presented so far are easily adaptable to a higher number of dimensions. Affine fractals, for instance, use matrices to transform the objects of the initiator. You should also note that there is no explicit reference to dimension for any of the *RWFaf_Object* derived classes. You can therefore use one, two, three, or however many dimensions you desire for the objects in the initiator, as long as the matrices have the corresponding dimensionality. So, you can create three-dimension analogs of the Sierpinski Gasket, Koch Curve, and any of the other affine fractals. Similarly, extending the fBM algorithm to three or more dimensions involves only slightly more effort, just as was done from one dimension to two.

One of the primary uses for the fBM-style fractals is in creating realistic models of rough surfaces, specifically mountainous terrain. In the next two chapters, you'll see how to incorporate the fBM algorithms into a general-purpose terrain-rendering program. These techniques let you combine real data acquired from digitized maps and photographs with fractal models to generate finer detail than is present in the original measured data. The flexibility and efficiency of the fBM algorithms make them ideal for texturing terrain surfaces, adding that final touch of realism that computer graphics artists are always trying to obtain.

Three Dimensions and Beyond

The previous chapters dealt almost exclusively with one- and two-dimensional fractal objects. But in this chapter, you'll learn how to extend the same techniques to create fractals in three or more dimensions. You have already seen one example of a three-dimensional fractal from Chapter 9. In that instance, you use two-dimensional fBM to create a three-dimensional mesh of heights suitable for modeling a rough surface.

Creating three-dimensional affine fractals is especially straightforward because the affine-fractal classes are based on matrix transformations. Because the vector and matrix classes support transformations in any number of dimensions, you can easily construct affine fractals of three or more dimensions using multi-dimensional matrices to define their respective generators. The tree and crater models of Chapter 7 are easily extended to three dimensions simply by using three-dimensional polygonal models for the tree branches and spheres instead of circles to create fractal clouds. This chapter also shows you how to efficiently handle some of the special problems of creating perspective fractal images. Finally, you'll combine the fractal clouds with some simulated lightning based on the one-dimensional fBM techniques of the previous chapter.

255

Multidimensional Affine Fractals

In Chapter 3, you saw how an *RWFgraph_Object* can be either two- or three-dimensional, depending on how you initially specify the object. You can, for instance, create an *RWFgraph_Point* using either a two- or three-dimensional vector to specify the initial position. If you initialize the point with a three-dimensional vector, the *RWFgraph_Point* object is treated as a three-dimensional object. Similarly, you can create three-dimensional polygons with the *RWFgraph_Polygon* class by initializing the polygon vertices either with explicit *x*-, *y*-, and *z*-coordinates or three-dimensional vectors. In addition, the member function *make3D()* can be used to make any *RWFgraph_Object* be treated as a three-dimensional object.

Except for a few specialized drawing routines, a three-dimensional object is treated the same as a two-dimensional object. You can scale, rotate, and translate a two- or three-dimensional graphics object using transformation matrices. Also, you can use three-dimensional transformations for the initiators and generators of an affine fractal just as easily you can two-dimensional ones. While the actual generation of a three-dimensional fractal is virtually the same as the two-dimensional one, there are a few additional computations you must make to produce a suitable perspective drawing of a three-dimensional fractal object. So we'll create a new base class for three-dimensional fractals called *RWFaf_3DObject*, which performs these extra functions.

RWFaf_3DObject is derived from the *RWFaf_Object* class. The simplest way to see how this class works is with an example. So let's construct a three-dimensional analog of the Sierpinski Gasket. Figure 10–1 shows the basic construction for this object. You start with a tetrahedron as the initiator. The generator produces four half-sized copies of the tetrahedron, one on top and three on the bottom, as shown in Figure 10–1. The process then proceeds to subdivide each of the new tetrahedrons, continuing indefinitely. This is analogous to the procedure for the two-dimensional Sierpinski Gasket, except the initiator is divided into four pieces instead of three. The figure at the fifth iteration is shown in Figure 10–2. Note that with this construction, each side of the three-dimensional object is a two-dimensional Sierpinski Gasket.

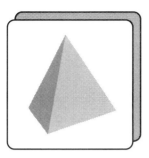  

Figure 10–1. Constructing a three-dimensional Sierpinski Gasket. Beginning with one tetrahedron, each iteration divides a tetrahedron into four half-sized tetrahedrons.

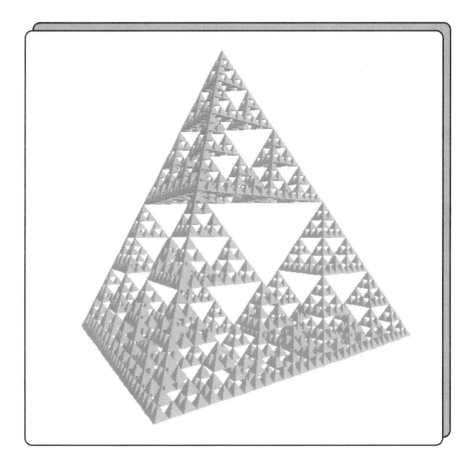

Figure 10–2. Three-dimensional Sierpinski Gasket at the fifth recursion level. Note that each side of the object is a two-dimensional Sierpinski Gasket.

The code to create the three-dimensional Sierpinski Gasket is a simple extension of the two-dimensional one. First, you must create a tetrahedral object consisting of four equilateral triangles. The *RWFgraph_ObjectList* is the easiest way to store a list of polygons. For convenience, the base of the tetrahedron lies in the x-y plane, while the tip lies along the z-axis. Now you just need the coordinates of the four vertices that define the tetrahedron, as shown in Figure 10–3. The tetrahedron is constructed to have sides of unit length.

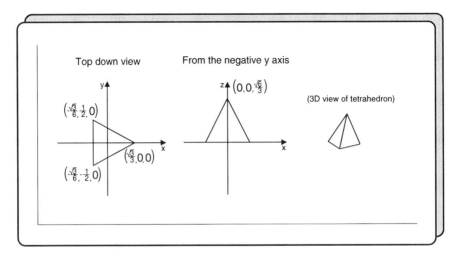

Figure 10–3. Defining a tetrahedron with sides of length one.

Given the vertex coordinates of the tetrahedron, you can define a tetrahedronal object as a simple collection of polygons. The following code segment illustrates how to construct the tetrahedron using the *RWFgraph_ObjectList* class:

```
//  Vertices are at: (0, 0, sqrt (6.0)/3.0),
//       (sqrt(3.0)/3, 0, 0), (-sqrt(3)/6, 0.5, 0)
//       (-sqrt(3)/6, -0.5, 0)

// Define the tetrahedron as an object list

// Declare a temporary polygon to hold the sides
RWFgraph_Polygon triangle, *poly;
// Declare the list to contain four polygons
```

```
RWFgraph_ObjectList tetra(4);
make 3D(); // Forces this to be 3-dimensional

// Define the principal vertex coordinates
const float xtri1 = sqrt(3.0) / 6.0;
const float xtri2 = -sqrt(3.0) / 6.0;
const float ytri = 05;

// First, create the bottom piece
triangle[0].setCoord(xtri1, 0, 0);
triangle[1].setCoord(xtri2,  ytri, 0);
triangle[2].setCoord(xtri2, -ytri, 0);
// Create a new polygon copy
poly = new RWFgraph_Polygon(3);
*poly = triangle;  // Copy the triangle
tetra[0] = poly;

// Now, create the three sides
triangle[0].setCoord(0, 0, sqrt (6.0) / 3.0);
triangle[1].setCoord(xtri1, 0, 0);
triangle[2].setCoord(xtri2, ytri, 0);
poly = new RWFgraph_Polygon(3);
*poly = triangle;  // Copy the triangle
tetra[1] = poly;

// Note that the first coordinate is always the tip,
// so you don't have to keep setting it
triangle[1].setCoord(xtri2, ytri, 0);
triangle[2].setCoord(xtri2, -ytri, 0);
poly = new RWFgraph_Polygon(3);
*poly = triangle;  // Copy the triangle
tetra[2] = poly;

triangle[1].setCoord(xtri2, -ytri, 0);
triangle[2].setCoord(xtri1, 0, 0);
poly = new RWFgraph_Polygon(3);
*poly = triangle;  // Copy the triangle
tetra[3] = poly;

// Tetrahedron stored in tetra is complete!
// You can now treat the tetrahedron as a single
// graphics entity
// Proceed with further processing
...
```

To help simplify the creation of the fractal objects of this chapter, the graphics object classes *RWFgraph_Tetrahedron* and *RWFgraph_Cube* are provided as standard graphics objects. The constructor for these objects generates a list of polygons, just as was done with the tetrahedron-generating code shown previously. These two classes are useful examples of how to create your own graphics objects as lists of polygons. You only need to derive your new object class from *RWFgraph_ObjectList* and define the constructor to create the appropriate set of polygons.

Given the tetrahedronal object, you can now create the three-dimensional Sierpinski Gasket. The generator consists of four transformations, each of which scales the base tetrahedron by half in all axes, and then translates the smaller copy to one of the four corners of the base tetrahedron. Our new base class for three-dimensional fractals is *RWFaf_3DObject*, which has all the same member functions as *RWFaf_Object* and works in an almost identical manner.

You can derive a class from *RWFaf_3DObject* to represent the three-dimensional Sierpinski Gasket in the same manner that the *RWFsg_Gasket* class of Chapter 6 is derived from the *RWFaf_Object* base class. The three-dimensional Sierpinski object class is called, naturally enough, *RWFsg_3DGasket*. The only differences between the definitions of *RWFsg_Gasket* and *RWFsg_3DGasket* are in the matrices that define the generators and action functions, which actually draw the object you use. The matrices in *RWFsg_3DGasket* are three-dimensional matrices, and there are four instead of three in *RWFsg_Gasket*.

As pointed out in Chapter 6, you could use the *RWFaf_Object* class to create fractal objects of any number of dimensions because there is no explicit reference to the dimensionality of the objects being drawn. However, there are two additional operations that the *generate()* function must perform to create a perspective drawing. The first addition operation passes a *RWFgraph_ViewingGeometry* structure, which defines the perspective view, to the drawing routines. The second addition has *generate()* sort the objects being drawn in back-to-front order for the particular view being generated. Passing a viewing geometry structure is a relatively easy modification. But sorting the objects requires a little more effort, as you'll see in the next section.

The action functions need the viewing geometry to draw the final three-dimensional rendering. Recall that the action functions for *RWFaf_Object* take two arguments: a pointer to the graphics object to process and the current recursion level. To generalize the action functions a little further, the *set3DAction* member function of *RWFaf_3DObject* lets you pass the address of a function that accepts three arguments instead of just two. The first two arguments are the same as the action functions for *RWFaf_Object*. The third argument is a reference to the *RWFgraph_ViewingGeometry* structure required for three-dimensional drawing. For the three-dimensional Sierpinski Gasket, the action function for drawing the tetrahedrons at the final recursion level is simply:

```
void RWFaf_3Ddraw(RWFgraph_Object *object, int level,
                  RWFgraph_ViewingGeometry &vg)
{
  if(object)
    object->draw(vg);
}
```

In order to pass the additional viewing-geometry structure, the *generate()* member function of *RWFaf_3DObject* uses an additional argument defining the viewing geometry for the three-dimensional case. The three-dimensional version of *draw()* therefore saves a pointer to the passed viewing-geometry structure before defining the action function with *setAction()*. The three-dimensional *draw()* function is defined as follows for the *RWFsg_3DObject* class:

```
class RWFsg_3DObject : public RWFaf_3DObject {
  private:
  protected:
  public:

    // The constructor defines the generator and initiator
    RWFsg_3DObject(void);

    // The drawing function also sets the action
```

```
    // and calls process()
    void draw(RWFgraph_ViewingGeometry &vg)
       {save_vg = &vg; set3DAction(&RWFaf_3Ddraw); process();};
};
```

The *generate()* member function for *RWFaf_3DObject* passes the saved pointer to the three-dimensional action function. The only other addition to *generate()* is to sort the transformed object copies into a proper back-to-front sorting order. In all other respects, *generate()* for *RWFaf_3DObject* is identical to *generate()* for *RWFaf_Object*. Even the stopping criteria based on object size can easily be modified to work for two- or three-dimensional generators.

Recall that the function *rwf_matGetGlobalScalingFactor()* uses the matrix determinant to determine the global scaling factor. The version in Chapter 6 took the square root of the determinant because only the two-dimensional matrices were being used. This can be generalized by using the inverse of the *n*th root of the determinant as the global scaling factor, where *n* is the dimensionality of the passed matrix. An easy way to find the *n*th root is with the C function *pow()*, using the power *1/n*.

Using the object class *RWFsg_3DObject*, you can now create images of the three-dimensional Sierpinski Gasket with the same ease as you would working in two dimensions. Furthermore, you have the same flexibility to color or manipulate the object by defining an appropriate action function to take whatever action you like when the object is drawn. Before examining other three-dimensional fractals, it is worthwhile to review some of the special issues surrounding the construction of three-dimensional objects.

Why Three Dimensions Are Special

In Chapter 3, you saw how to define and create three-dimensional objects using the *RWFgraph_Object* class. For the most part, two- and three-dimensional objects can be treated in an identical manner. There are, however, a few additional considerations you must be aware of when constructing a three-dimensional object.

Facing the right way

First, defining three-dimensional objects as lists of polygons requires you ensure that the polygons face the correct way. For an object such as the tetrahedron, you want to make sure the polygons face outward, away from the center of the object. Three-dimensional polygons are considered to be one-sided entities lying in a plane. A polygon can therefore be facing one of two directions relative to the plane it is in. If a polygon is facing away from the eyepoint when the polygon is rendered, then that polygon is not drawn. This rendering technique is referred to as *back-face removal*. (You can learn more about it in the sections on perspective rendering in Chapter 6 of *Computer Graphics: Principles and Practice*, which is listed in this book's bibliography). The direction a polygon faces is determined by its *surface normal*, or a vector that is perpendicular to the plane on which the polygon lies. You can generate the surface normal by examining the order in which the vertices are defined. Figure 10–4 shows you how to construct the surface normal using the *right-hand rule* on the vertices. The important point is to make sure you define the vertices counterclockwise for the direction you want the polygon to face. If you examine the code defining the tetrahedron, you'll see that it does just that for each face.

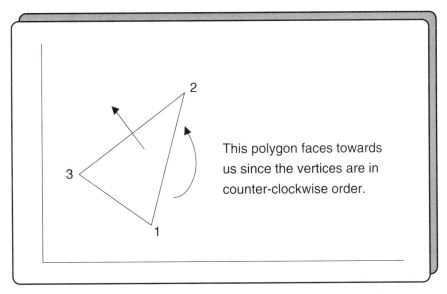

Figure 10–4. Using the right-hand rule to define the direction a polygon faces. The vertices must be defined counter-clockwise for the direction you want the polygon to face.

Object sorting

The second issue concerning three-dimensional objects has to do with constructing collections of objects. As shown in Chapter 3, you can use the *RWFgraph_ObjectList* class to define a complex object composed of simpler pieces. However, for the purposes of the software in this book, we must impose one additional restriction: Each object in an *RWFgraph_ObjectList* must not intersect any other object in the list. This restriction is imposed by the fairly simplistic three-dimensional rendering algorithms used in this book. The perspective rendering algorithm uses the painter's algorithm to draw multiple objects. Essentially, the *painter's algorithm* sorts a list of objects by their distance from the eye-point, and then draws the objects in back-to-front order. Drawing objects from back-to-front ensures that the nearer objects properly cover objects that are further away.

To implement the painter's algorithm, you must determine when one object is in front of another object. The simplest criteria for determining the drawing order uses a single *(x,y,z)* reference point for an object. Whenever a list of objects is drawn, each object's reference point is projected into the screen coordinate system in which *x* and *y* correspond to the *x*- and *y*-screen coordinates, and *z* corresponds to the distance from the viewing plane to the reference point. Given the *(x,y,z)* coordinate of each projected reference point, you can now sort the objects from back-to-front, drawing the objects with the most distant reference point first and the one with the nearest reference point last. This technique for sorting objects, however, does have its limitations. The primary limitation is that none of the sorted objects can intersect with one another, which means a portion of one object cannot penetrate any surface of another object. Although this is not a concern for rendering the fractal objects in this book, it can cause problems in more complex graphics environments that have many different objects, such as objects floating in a pool of water.

Each of the defined graphics objects, *RWFgraph_Point*, *RWFgraph_Polygon*, *RWFgraph_Circle*, and so on, defines a reference point whenever you set the coordinates of the object. *RWFgraph_Polygon*, for instance, defines the reference point as the average of the vertex coordinates. *RWFgraph_Circle* defines the center of the circle as the reference point.

You may use the member function *getReferencePoint()* to retrieve the *RWFvec_Vector* vector containing the current reference point. However, you will seldom need to use this function explicitly in your code as the reference point is really only needed by the object-sorting routines.

As mentioned earlier, the *generate()* member function of *RWFaf_3DObject* must sort the transformed objects before drawing them. Consider the portion of *generate()* for *RWFaf_Object* that performs the recursive calls for each iteration:

```
int next_level = level + 1;
for(int i=0; i < numTransforms(); i++) {
  // OK, go to the next recursion level
  generate(pmatrix * transforms[i], next_level);
}
```

Each transformation in the generator is applied in the order you originally specified. For two-dimensional drawings, there is no need to compute the transformations in any specific order. However, in the three-dimensional version of *generate()*, you must apply the transformations in the proper order to draw the transformed initiators from back to front. To do this, you must sort the transformations before making the recursive call to *generate()* with the new matrices. Sorting the matrices involves the following steps:

1. compute *pmatrix* * *transforms[i]* for each transformation matrix;

2. apply *pmatrix* * *transforms[i]* to the reference point for the initiator; and

3. sort the transformed reference points from maximum z to minimum z.

The function *rwf_graphSortMatrices()* shown in Listing 10–1 performs this operation on the table of matrices that defines the generator in *RWFaf_3DObject*. Instead of actually sorting the table of matrices, you can create a table of indices that specify the order in which to apply the transformations instead. *rwf_graphSortMatrices()* performs

this operation using a temporary table to store the distance of each transformed reference point from the eyepoint. *generate()* passes a table of *int*s in which to store the sorting order.

rwf_graphSortMatrices() uses the *RWFgraph_ViewingGeometry* member function *getProjectedCoordinates()* to transform the reference points into the appropriate screen coordinates. Once you have the transformed point, you can simply compute the distance from the reference point to the eyepoint. The table of z-values is sorted using a simple bubble-sort algorithm that compares the z-coordinates for each pair of transformations. If the reference points are in the wrong order, elements in the sorting-order table are swapped. When the sort is complete, the recursive calls to *generate()* can be made, which effectively draws the fractal object in back-to-front order.

Listing 10–1. The function *rwf_graphSortMatrices()* sorts a table of matrix pointers into a suitable drawing order for the *generate()* member function of *RWFaf_3DObject*.

```
// Define the sorting-order table
typedef RWFlist_SimpleTable<int>
        RWFlist_SortingOrderTable;
// Define a type to hold eyepoint distances
// These are the value you sort on.
typedef RWFlist_SimpleTable<float>    RWFlist_RTable;

void
rwf_graphSortMatrices(RWFgraph_ViewingGeometry &vg,
                      RWFmat_Matrix &global_matrix,
                      RWFvec_Vector &ref_point,
                      RWFmat_MatrixTable &mtable,
                      RWFlist_SortingOrderTable &order)
{
  int n = mtable.size();
  // Create a table to hold the projected z-coordinates
  // No need to constantly create and destroy it; it can
  // remain static.
  static RWFlist_ZTable rtable(n);
  static RWFvec_Vector tvec(3);
```

```
for(int i=0; i < n; i++) {
  // Transform the reference point
  tvec = global_matrix * mtable[i] * ref_point;
  // Transform the reference point from world
  // coordinates
  tvec = vg.getProjectedCoordinate(tvec);
  // Now get the distances
 rtable[i] = tvec.length();
  order[i] = i; // Set the default order
}


// Sort the distances using a bubble sort
int sorted = 0;
int limit = n;
int index1, index2;
while(!sorted) {
  sorted = 1;
  limit--;
  for(int i=0; i < limit; i++) {
    index1 = order[i];
    index2 = order[i+1];
    if(rtable[index1] < rtable[index2]) {
      sorted = 0;
      order.swap(i, i+1);
    }
  }
}


// The correct order for drawing objects is now stored
// in the order array
}
```

Note that there is an additional argument to *rwf_graphSortMatrices()* of a global matrix that multiplies each matrix in the passed matrix table. This extra argument is necessary because each recursive call to *generate()* requires multiplying all the matrices in the generator by the current matrix. Rather than having to generate a new table of matrices with this multiplication already computed, *rwf_graphSortMatrices()* is simply passed

the single multiplying matrix and applies this matrix to each matrix of the generator.

The modified version of *generate()*, which sorts the transformations prior to making the recursive calls to *generate()*, is shown in Listing 10–2. You should also note that the same sorting problem occurs when defining a list of objects as a single *RWFgraph_ObjectList* object. The three-dimensional version of *draw()* for *RWFgraph_ObjectList* also sorts the list of objects before drawing them on the screen.

The sorting operation is slightly different from that of *rwf_graphSortMatrices()* because each object in an object list has its own separate reference point, instead of using a common reference point for all the objects (each recursive call to *generate()* creates a scaled copy of the base object, so there is only one reference point to transform). In all other respects, though, the sorting algorithm is the same as the one shown in Listing 10–1. The reference point for an entire *RWFgraph_ObjectList* object is just the average of all the reference points for the objects in the list.

Listing 10–2. The *generate()* member function for the *RWFaf_3DObject* class.

```
void
RWFaf_3DObject::generate(RWFmat_Matrix &pmatrix,
                         int level)
{
  // Reached max recursion level yet?
  if(level >= max_level) {
    base_object->setMatrix(pmatrix);
    (*action_3Dfunc) (base_object, level, *save_vg);
    return;
  }

  // Now, is the object small enough?
  float scale = rwf_matGetGlobalScalingFactor(pmatrix);
  if((scale * cur_object_size) <= min_object_size) {
    base_object->setMatrix(pmatrix);
    (*action_3Dfunc) (base_object, level, *save_vg);
```

```
    return;
  }


  // Sort the objects
  // First, create the order table
  int numtrans = transforms.size();
  RWFlist_SortingOrderTable order(numtrans);


  // Sort the objects
  rwf_graphSortMatrices(*save_vg, pmatrix,
                    base_object->getReferencePoint(),
                    transforms, order);


  // OK, draw the objects in the correct order
  int next_level = level + 1;
  int index;
  for(int i=0; i < numtrans; i++) {
    // OK, go to the next recursion level
    index = order[i];
    generate(pmatrix * transforms[index], next_level);
  }
}
```

Assorted Three-Dimensional Fractals

With the *RWFaf_3DObject* class, you can now easily create three-dimensional affine fractals. For example, a three-dimensional equivalent of the Sierpinski Carpet is the Menger Sponge, discovered and researched by the Austrian mathematician Karl Menger. The construction of the Menger Sponge is very similar to that of the Sierpinski Carpet. You start with a single cube, which is initially sliced into three uniform pieces in the x-, y-, and z-axes. This divides the initial cube into 27 one-third sized cubes. The generator for the Menger Sponge removes the center cube and the cube at the center of all six sides. The process is then repeated on all the remaining cubes. The resulting object at various recursion levels is shown in Figure 10–5. Note that just as the three-dimensional Sierpinski Gasket has a two-dimensional Sierpinski Gasket on each side, the Menger Sponge produces a Sierpinski Carpet on all six sides of the original cube.

269

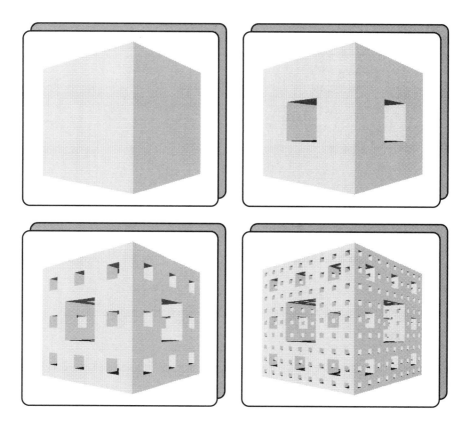

Figure 10–5. The Menger Sponge is the three-dimensional analog of the Sierpinski Carpet.

You can create your own interesting combinations of three-dimensional fractal objects using creative combinations of action functions. In Chapter 6, you created a Sierpinski Carpet made up of Sierpinski Gaskets. Figure 10–6 shows the three-dimensional equivalent, a Menger Sponge filled with three-dimensional Sierpinski Gaskets. The only coding difference between Figure 10–5 and Figure 10–6 is that the action function draws a *RWFsg_3DGasket* instead of a cube when the final recursion level of the sponge is reached. Any fractal object derived from *RWFaf_3DObject* may be used just as any other graphics object, allowing you to combine fractal objects in interesting ways, as shown in Figure 10–6.

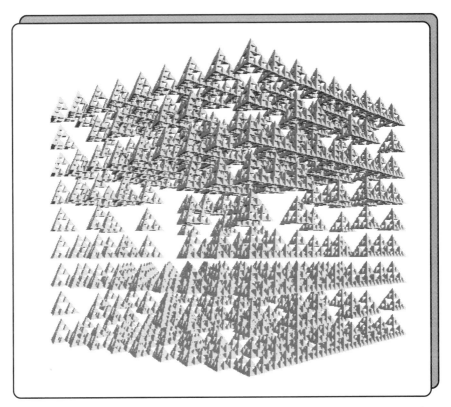

Figure 10–6. A Menger Sponge constructed from three-dimensional Sierpinski Gaskets.

Reverse Three Dimensions

There are actually two different ways to draw objects with the *RWFaf_Object* class. The first is the forward method, which draws an object only at the final recursion level. The second is the reverse method, which draws an object at each recursion level. The reverse method works well in two dimensions because it acts to erase portions of the original figure. In fact, you can create an inverse of a particular fractal object not by erasing the original figure, but by simply drawing another object in the "holes" of the initiator. You can implement the equivalent of the reverse-generation method in three dimensions. The erase initiator specifies what object to draw in the holes of the initiator at each recursion level. You can, for instance, construct an inverted Menger Sponge by drawing an object such as a cube or sphere in the holes of the sponge. The inverted Menger Sponge is shown in Figure 10–7.

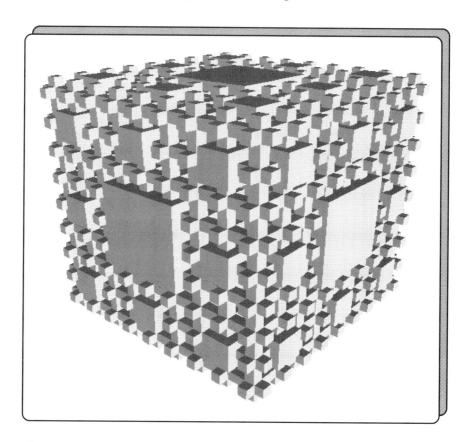

Figure 10–7. An inverted Menger Sponge. This object uses the *process_reverse()* method to draw cubes in the holes of the Menger Sponge of Figure 10–5.

The *process_reverse()* member function of *RWFaf_3DObject* is the same as the *process_reverse()* member function of *RWFaf_Object*, except the three-dimensional version does not draw the initial object first. The *generate_reverse()* function requires the same modifications that the *generate()* function does for the three-dimensional case; namely, the objects must be properly sorted. The transformed copies of the initiator must be sorted into back-to-front order, as do the multiple objects in the erase initiator. The only major difference between *generate()* and *generate_reverse()*

is that both the erase initiator and the transformed copies of the base initiator must be sorted together as one collection of objects, and then drawn in back-to-front order. When you specify the erase initiator with *setEraseInitiator()*, the transformation matrices for the erase initiator are added to the matrix table that defines the generator transformations, so they can all be sorted together. The three-dimensional version of *generate_reverse()* is shown in Listing 10–3.

Listing 10–3. The *generate_reverse()* member function for the *RWFaf_3DObject* class.

```
void
RWFaf_3DObject::generate_reverse(RWFmat_Matrix &pmatrix,
                                 int level)
{
  // Reached max recursion level yet?
  if(level >= max_level)
    return;

  // Now, is the object small enough?
  float scale = RWFmat_GetGlobalScalingFactor(pmatrix);
  if((scale * cur_object_size) <= min_object_size)
    return;

  // Sort the objects
  // First, create the order table
  // Must use the actual table to get all transformations
  int numtotal = transforms.size();
  RWFlist_SortingOrderTable order(numtotal);

  // Sort the objects
  rwf_graphSortMatrices(*save_vg, pmatrix,
                        base_object->getReferencePoint(),
                        transforms, order);

  // OK, draw the objects in the correct order
  int next_level = level + 1;
  int index;
  // Get the number of transformations of the generator
```

273

```
for(int i=0; i < numtotal; i++) {
  // OK, go to the next recursion level
  index = order[i];
  if(index < numBase) {
    // This is a base-generator transformation
    generate_reverse(pmatrix * transforms[index], next_level);
  } else {
    // This is an erase object to draw
    int j = index - numBase;
    RWFmat_Matrix save_matrix;
    save_matrix = erase_object[j]->getMatrix();
    erase_object[j]->setMatrix(pmatrix * save_matrix);
    (*action_3Dfunc) (erase_object[j], next_level,
                      *save_vg);
    erase_object[i]->setMatrix(save_matrix);
  }
}
}
```

As discussed in Chapter 6, using the reverse method has several advantages over the forward method. With the reverse method, for instance, you can easily color the objects based on the current recursion level. Color plate 6 provides a more colorful example of the possibilities in which a Menger Sponge is constructed from cubes colored according to their recursion level. At the first recursion level, colorful three-dimensional Sierpinski Gasket is drawn in place of the cubes. The possible combinations of fractal objects are limited only by your imagination.

Trees

The *RWFtree_Object* class of Chapter 7 is easily adapted to three dimensions. The class *RWFtree_3DObject*, derived from *RWFaf_3DObject*, defines a class for generating trees in three dimensions. *RWFtree_3DObject* is identical to *RWFtree_Object* in all respects and shares the same member functions and operations. But instead of using a unit line segment for the base initiator, *RWFtree_3DObject* uses a unit cube. The initial cube is, of course, usually stretched along one dimension to create a rectangular branch, unless you want very blocky trees! A simple modification that you can try is to replace the rectangular branch with a cylindrical one by using a unit cylinder as the base branch object.

The *generate()* and *generate_reverse()* member functions for *RWFaf_3DObject* provide the same feature that lets you define an optional matrix-randomizing function. Of course, now you have the option to introduce more random variations by considering three, instead of two, dimensions. In both *generate()* and *generate_reverse()*, the transformations are randomized prior to the transformation sorting operation. The compatibility between *RWFtree_Object* and *RWFtree_3DObject* even lets you use the same *RWFtree_BranchData* class to define the attributes for creating new branches. The definition of *RWFtree_BranchData* is:

```
class RWFtree_BranchData {
   public:
   int id;
   RWFrand_GaussianRV length, angle;
   RWFrand_UniformRV  offset, side;

   RWFtree_BranchData(void);
};
```

In the two-dimensional case, the random variable *side* determines which side of the parent branch the new branch should be placed. In the three-dimensional case, *side* determines the angle with respect to the main axis of the parent branch, and can therefore take on any value from 0 degrees to 360 degrees. The random variable *offset* determines where to start the new branch along the axis of the parent branch. By convention, the tree is considered to grow upwards (in the *z*-direction). A sample three-dimensional matrix-randomizing function for three-dimensional branch generation is shown in Listing 10–4.

Listing 10–4. A sample three-dimensional matrix-randomizing function for three-dimensional branch generation.

```
int
RWFtree_3DFindBranchMatrix(void *data,
                           int level,
```

275

```
                                    RWFmat_Matrix &bmatrix)
    {
      RWFtree_BranchData *branch = (RWFtree_BranchData *)data;
      float factor;

      bmatrix.Identity();
      factor = branch->length.next();
      // Scale only in the z-direction
      bmatrix.scale(1.0, 1.0, factor);
      factor = branch->angle.next();
      // First, rotate about the y-axis
      bmatrix.rotate(0.0, factor, 0.0);
      // Use the side parameter to determine a rotation
      // angle about the z-axis
      // Now, rotate about the z-axis
      factor = branch->side.next();
      bmatrix.rotate(0.0, 0.0, factor);
      // Finally, translate the branch along the z-axis
      factor = MAX(MIN(branch->offset.next(), 1.0), 0.0);
      bmatrix.translate(0.0, 0.0, factor);

      return 1;
    }
```

Cloudy Days

You can model another familiar outdoor object, the cloud, by three-dimensional fractals. Using a variation of the *RWFtree_3DObject* class, you can create an attractive cloud model using scaled spheres. Unlike the normal tree-drawing class, you need to use the *process()* member function to draw the spheres only at the final recursion level. The basic cloud begins with a single sphere, which you normally scale in *x* and *y* to flatten it slightly. The initial scaled sphere is then randomly scaled down and copied a number of times with different orientations and slightly offset from the center of the parent sphere, as shown in Figure 10–8. The process is just a three-dimensional version of the cratering procedure of Chapter 7. You continue the process until a final recursion level is reached, or the scaled spheres are a pixel or less on the screen, and then draw the scaled

276

spheres. The class *RWFtree_Cloud* and its associated matrix-generating function *rwf_tree3DFindCloudMatrix()* provides a suitable default set of parameters for adding clouds to your own programs. Color plate 7 shows an example of a cloudy sky created with this technique.

Figure 10–8. Creating a cloud as a collection of scaled spheres.

The construction of the cloud can sometimes violate our previously stated rule that the transformed copies of objects must not intersect. But violating this rule does not have an impact on the final cloud image because of the objects' uniformity, which are spheres that make up the cloud in this instance. They are all basically the same color, and the order in which they are drawn does not have a noticeable visual impact on the final image. With an object composed of more individually discernible features, a violation of the back-to-front drawing order can be more noticeable.

Color plate 8 combines the clouds with some simple trees to create an image of an overcast day in a nearby forest. To create a more realistic appearance in the clouds, the color of each individual sphere is a function of its height above the ground. A darker gray is used for the lower parts of the cloud, which gradually increases to a lighter gray toward top. Simply by changing the intensity and magnitude of this color, you can create the visual appearance of anything from storm clouds to white clouds.

A Stormy Demonstration

The demonstration program *storm.exe* illustrates how color affects your perception of clouds, as well as the ability to create all sorts of interesting cloud types. This program creates clouds based on the parameters you enter. You set the relative size of the cloud by entering x- and y-scale factors (relative to the z-scale factor set at 1.0). You may also select the standard deviation of the offset (how far each copy is from its parent's center), the rotation angles (relative to the orientation of the parent), and the size scale factors (always between 0.0 and 1.0). Once the cloud scene is created, *storm.exe* will cycle through the color palette to create the illusion of clouds moving in both a sunny and an overcast environment.

To enhance the storm simulation, you can add a lightning effect between the clouds using the one-dimensional fBM routine from Chapter 8. A lightning bolt is modeled as a path from a point in one cloud to a point in another cloud. The *rwf_fbm1DGenerate()* function computes deviations from a straight path between these two points. The lightning bolt is drawn simply by connecting the points along the modified path. To speed up the demonstration, several passes of one-dimensional fBM are precomputed. *storm.exe* randomly selects one of these precomputed data sets and uses it to plot the path of the lightning. The result is quite an interesting demonstration.

Modeling the Rest of the World

As you have seen, all the fractal algorithms developed in the earlier chapters are easily extensible from two dimensions to three or more dimensions. The only significant modifications to the fractal algorithms allow for correct perspective display of three-dimensional objects, as the most complex issue is drawing the pieces in back-to-front order correctly. The fractal-generating techniques are basically identical in all dimensions and involve only the use of matrix transformations of greater dimensionality.

By extending the tree- and crater-generating fractal classes, you now have suitable methods for modeling plants, trees, and clouds. Now all you need is a method for generating the underlying terrain, and you can even create a model of the whole world. And in the next chapter, you'll learn how to do just that using two-dimensional fBM to create realistic models of rocky mountains, oceans, lakes, forests, and whatever else you want. You'll then see how many of the techniques from both this and the next chapter are combined to create the ultimate virtual reality for the demanding real-time world of flight simulation.

Fractal Life Savers

Creating realistic terrain images has become one of the most popular applications for fractals today. Since the publication of Mandelbrot's *The Fractal Geometry of Nature*, many computer graphics artists and programmers have used fractal techniques to create an astonishing variety of images of locations both real and imaginary. In fact, fractals were catapulted to movie stardom when Loren Carpenter, Alain Fournier, Don Fussell, and other members of Lucas Film Productions used fractals to create the Genesis planetary evolution sequence in the movie "Star Trek II."

Fractal models help solve two fundamental problems in computer graphics: the previous inability to create realistic images of natural phenomenon and the previous inability to efficiently generate those images without the need of an inordinately large amount of data or additional computation. You have already seen in the previous chapters how to create images of trees, plants, clouds, and other naturally occurring objects using fractal models. In this chapter, you'll see how to use the fBM techniques of Chapter 9 to model a terrain surface complete with hills, mountains, lakes, and oceans. By combining both the continuous and discrete fBM methods, you can create very realistic images of actual places using measured data acquired from maps, satellite statistics, and aerial photography. The scenes are realistic enough to use in one of the most demanding computer graphics applications, real-time image generation for a flight simulator. Several of the color plates show how the fractal-terrain-generating techniques of this chapter can produce rich, realistic scenes that would be difficult, if not impossible, to produce any other way.

Mountainous Problems

To understand some of the problems encountered in generating terrain images, let's first consider how to create a model of a single mountain. Until the introduction of fractal models, computer graphics was primarily concerned with creating images of smooth geometric shapes, such as spheres, cylinders, and polygons. Creating a complex shape consists of combining simpler shapes, just as you did in Chapter 3. While such smooth and regular shapes are quite suitable for modeling mechanical objects like machine parts, spheres and cylinders are not very useful in modeling rough and irregular objects like hills and mountains.

Most computer-graphics models consist of collections of polygons primarily because you can approximate virtually any type of object to any desired level of accuracy by using enough polygons. Modeling an irregular shape, such as a mountain, may require thousands of polygons to recreate all the jagged edges and surfaces. If you have ever tried to create such a model, you probably quickly recognized the need to come up with an automated means of generating the polygons in your mountain model. Defining the coordinates of the vertices for thousands of polygons is a difficult and time-consuming task even with the best modeling programs.

Given that you need an automated means of producing a mountain model, let's see what characteristics such an algorithm should have. First, it should be able to produce a model at any desired scale, allowing you to approximate anything from low hills to Mount Everest. Second, you should be able to easily control the algorithm so you can create a model of a particular mountain such as Mount Everest, rather than a generic mountain.

Typically, you do this by creating a simple geometric model of your specific mountain that consists of a small number of polygons (for instance, 100 to 200) using a suitable modeling program and working with photographs or other data that defines the outline of the mountain. Your automated mountain generator starts with this initial low-resolution model and then breaks the polygons of the initial model into smaller ones, introducing random variations to create natural-looking rocks, snow, grass, or whatever features are on your particular mountain.

In most cases, you do not want or need to reproduce an exact model that includes the smallest rocks and pebbles on the mountain. You simply need to create a model that looks close enough to the original at reasonable levels of detail. So your automated mountain generator should be able to take an existing simple model and produce a more detailed model that matches the less detailed original model, but has more nooks and crannies. This is the second criteria for automated mountain production in which the algorithm should be able to start with an initial model and produce a more detailed model in a controlled fashion. The algorithm is said to be *consistent* because the different resolution models match up with one another.

So now, you have a wonderfully detailed model of a mountain, consisting of perhaps thousands of polygons. With a good rendering program and a fast computer, you can create an image of a mountain in a reasonable amount of time. Suppose you want to create a simulated flyby of a mountain range such as the Andes. You now need a database consisting of many mountains. Creating such a database should be no problem because you can make as many mountains as you like with your new algorithm. Of course, the database will probably become quite large because of the large number of mountains. Depending on the amount of detail you desire, you might have a database consisting of several hundred thousand polygons, which all must be stored, retrieved, and processed to create a picture. Your image generation for the simulated flyby now requires more time than it did for the single mountain image. To generate the flyby sequence, you have the choice of either using less polygons per mountain, which creates less detailed images but generates the sequence much faster, or using more detailed models that take longer to generate the sequence. With a little analysis, however, you can significantly reduce the number of polygons you must process when rendering a particular image.

Multiple Levels of Detail

In a typical view of a mountain range, probably only one or two of the mountains are close enough to see any real detail. The rest of the range is too far away to see any significant detail. The mountain models that are far away do not need to be as detailed as the close-up mountains. So one way to reduce the total number of polygons that must be processed is to use lower resolution models for the mountains that are further away. For instance, the initial 100 to 200 polygon model might be perfectly adequate for viewing the mountain from ten miles away. But it is not adequate when you are flying directly over the mountain. One solution to the polygon processing problem is to have multiple, consistent models with a varying number of polygons. An object with multiple representations using different numbers of polygons is said to have *multiple levels of detail*. The rendering program can determine which resolution model (number of polygons) to use for a particular image by examining how far away the mountain is from the viewer. If it is far away, then use the lowest resolution model. If the mountain is close, use a higher resolution model. By using various level-of-detail models, you can greatly reduce the number of polygons required to create a particular scene. Figure 11–1 shows a sample sequence of various resolution models of the same simulated mountain with increasing resolution from left to right. Although each succeeding model matches the previous model, it provides more detailed features.

Despite the enormous advantage that multiple level-of-detail models provide in reducing the number of polygons you would need to render, there are still a few other considerations of which you should be aware. First, you still must be able to store and access the models at all the various resolutions, including the highest resolution. This may require a great deal of memory and disk storage for the thousands of polygons defining your mountain range. The second problem occurs when you are creating an animated sequence, such as a simulated flyby. As the eyepoint moves through your database, the rendering algorithm decides which level-of-detail model to use. At some point in the motion, the models will be switched, either from a lower to a higher resolution model (movement closer to a particular mountain) or vice versa (movement away from a mountain). Unless you are very careful in constructing the various level-of-detail models, the point at which the switch from one model to another occurs will be very noticeable in the final animation sequence. The only way to ensure smooth transitions between the levels of detail is to have a lot of different levels with only slight variations between them, so the transition from one level to another is not so noticeable. So another criteria for automated model generation is the ability to create multiple level-of-detail models at many different resolutions that are consistent with one another.

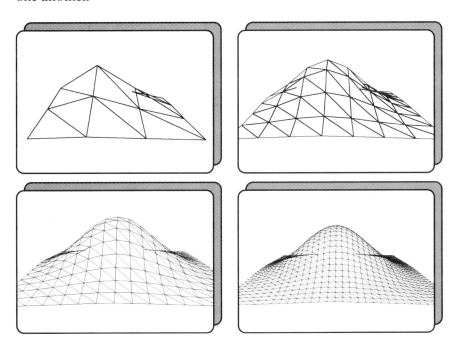

Figure 11–1. Multiple level-of-detail models of the same mountain.

You can make a further refinement to level-of-detail modeling by observing that even within the same mountain, you may not need the same detail on one part of the mountain as another. If you are standing on top of the mountain, for instance, you need the highest level of detail for the closest features. But the base of the mountain does not require the same resolution, especially if it is a tall mountain. So in some instances, you might also want to refine your model to have greater resolution of one part rather than another. However, incorporating multiple levels of detail for different parts of the mountain requires even more sophistication in the level-of-detail algorithm and more storage for the extra models. Clearly, managing multiple level-of-detail models can quickly get out of hand.

Storing the World

An important consideration when building a complicated polygon database is the amount of storage required for the models. You can easily estimate how much storage a particular database will require by counting its polygons. With the *RWFgraph_Polygon* type, each polygon is stored as a list of three-dimensional vectors. Each three-dimensional coordinate requires three *float* values that occupy 12 bytes. If the database consists of nothing but triangles, you'll need to store at least 36 bytes per triangle. In addition to the vertex information, there may also be some ancillary information stored about the polygon, such as its color and other attributes. In general, a minimum of 40 bytes per polygon should be stored. So a 5,000-polygon database of a mountain requires at least 200,000 bytes of storage. Multiple level-of-detail models of the same mountain might require at least another 200,000 bytes of storage. A mountain range consisting of 30 mountains would require almost 6 megabytes of storage. And keeping all the models in memory for a DOS program is problematic at best. A detailed model of a complex terrain environment may require even more entities to model trees, lakes, oceans, beaches, and other features you encounter in real land; each object could possibly require multiple levels of detail. There is, however, an alternative to storing all the polygon lists.

Fractals to the Rescue

Instead of using the automated mountain generator to create a complete list of polygons for the entire mountain, you can incorporate the mountain generator directly into the rendering program. Use the simple 100 to 200 polygon models to define the base shape of the mountain, and use the generator to create the desired level of detail for the particular view. This obviates the need for massive amounts of additional storage, either on disk or in memory. An algorithm for generating an object database dynamically is called a *procedural* model because it defines the object not just as a list of primitive objects, but by its method (or procedure) for generating detailed models from a small set of parameters as well. There are many types of procedural object models that include fractals. For instance, you can easily define an algorithm to generate a polygonal description of a sphere by dividing the sphere into uniform angular pieces, as shown in Figure 11–2. Using the sphere-generating algorithm, you can create as many polygons as you need to achieve a desired resolution. If the sphere is small or far away, you might only use angular steps that are 10 degrees apart. But a close-up rendition of the sphere might require steps that are 1 degree or smaller. The point is that you do not need to store huge numbers of polygons to create a detailed model of a sphere. You only need to specify the desired radius, location of the center, color, and other such attributes as well as the procedure for generating the polygons from these parameters.

To be effective, any procedural object model must be efficient, compact, and provide a reasonable representation of an object at different scales, as discussed previously. A procedural model must be able to generate consistent models at any desired level of detail. You must be able to specify the model with a small set of parameters, such as the center and radius of a sphere. As you'll see later in this chapter, it is also highly desirable to be able to compute different levels of detail for different parts of the same object. Finally, the procedure must be efficient, so that it may be directly incorporated into the rendering program without inducing a lot of extra computational overhead. If generating the list of polygons takes a long time, then you'll negate the advantage of using multiple level-of-detail models in the first place.

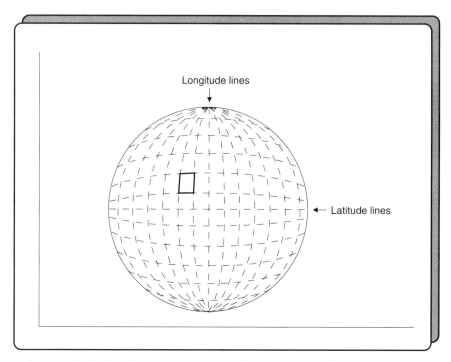

Figure 11–2. Creating polygons to define a sphere. With a procedural model, you can generate any number of polygons for the sphere.

All this, of course, leads us to the idea of using fractals as an ideal procedural model for many types of naturally occurring objects. For instance, the tree model from Chapter 7 lets you create trees with any desired level of branching, effectively corresponding to different levels of detail. For a tree viewed from 100 feet away, you probably only need two or three levels of branching. As you move closer, you can generate more branches with greater recursion levels. You can increase the detail in small steps, by stepping through the recursion one level at a time. Furthermore, you can create a tree of any size, and by fine-tuning the small number of branching parameters, you can create many different types of trees. So the tree fractal satisfies all the desirable criteria for a procedural model. The same comments apply to the crater and cloud modeling of the previous chapters. Now all you need is a suitable procedural model for terrain.

You have already seen one such suitable method for generating rough surfaces, the fBM algorithms of Chapter 9. But that method is by no means the only one. You can create random surfaces in a great variety of ways, but the fBM algorithms have all the characteristics required of a procedural algorithm. First and foremost the surfaces they generate look like rough terrain. The rough features of a mountain look similar to the mountain itself, just at a different scale. You would therefore expect an algorithm based on self-similarity (like fBM) to be able to reproduce the features of a self-similar object such as a mountain. The fBM algorithms also satisfy the other criteria for a procedural model (as do all the fractal models), such as requiring only a few parameters to define a surface (the values at the four corners, the initial standard deviation, and the fractal dimension H). By selecting the appropriate recursion level, these algorithms also can generate any desired level of detail.

Matching Reality

While the fBM algorithms described in Chapter 9 provide a suitable procedural model for generating a random terrain surface, you cannot use them to create a specific terrain surface. You can only specify the initial four corners of the grid in the algorithm. All the internal points are generated by the algorithm. You can, however, incorporate the fBM algorithms with data that defines a specific terrain surface to make a more complete and useful model.

Digital maps

Our method for defining terrain originally comes from using digital satellite data. Satellites such as LANDSAT are constantly circling the Earth and sending back digitized images of the planet's surface. These images are organized like any other digital picture, as an x-y digital raster image. Each pixel of the image corresponds to a rectangular area on the ground. Depending on the satellite, the resolution of the pixel can be anywhere from 100 meters to 5 meters per side. So a digitized-satellite image provides an image of a relatively large area on the ground with fairly coarse resolution. Using the raw satellite data, you can produce a digital map of a particular area, identifying pixels as members of a particular object class, such as water, pine tree, oak tree, road, or building. So from the original unprocessed satellite data, you can produce a new image called a *classified* image, with the values at each pixel indicating to which type of terrain feature the corresponding area on the ground belongs. A typical classified map is shown in Color Plate 11, where color is used to identify the various classes.

You can also acquire the data for a digital map from other sources. You can, for example, directly digitize a map using a large digitizing tablet. This requires an operator to identify regions on the map as belonging to a particular object class. Digitizing maps is a useful way of augmenting a classified image generated from satellite data. Often, parts of a region in a satellite image are obscured by clouds, tree cover, or other features that can be identified and entered directly from a map of the region. Another source of high-resolution information is digitized aerial photography, taken from a high-altitude aircraft. Using a digital scanner, you can digitize the aerial photograph and process it in a similar manner as the satellite data to produce a more detailed classified image.

In addition to classifying a terrain image into various groups, you can also acquire other digital information about a geographic area, including elevation data that defines the height of the terrain above sea level. The most common form of elevation data is topographic maps that show contours of constant elevation. Digitized elevation data is available from a number of government sources, including the Defense Mapping Agency. There are also a number of commercial firms that specialize in acquiring such data for a specific region.

Wherever the data comes from, you need a digital raster elevation map of a region for terrain modeling. Just as the pixels in a digital-class map identify the terrain type, the pixels in a digital elevation map indicate the height above sea level for that region. Typically, the resolution of the elevation data and the classified data do not initially match one another. But by resampling the two raster data sets, you can create a combined raster data set that provides both the height and terrain classes at the same x- and y-spacing across the desired area.

A raster-terrain data set containing both height and terrain class information is the principal means for capturing a specific terrain region in digital form. However, the resolution of such a database is limited not just by the imaging resolution of the particular satellite being used. The total number of pixels in a raster-terrain database depends on the area size you want to cover and the resolution of the satellite imagery. To cover a 50 mile by 50 mile area with 30 meter resolution pixels requires about 2,500 by 2,500 pixels. Higher resolution, say 10 meter pixels, requires nine times as much data to cover the same area on the ground. A 1 meter pixel database would take 900 times as much storage as the 30 meter resolution data! A raster-terrain data set requires a lot of disk storage. Even 10 meter pixels provide very coarse resolution if you want to create an image from a ground-level perspective.

So you're quickly in the massive database dilemma discussed earlier. Gathering enough data at sufficient resolution to create a picture from ground level—such as standing on the mountain top—requires much higher resolution and, consequently, more storage in the database than you could hope to use, much less process. A procedural modeling approach is definitely the preferred method for solving this modeling problem.

Fractal terrain

The solution to our database storage and rendering problem is now fairly straightforward. The raster-terrain database defines a grid of pixels over the terrain. For every pixel in the grid, you have both the height and terrain class of the area covered by each pixel. Figure 11–3 shows such a raster grid. The grid effectively divides the terrain into a series of rectangles, called *grid cells*, whose heights and terrain classes are known at the corners or each rectangle. The fBM algorithms of Chapter 9 are now applicable for subdividing each of the individual rectangles, as shown in Figure 11–3. So you use the low-resolution terrain data acquired from satellites, maps, aerial photography, or other sources to define the global characteristics of the terrain, and the fBM algorithms to create the detailed model. By combining the procedural fractal model with the measured terrain data, you create a very powerful

technique for creating images of real places. Let's see how to implement this technique using the fractal and graphics classes developed so far.

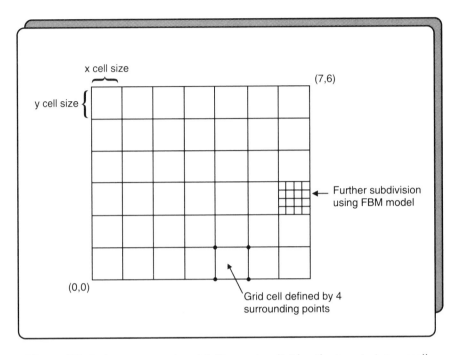

Figure 11–3. A raster-terrain grid. The raster divides the terrain into small rectangular areas. Each rectangle can be further subdivided using the fBM algorithms in a procedural model.

In order to draw our terrain image, you need an object to represent a rectangular grid of points. The *RWFgraph_Grid* class serves this purpose. The *RWFgraph_Grid* class is derived from *RWFgraph_Object*. Being a graphics object means you can use and draw an *RWFgraph_Grid* like any other graphics object. A *RWFgraph_Grid* is a grid of *RWFgraph_GridElement* entries. A grid element is simply defined as:

```
class RWFgraph_GridElement {
public:
int class;      // Class value for this pixel
float h;        // Height above sea level
};
```

RWFgraph_Grid behaves like a matrix object in many ways. You can easily work with the height or class of any particular pixel. In particular, you can use the subscript operator *[]* to access any particular pixel just as you can with a matrix. So, to find the class or height at a particular location, you would use the following code:

```
RWFgraph_Grid terrain(32, 32);

// Load the grid
...
// Process pixels
int numrows = terrain.nrows();
int numcols = terrain.ncols();
for(int j=0; j < numrows; j++) {
  for(int i=0; i < numcols; i++) {
    terrain[j][i].class = new_class;
    terrain[i][j].h    = new_height;
  }
}
```

As with the matrices, you may define a grid of any size that will fit in memory. In addition to defining the height and class of each pixel, you must define the size of the terrain pixels to indicate what the resolution of the data is. If you are using 30 meter data, you would define the size of each pixel as 30, using the *setPixelSize()* member function, for instance. The default grid cell size is a size of 1.0 for each grid cell. The grid is assumed to be oriented with the element at (0,0), located at the origin, as shown in Figure 11–4. You can easily change the orientation of the grid by specifying a transformation matrix, just as you can with any graphics object. Not e that unlike a matrix, you access an (x,y) pixel in the grid with a subscript as *grid[x][y]*, rather than the reverse used with matrices.

Ignoring the inclusion of the fBM algorithms for the moment, the *draw()* member function for *RWFgraph_Grid* draws a grid by dividing each rectangle in the grid into two triangles, as shown in Figure 11–4. You cannot draw each rectangle as a single polygon because each corner may be a different height, resulting in a nonplanar four-sided polygon.

A triangle, however, is always planar. The choice of which diagonal to divide the rectangle with is arbitrary. In most cases, the choice is irrelevant, but in some circumstances it can make a slight difference in the resulting image, as shown in Figure 11–4.

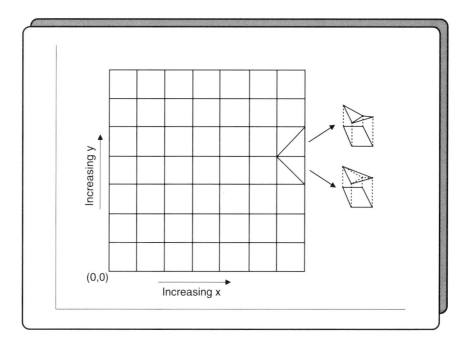

Figure 11–4. The default orientation and location of a grid. The lower-left corner corresponds to the element at row 0; column 0 is located at the origin. The *draw()* function divides each rectangle into two triangles. There are two possible choices for dividing each rectangle, which occasionally results in a different appearance of the final image.

Another way to divide a grid cell into suitable triangles is to compute the center point of the grid cell as the average of the four corners. You then divide the grid cell into four triangles, using each pair of grid-cell corners and the computed center point. This solution to drawing the four-sided grid cell, however, creates twice as many triangles to draw the same grid cell. In most applications, dividing the grid cells along a diagonal is sufficient. The x- and y-coordinates of grid element (i,j) is simply $(i*x\_cell\_size,$ $j*y\_cell\_size)$, where x_cell_size and y_cell_size are the (x,y) dimensions, respectively, of the grid pixels. The z-coordinate is just the height h stored for that particular element of the grid. Given the three-dimensional coordinates of each element of the grid, you can easily construct the triangles for drawing the grid.

Drawing the grid is relatively straightforward. There is only one complication—ensuring that the generated triangles are drawn in a back-to-front order. Without considering the drawing order, you would normally process the grid in a simple raster-scan order one row at a time. To draw the triangles in the proper order, however, requires determining whether to process in the normal row order or column order, and whether to scan through the grid from top to bottom, bottom to top, left to right, or right to left. Figure 11–5 shows how to determine the scanning order on the current viewing direction relative to the grid. The *RWFgraph_Grid* member function *findScanningOrder()* returns values, indicating which processing order to use, as shown in Figure 11–5. Listing 11–1 which shows a simplified version of the *draw()* function for the grid illustrates how the grid elements are processed.

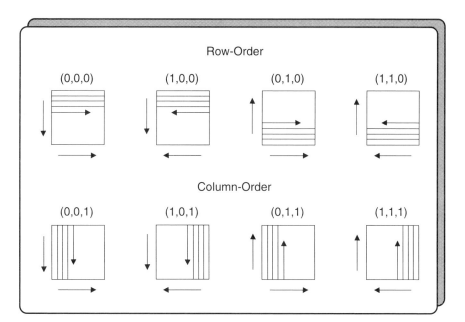

Figure 11–5. To ensure that the grid is rendered in back-to-front order, you select the scanning direction through the grid based on the orientation of the view. There are eight possible combinations of scanning orders.

Listing 11–1. A simplified *draw()* function for *RWFgraph_Grid* that draws the grid using the same color for each polygon. Only the code for the scanning order of Case 6 from Figure 11–5 is shown, as the other cases use nearly the identical code.

```
// Grid-drawing routine using a constant color
// for all polygons and no fBM support

void
RWFgraph_Grid::draw(RWFgraph_ViewingGeometry &vg)
{
  RWFgraph_Polygon triangle(3);
  float x1, y1, x2, y2, z1, z2, z3, z4;

  int numrows = nrows(); // Same functions as the matrix class
  int numcols = ncols(); // for consistency
   triangle.setMatrix(getMatrix());
  // For the moment
   triangle.setColor(getColor());

int left_to_right, top_to_bottom, column_order
// Now simply loop through all the elements
  // of the grid
  // Only one case is shown;
  // all the other cases are basically the same

  int scanning_order = findScanningOrder(vg, left_to_right, top_to_bottom, column_order);
  // This section corresponds to Case ( of Figure 11-5
  // Scan in row order, bottom to top, left to right
  for(int j=0; j < numrows-1; j++) {
    y1 = j*y_cell_size;
    y2 = y1 + y_cell_size;
    for(int i=0; i < numcols-1; i++) {
      x1 = i*x_cell_size;
      x2 = x1 + x_cell_size;
      // Fetch the z-coordinates at the four corners
      /*
```

```
    (x1,y2) z12------z22 (x2,y2)
            |      / |
            |     /  |
            |    /   |
            |   /    |
            |  /     |
            | /      |
    (x1,y1) z11------z21 (x2,y1)
    */


    z11 = ((*this)[i][j]).h;
    z12 = ((*this)[i][j+1]).h;
    z21 = ((*this)[i+1][j]).h;
    z22 = ((*this)[i+1][j+1]).h;
    // Construct the first triangle
    triangle[0].setCoord(x1, y1, z11);
    triangle[1].setCoord(x2, y1, z21);
    triangle[2].setCoord(x2, y2, z22);
    triangle.draw(vg);
    // Construct the second triangle
    triangle[0].setCoord(x1, y1, z11);
    triangle[1].setCoord(x2, y2, z22);
    triangle[2].setCoord(x1, y2, z12);
    triangle.draw(vg);
  } // End of x (column) loop
 } // End of y (row) loop

 } // Finished!


 } // Return
```

Roughing Things Up

You now have a method for drawing a raster-terrain database, given the height at each point on the grid. You can now proceed to incorporate the fBM algorithms to produce finer detail for each of the grid cells. In Listing 11–1, each grid rectangle is simply broken into two triangles and each triangle is drawn. Instead of doing that, you can simply use the *rwf_fbm2DGenerate()* function to subdivide the grid rectangle into another, finer grid. In order to use *rwf_fbm2DGenerate()*, you need a two-dimensional array in which to store the new grid values as well as the settings necessary for the initial standard deviation and the number of recursion levels. For the moment, let's use a constant recursion level, initial standard deviation, and fractal scale for all grid pixels. Given *rwf_fbm2DGenerate()*, it is now fairly straightforward to modify the code for *draw()* in Listing 11–1 so it subdivides each grid cell.

There is, however, one unresolved issue originally discussed in Chapter 9, namely, ensuring that the fBM algorithm always produces the same set of z-values for the same grid cell. Because you can potentially scan the grid in any of eight ways, you must ensure that the same sequence of random variations is used for a given grid cell, independent of the scanning order. Furthermore, recall that the two-dimensional fBM algorithm uses a one-dimensional fBM to generate the heights along the edges of the cell. As shown in Listing 11–1, each grid cell is processed independently; that is, you draw each grid cell without referring to the neighboring grid cells. As you step through the grid cells, you must make sure that adjacent grid cells use the same fBM algorithm along the shared edges; otherwise, you'll have a mismatched edge between grid cells. Figure 11–6 illustrates this potential problem.

Ensuring consistency of the grid cells requires initializing the random-number generator with the same seed for the same set of grid cells. The simplest way to do this is to assign a common seed to each element in the grid. The two-dimensional fBM algorithm uses the sum of the four seed values for the corner elements as the initializing seed for the random-number generator. The one-dimensional fBM algorithm uses the sum of the seeds at the endpoints as the initializing seed. Because the random-number seed is based on the sums of the seed values at the corners, the order in which you process the grid cells does not matter. The same two-dimensional fBM values will be generated for the same seed values at the corners. It does not really matter what seed values you assign the grid elements, so a simple function of the row and column index for the element will suffice. To support specifying the seed values at the corners, we have provided a new version of *rwf_fbm2DGenerate()* in which you pass an additional four-element array of *long* values containing the seeds at each corner. Listing 11–2 shows the modifications needed to incorporate two-dimensional fBM into the grid-cell processing algorithm of Listing 11–1.

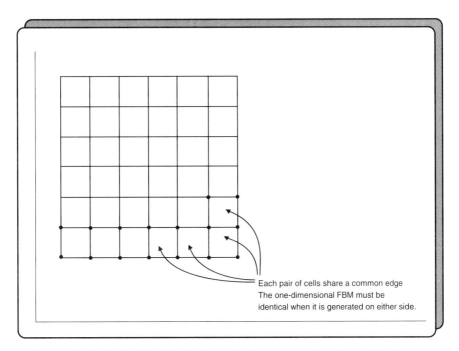

Each pair of cells share a common edge
The one-dimensional FBM must be
identical when it is generated on either side.

Figure 11–6. Each grid cell is independently processed as the grid is drawn. You must ensure that the same set of z-values are generated for each cell, regardless of the order in which the cells are processed. Furthermore, you must ensure that the shared edges generate the same one-dimensional fBM values.

Listing 11–2. Incorporating two-dimensional fBM in the *draw()* function from Listing 11–1.

```
// Again, only considering Case (1,0,0)
// left-to-right, bottom-to-top, row order scan

// Totally arbitrary constant
#define BIG_CONSTANT 1010101

// The zfbm array is a private temporary array
```

```
// allocated when the member function
// setRecursionLevel() is called.
float zcorners[4];
long  seed_corners[4];

// Processing the grid cell from (i,j) to (i+1, j+1)

zcorners[0] = ((*this)[i][j]).h;
zcorners[1] = ((*this)[i][j+1]).h;
zcorners[2] = ((*this)[i+1][j]).h;
zcorners[3] = ((*this)[i+1][j+1]).h;

// Now compute the seeds at the corners
// You can use any method you like as long as
// it is consistent. In this case, we simply
// computer (j+1)*BIG_CONSTANT + i for element (i,j)
seed_corners[0] = (j+1) * BIG_CONSTANT + i;
seed_corners[1] = seed_corners[0] + 1;
seed_corners[2] = seed_corners[0] + BIG_CONSTANT;
seed_corners[3] = seed_corners[2] + 1;

// Now you can subdivide the grid cell
rwf_fbm2DGenerate(zcorners, seed_corners, NULL, stdev,
                  level_scale, nlevels, zfbm);

// Ok, now process the new subgrid
int nsubgrid = 1 << nlevels;
float y_subcell = y_cell_size / (float)nsubgrid;
float x_subcell = x_cell_size / (float)nsubgrid;

int zindex1, zindex2;
for(int k=0; k < nsubgrid; k++) {
  y1 = j*y_cell_size + k*y_subcell;
  y2 = y1 + y_subcell;
  // There are (nsubgrid+1) elements per row of zfbm
  zindex1 = k * (nsubgrid + 1);
  zindex2 = zindex1 + nsubgrid + 1;
  for(int l=0; l < nsubgrid; l++) {
    x1 = i*x_cell_size + l*x_subcell;
```

```
    x2 = x1 + x_subcell;
    // Fetch the z-values
    z11 = zfbm[l][k];
    z12 = zfbm[l][k + 1];
    z21 = zfbm[l +1][k];
    z22 = zfbm[l +1][k + 1];
    // Construct first triangle
    triangle[0].setCoord(x1, y1, z11);
    triangle[1].setCoord(x1, y2, z21);
    triangle[2].setCoord(x2, y2, z22);
    triangle.draw(vg);
    // Construct the second triangle
    triangle[0].setCoord(x1, y1, z11);
    triangle[1].setCoord(x2, y1, z22);
    triangle[2].setCoord(x1, y2, z12);
    triangle.draw(vg);
  }
}
```

Figure 11–7 shows an example of generating a mountain using the grid data type. The initial grid is a 64-by-64 element that uses a two-dimensional Gaussian function to generate the rough hill shape. The hill is then refined in successive steps by using the fBM algorithm to add finer and finer details to the individual grid cells. Note that the final figure looks much more like a rough hill than the initial figure. By using the procedural method to generate the finer steps as needed, you increase the effective resolution of the database from the original 64-by-64 grid size to 1,024 by 1,024, using four recursion levels (these four recursion levels divide each original grid cell into a 16-by-16 subgrid, which increases the displayed resolution). The procedural method provides a more compact way to represent a complex object, such as a tree or mountain, than a simple polygonal or geometric description.

Figure 11–7. Generating a simple mountain starting from a two-dimensional Gaussian Curve.

Adding Color and Other Features

So far, you have not had to use the class information provided in our terrain database. You can use the class identifier to control a number of attributes for the terrain image. For example, you can create a table of the various colors to use for each class, assigning blue to water, green to grass, white to snow, and so on. Furthermore, you can specify other attributes by class such as the initial standard deviation and fractal dimension H to use for each terrain type. The most convenient way to represent these elements is in a table, using the following class to specify these various attributes by class:

```
class RWFfbm_ClassTableElement {
public:
int red, green, blue;  // Color of the class
```

```
float stdev;            // Initial standard deviation
float level_scale;      // (0.5)^H

// Initial constructor
RWFfbm_ClassTableElement(void)
  {red = green = blue = 255; stdev = 1.0;
   level_scale = sqrt(0.5);};

void setColor(int r, int g, int b)
  {red = r; green = g; blue = b;}
void setStandardDeviation(float new_stdev)
  {stdev = new_stdev;};
void setFractalDimension(float H)
  {level_scale = pow(0.5, H);};
};


// Define a table for these entries
typedef RWFlist_SimpleTable<RWFfbm_ClassTableElement>
        RWFlist_ClassTable;
```

You can now specify attributes such as color, fractal dimension, and so forth on a class-by-class basis by creating an *RWFlist_ClassTable*. The *RWFgraph_Grid* member function *setClassTable()* assigns a class table to use when the grid is drawn. Instead of using a global value for the standard deviation, color, and fractal dimension, the class value of the grid cell lets you select the appropriate value for a given terrain type. Now your terrain grid can truly represent a variety of terrain types all within the same database.

The only remaining issue to resolve before completing the terrain-rendering algorithm is handling the boundaries between different classes. This is where the discrete two-dimensional fBM algorithm comes in. Just as the heights are randomized, you can also randomize the boundaries between classes using the discrete fBM function *rwf_fBM2DDiscreteGenerate()*. Just as was done with *rwf_fBM2DGenerate()*, we have provided a version of *rwf_fBM2DDiscreteGenerate()* with which you pass the random-number seeds to use at the corners, thus ensuring consistency when processing the individual grid cells. The only code change required to Listing 11–2 is to randomize both the z-values and the class values. As each triangle is generated for the subcells, the triangle color is set according to the entry in the class table for the class of the lower-left corner of the subcell. So you not only randomize the heights, but you randomize the boundaries between the various classes, adding a great deal more realism to the image as well. Color plate 8 illustrates the effect of randomizing class boundaries using the mountain from Figure 11–7. Four classes were used for the mountain, based on the height of each pixel. The color plate shows water at the base, a forest (green) along the foot of the mountain, bare rock moving up the mountain, and snow on top. The fractal clouds and trees provide the final touch for your terrain image. The demonstration program described at the end of this chapter lets you adjust the various parameters to create mountains of your very own.

Another issue with the boundaries between different terrain types (different classes) is deciding which values to use for the standard deviation and fractal dimension when generating the new height values. Recall that *rwf_fBM2DGenerate()* only uses a single value for each of these parameters. At the boundaries between classes, you'll have grid cells that have different class values at each corner with potentially different fractal dimensions and standard deviations. You must generate a single value from the multiple classes at the corners. The simplest rule is just to pick one of the corners (in our case, we always use the class of the lower-left corner of the grid cell) and use the values for that corner. Other approaches are to use the average values, the minimum or maximum values, or to have priorities between classes that specify which class to use when there is a choice. Whatever method you choose, you must at least ensure that it is consistent, so that the same values are used for the same grid cell.

Choosing the Recursion Level

Just as was done for the fractal objects of the previous chapters, you can choose the recursion level to use when drawing a terrain grid. Basically, you want to avoid doing any more work than you have to, so you'll generally want to use the minimum number of recursions that you can get away with. In the two-dimensional case, you simply let the recursion proceed until a subpixel level is reached. For the terrain grid, you do a very similar feature, except that the maximum recursion level is precomputed. The simplest technique is just to project the corners of the terrain grid onto the screen and look at the size of the projected area on the screen, as shown in Figure 11–8. You can then use as many recursion levels as needed to achieve subpixel resolution. If your grid is 64 by 64 and the projected region on the screen is 512 by 512, for instance, then you need 512 / 64 = 8 further subdivisions of the grid. In this case, eight subdivisions corresponds to three recursion levels. Because this is only an approximation to the number of subdivisions you need, it is a good idea to go one extra recursion level (in this case, four). The *RWFgraph_Grid* member function *setRecursionLevel()* automatically sets the required recursion level based on the current viewing geometry.

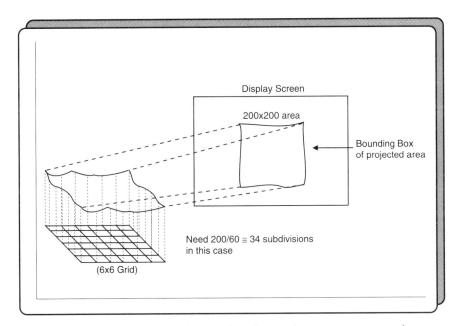

Figure 11–8. By projecting the initial grid onto the screen, you can determine the number of the minimum recursion level required to achieve subpixel resolution in the final image.

While it is beyond the scope of this book, you can also significantly improve the rendering for the grid by determining the recursion level on a grid-cell-by-grid-cell basis. You can use the same technique previously described to project each grid cell onto the screen and to determine how

many levels in which to divide the grid cell. The difficulty is that you must be very careful about handling the boundaries between grid cells to ensure that if two adjacent grid cells use different recursion levels, they will still correctly match up. Once you solve this problem, however, you can substantially improve the rendering time for a terrain image. Only the grid cells close to the eyepoint will be subdivided with a large number of recursion levels. Most of the grid cells will be far enough away from the eyepoint that little or no subdivision is required, which significantly reduces the amount of time it takes to draw them.

More Fractal Terrain

You now have a means for generating images of a landscape containing different types of terrain with realistic boundaries and surface textures captured from actual maps and photographs. There are many ways to build upon the methods presented so far. Instead of just altering the height of the surface with the fractal subdivision, for instance, you could directly modulate the surface color to texture a flat surface. Consider the two-dimensional fBM algorithm as a way to randomize any set of continuous values, whether it is terrain height, color, temperature, or any other physical parameter. With more sophisticated rendering packages, you can use the same fractal methods in this chapter to modulate other attributes such as transparency and surface reflectivity. The fBM algorithms, and procedural modeling techniques generally provide an elegant and efficient means of adding lifelike variations and textures to objects.

As an example of how color texture can vastly enhance the realism of a scene, Color Plates 12, 13, and 14 show some representative scenes from a unique real-time image generator for flight simulation manufactured by IVEX Corp. of Atlanta, Georgia. The terrain database for a flight simulator must cover an extensive area (typically 50 by 50 miles), but it must also be quite detailed, especially in the area around the runway. Using the fractal procedural modeling techniques described in this chapter, the IVEX database covers the entire training area and still provides textured details down to subinch resolution on the runway. The IVEX database is a perfectly flat plane that uses color texture to create the illusion of waves on lakes and oceans, grass around the runways, and small hills in the surrounding area.

The fBM algorithms are an excellent model of many textures, including the concrete and asphalt texture used for the runways and taxiways. Even the skid marks and runway markings use fBM texturing of transparency to make them appear as if they have been painted over the concrete surface. By combining digitized map and satellite data with the fBM procedural models, IVEX can create a realistic database that accurately recreates the appearance of airfields around the world.

Mountain Maker

The program *mountain.exe* lets you explore the effect of adjusting the fractal parameters for the mountain type of Figure 11–7. You can adjust the fractal parameters of each class and adjust the color. In addition, you can choose from several different starting shapes for the mountain to see how the initial terrain data influences the final image. The program *mountree.exe* creates the image shown in Color Plate 8 using the terrain generator, trees, and clouds to make a more complete scene.

Modeling the Whole World

The fractal techniques of this and the previous chapters provide you with a powerful set of modeling tools for synthesizing images of the world around you. Despite the rather prodigious hype, fractals are not always suitable models for every type of object or every type of natural phenomenon. Fractal models are an important tool because they accurately model the self-similarity found in many natural objects. By combining a statistical fractal model with actual measured data from the real world, you can create a more accurate and efficient terrain model for use in rendering scenes in your flight simulator. The terrain-grid data type acts as a global definition of the terrain, defining the overall structure and significant features, which may or may not be fractal in nature. The fBM procedural models essentially define the fine detail and the atomic structure of the data. The terrain-rendering algorithms presented in this chapter let you combine the two distinctly different models together in a consistent and integrated way.

Another way to look at procedural models is as a very compact way to store a database. Instead of storing huge amounts of polygon data for a terrain database, you store a few parameters and the definition of the procedure for recreating the full object-definition from those parameters. So procedural modeling can also be considered a way to significantly reduce, or compress, the amount of data you should store to define a database. In the next chapter, you'll see how this notion of data compression led Dr. Michael Barnsley, CEO of Iterated Systems Inc., and others to develop some general purpose methods of image compression based on storing fractal models, rather than simply storing raw pixel data. These methods of data compression have led to some of the more interesting and commercially viable applications of fractals.

Fractal-Image Compression

In the previous chapters, you learned how to construct complex objects such as trees and clouds using a very small data set (the initiator) and some very simple rules (the generators). The fractal definition of a tree is much more compact than the alternative method of storing the position of every trunk, branch, and leaf of the tree. The same is true for any self-similar object: If you know the generators for the object, then you need only store the initiator and generators, and you can easily reconstruct an image of the object at any desired resolution. You have already seen several methods in the previous chapters for constructing a self-similar object from its generators. In this chapter, you'll learn an approach to solving the reverse problem, namely, finding approximations to the generators for a self-similar object when given a digital image of the object.

The notion of storing the generators for an image (rather than the image as a raster array of individual pixels) has led to new developments in *image compression* (the reduction of the amount of data used to store an image). With the advent of high-definition television (HDTV), high-resolution satellite imagery, and animated multimedia graphics, there is a

309

tremendous amount of digital-image data being processed today. Efficient image compression is essential to being able to store, broadcast, and process high-resolution digital images. *Fractal-image compression*, as it is now known, offers many new possibilities of maintaining and archiving images using far less storage than alternative compression techniques.

Image Processing

But before looking at various image-compression methods, you must first be able to read and manipulate an image in your program. The software that accompanies this book lets you work with PCX-format data files. In fact, several example images are provided on the disk, and there are many commercial programs, such as HiJaak PRO from Inset Systems, that convert images from your favorite format to PCX format. All the PCX files are treated as 8-bit gray-scale images. Working with the image files is relatively straightforward. The basic pixel data type is defined as:

```
typedef unsigned char RWFpixel;
```

Pixel values always range from 0 to 255. A rectangular block of pixels is stored in an *RWFgraph_PixelBlock* object, a class derived from *RWFgraph_Object*. You can therefore treat a block of pixels like any other graphics object if desired. To access an individual element, you use the member function *getPixel()*, which takes as arguments an *x* and *y* position in the pixel block. As with other graphics objects, you use the *draw()* member function to draw the pixel block on the screen. You can specify the size of the pixel block either through its constructor (like declaring a matrix) or explicitly via the *setSize()* member function.

Accessing a PCX file is simple. You must first open the PCX file with a call to *rwf_pcxOpen()*, passing the name of the file to open. This function returns a pointer to a *RWFpcx_File* structure, which serves the similar purpose to a C *File*. Once a file is opened, you can determine the size of the image in the file using the *getSize()* member function. To read in a block of pixels from a file, you can use the *RWFpcx_File* member function *readBlock()*. You pass *readBlock()* the *(x, y)* of the upper-left corner of the block to read. The *readBlock()* function will then fill the block with pixels from the file. If the block extends beyond either file boundary, then the portions of the block beyond the edge of the file are filled with zero. To open an image file and read in the entire contents, for example, you would use code such as the following:

```
RWFpcx_File *pcxfile;
RWFgraph_PixelBlock pixrect;
int xsize, ysize;

// Open the file
pcxfile = rwf_pcxOpen("test.pcx");
if(!pcxfile) {
  // An error occurred, abort the operation
  exit(1);
}

// OK, how big is the file?
pcxfile->getSize(xsize, ysize);
// Make the pixel block the same size as the image
pixrect.setSize(xsize, ysize);
// Read in the entire image
pcxfile->readBlock(pixrect, 0, 0);
// All set to go, pixrect has been filled
// For example, you can now draw it on the screen
pixrect.draw();
```

You can also use the *RWFgraph_PixelBlock* member function *getFromFile()* to perform the exact operation as *readBlock()*. In addition, the *RWFgraph_PixelBlock* member function *getFromScreen()* will read a block of pixels from the graphics screen.

As with any other graphics object, you can use matrix manipulations to translate, scale, and rotate the image. However, drawing a transformed image is relatively slow because the implementation requires performing a matrix multiplication to determine the mapping from output pixel to input pixel under the transformation. For the purposes of this chapter, you only need to use a few specific transformations that you can optimize to significantly improve the overall performance of the algorithms.

In particular, you'll need to be able to rotate a pixel block by 90-degree increments and reflect it (draw right to left rather than left to right). The member function *setScanningOrder()* lets you specify which corner of the pixel block to start with when drawing or manipulating the pixel block, and it specifies whether to process the block in row or column order. *setScanningOrder()* takes three arguments, each with a value of either zero or one. The first argument determines whether to scan left to right (zero) or right to left (one). The second argument determines whether to scan top to bottom (zero) or bottom to top (one). The third argument specifies whether to scan in row order (zero) or column order (one). Figure 12-1 shows how the eight possible settings of the arguments to *setScanningOrder()* affect the display of a pixel block.

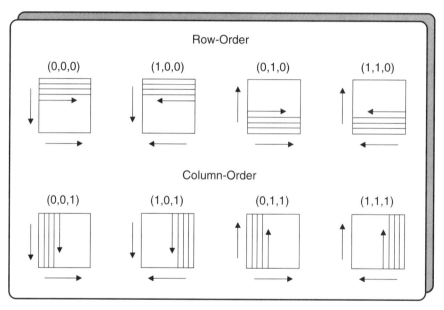

Figure 12-1. There are eight possible ways to access the pixels in a pixel block using the *setScanningOrder()* member function.

The scanning order affects all operations for the pixel block. In particular, the *getPixel()* member function always accesses elements of the block according to the scanning order. Consider a block that is 256 columns by 256 rows large, for instance. If the scanning order is set to (1, 1, 0), then *getPixel(0, 0)* will return the pixel at location (255, 255) in the original image. *getPixel(1, 0)* will return the pixel from location (254, 255) because the scanning order (1, 1, 0) effectively reflects the block around both the *x*- and *y*-axes. If the scanning order were (1, 1, 1) instead of (1, 1, 0), then *getPixel(1, 0)* would return the pixel from location (255, 254) in the original file because scanning-order seven specifies that pixels are accessed in column order, rather than the normal row order. The scanning order plays an important role in letting you compare rectangular regions of one image with another, as you'll learn in a later section about fractal-image compression.

All the member functions for *RWFgraph_PixelBlock* are listed in Table 12-1. Note the addition of the *draw()* member function with explicit *x*- and *y*-offsets to draw a block at a specified location on the screen. This version of *draw()* is much faster than positioning the pixel block with matrix transformations because it avoids the matrix-multiplication operation for each pixel.

Table 12-1. Member functions for the *RWFgraph_PixelBlock* class

Member Function	Description
void setSize(int xsize, int ysize)	Sets the size of the pixel block to the passed values
void getSize(int &xsize, int &ysize)	Returns the current size of the pixel block
void setScanningOrder(int leftright, int bottomtop, int rowcolumn)	Sets the scanning order for the pixel block with each argument having a value of 0 or 1. Determines which corner is mapped to location (0,0) and whether the block is accessed in row or column order
void setScanningOrder(int order)	Sets the scanning order using the low-order 3 bits in the passed argument
void getScanningOrder(int &leftright, int &bottomtop, int &rowcolumn)	Returns the current scanning order

Table 12-1. *continued*

Member Function	Description
RWFpixel getPixel(int x, int y)	Returns the pixel at location *(x, y)* relative to the current scanning order
void setPixel(int x, int y, RWFpixel p)	Sets the pixel at location *(x, y)* to the value passed in p
void getFromScreen(int x, int y)	Reads in a block of pixels from the screen, starting with the upper-left corner at *(x, y)*
void getFromFile(RWFpcx_File *pfile, int x, int y)	Reads in a block of pixels from a PCX file
void getFromBlock(RWFgraph_PixelBlock &inblock, int x, int y)	Copies a block of pixels starting at (x, y) from another pixel block
void copyToBlock(RWFgraph_PixelBlock &outblock, int x, int y)	Copies the pixel block to another pixel block, starting at *(x, y)* in the output pixel block. The output block must be larger than the input block.
void draw(int x, int y)	Same as *draw()*, except this version draws the pixel block with the upper-left corner starting at *(x, y)* on the screen
void remapIntensity(float contrast, float offset)	Rescales the intensity values of every pixel using the equation: *new = contrast∗old + offset*.
float compare(RWFgraph_PixelBlock &pblock, float &c, float &b, int &scan_order)	Compares two pixel blocks of the same size, returning the error between the two and the optimum contrast, brightness, and scan-order settings.

314

Now that you can read and access image data in pixel form, let's see how you might go about representing the image using methods other than simply storing pixels.

General Compression Techniques

With the huge amount of digital data being processed today, it is not surprising that there are tremendous development efforts in the general field of data compression. Data compression is rapidly becoming an integral part of many types of database and spreadsheet applications, as well as being embedded in the operating system itself (such as Microsoft DoubleSpace for MS-DOS). As computer graphics and high-resolution video cards have become standard on most computers, so has the need to store greater amounts of image data. Storing images efficiently is a particularly important problem because the amount of storage required increases rapidly with greater image resolution. For instance, a 512-by-512 image with 256 colors (8-bits) per pixel takes 0.25 MB of storage, whereas a 1,024-by-1,024 image requires 1 MB of storage. If you want to store true-color images (24 bits per pixel), you need 3 MB per 1,024-by-1,024 image. You quickly use up a lot of disk space with just a few images. Things get even worse when you consider digital multimedia applications, applications that present short animated sequences. Even at relatively low resolution (320 by 256 = .08 MB) and a low update rate (say, 10 frames per sec), a 10-second animation sequence requires 8 MB of storage. Clearly, any method of reducing the storage requirements for imagery is important.

Most compression techniques work by creating a list, or *dictionary,* of the common sequences of data in a file. Compressing a text document, for instance, might work by having the dictionary store common words such as *the* or *an* and replacing them with a simple index into the dictionary. For language documents, storing the dictionary and the indexes into the dictionary can result in a significant reduction in the total data amount needed to store the document because typical text uses a relatively small vocabulary, and therefore only requires a small dictionary. A dictionary compression technique works well when the data has many fixed repetitive patterns, such as a language in which the same words occur repeatedly. Such a compression technique does not work as well when repetition does not occur frequently in the file being compressed.

Digital images offer a different type of compression challenge because images do not have the same properties as a text file. One simple image-compression method is called *run-length encoding*. Basically, you simply raster scan the image looking for long runs of the same pixel value. Instead of storing the entire run as individual pixels, you store a pixel count and the common pixel value, thus representing the entire run with just two values. This works well for images with uniform backgrounds or large uniform regions, such as an object drawn against a black background. It does not work well, however, when there are no long runs of common pixel values. In fact, you can end up actually increasing the amount of storage for an image in the run-length-encoded form if there are no runs of pixels with the same data value, because you then must store a count of one and the pixel value for every pixel in the image. Run-length encoding is not a very good general-purpose solution for compressing image data.

The main problem with run-length encoding is that it only treats the image one dimensionally; meaning, it only looks along scan lines. Images are fundamentally two-dimensional objects and should be processed that way. Another type of encoding scheme for images is to extend the dictionary idea from one to two dimensions. You scan the image looking for square or rectangular regions that occur repeatedly throughout the image. In most images, however, you will not actually find regions that match pixel for pixel exactly, but you might find regions very close in intensity. You therefore relax the criteria of requiring an exact match and settle for regions that have very similar values.

You'll see what we mean by "similar" in a moment. You can encode the image by dividing it into rectangular regions (for instance, into regions of 8-by-8 pixels) and either adding the region to the dictionary, or identifying the region as a copy of another region already in the dictionary and simply assigning it the same dictionary index. So, you can store an image as a dictionary of small regions with a map that says which region in the dictionary to use for each output region. To clarify the terminology, the dictionary for an image is referred to as a *region dictionary*. The region dictionary is simply a table of small pixel blocks that define regions of the image. Figure 12-2 shows how both the encoding and decoding process works for the dictionary image-compression scheme.

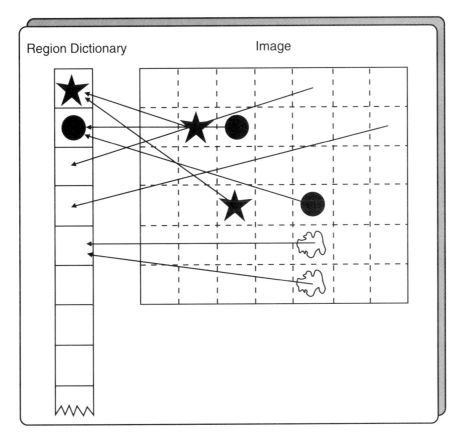

Figure 12-2. Encoding and decoding an image using a region dictionary.

The dictionary method is an improvement over run-length encoding, but this method still has a few problems. Using a fixed-region size and reference grid, as shown in Figure 12-2, is a serious limitation. Most images do not simply divide themselves up nicely along grid boundaries. Furthermore, this approach does not take advantage of the self-similarity of many images, in which one part of an image is similar to another, but at a different scale. In encoding a picture of a mountain, for instance, it would be more desirable to have the program attempt to recognize that the whole image of the mountain is very similar to portions of the mountain ridges. Finally, although there are no explicit directions about how to compare two regions for similarity, you must also allow for the possibility that two regions can be very similar geometrically but have different brightness and contrast settings, such as part of one image being in the shade. To make the region dictionary a more practical compression scheme, you'll want to generalize this process to create a more flexible dictionary structure for the image.

Fractal Compression

The major requirement for constructing any fractal object is to identify the self-similar features of the object. For instance, the tree models of Chapter 7 require you to define a set of branching characteristics that determine how to transform the parent branch to create sibling branches. The main way of acquiring such branching information is to take measurements of real plants and trees. In most cases, it is desirable to automate the measurement process, that is, to get the branching information directly from another source, such as a picture of the desired plant or tree type. Notice that once you have the correct branching information, you can reconstruct the complete image of the tree via only the branching information. Now the trick is to come up with an automated method for identifying the self-similar features in an image.

Compressing a terrain map

You have actually already seen one type of fractal-image compression. In Chapter 11, you used digitized terrain maps and fBM modeling to create much higher resolution images of a terrain area than the original digitized map data. As seen in the color plates, you can create very detailed maps starting with low-resolution data and augmenting it with the fBM models. This type of terrain modeling represents a means of substantially compressing the amount of data in a detailed map. For instance, the flight-simulator databases shown in the color plates typically use a 2,048-by-

2,048 digitized map grid to model a 50 mile-by-50 mile ground area. The fBM interpolation technique essentially provides up to 128-by-128 sub-pixels for each grid cell in the original database. This creates an effective digital map of 262,144-by-262,144 pixels. (This is 128 times the original database resolution in both x and y—quite a large number of pixels!) However, storing this database requires only the original resolution data and some very small tables, which result in an effective compression ratio of approximately 16,000:1. This level of compression would be quite good if you could achieve it on an arbitrary image. However, as with most things in life, there is a catch.

The terrain-mapping method first requires an original digitized map that must be generated from satellite data or digitized aerial photography. The process of classifying the terrain into its component elements such as grass, forest, sand, and water to generate the map of classes is a non-trivial—and not always accurate—process. Classifying arbitrary images into their constituent components is even more difficult, especially if you try to automate the process. The most fundamental limitation is in the fBM models themselves. While these models produce suitable random boundaries for typical terrain features, they are just not adequate for modeling other objects with totally different types of self-similarity, such as a face, flower, or building. As such, the fBM method of the previous chapter is not a suitable general-purpose image-compression method, so you must look to other approaches.

Fractal Encoding

Using a dictionary for cataloging the regions of an image is not a bad approach if you expand the definition of similarity. First, however, let's clarify what is meant by two regions being similar. One of the simplest definitions is just to compare two regions on a pixel-by-pixel basis. If the pixel values are the same for all pixels in the pixel block, then the two regions are identical. If the values are "close" to one another, then the regions are similar. A common method for measuring how different the two regions are is with the following error estimate:

$$E = \left[\sum_{j=0}^{nrows-1}\sum_{i=0}^{ncols-1}(p1_{ij} - p2_{ij})^2\right]/(nrows * ncols)$$ **(Equation 12–1)**

The variables *p1* and *p2* represent the two pixel blocks being compared and *nrows* and *ncols* are the number of rows and columns in the pixel blocks respectively. Essentially, you are computing the average square of the difference in pixel value across the entire pixel block. When *E* is small, the pixel blocks are very similar. When *E* is large, the pixel blocks have very different pixel values.

Intensity matching

As stated earlier, you will probably want to generalize the definition of the image dictionary to account for regional similarities in two ways: regions can be similar at different scales and regions can simply have a different brightness and/or contrast level. Let's look at the latter problem first. Basically, what you want to find is a contrast multiplier *c* and an offset level *b* that minimizes the error estimate *E* in the following revised version of Equation 12-1:

$$E = \left[\sum_{j=0}^{nrows-1}\sum_{i=0}^{ncols-1}\left((c * p1_{ij} + b) - p2_{ij}\right)^2\right]/(nrows * ncols)$$ **(Equation 12–2)**

You can determine the best values for *c* and *b* by computing the partial derivatives of *E* with respect to *c* and *b* and setting these partials to zero. The resulting equations for *c* and *b* are as follows (see Appendix A of *Chaos and Fractals*, Springer-Verlag, 1992, for a more detailed derivation):

$$c = \frac{\left(\sum_{j=0}^{nrows-1}\sum_{i=0}^{ncols-1}p1_{ij} * p2_{ij}\right) - \left(\sum_{j=0}^{nrows-1}\sum_{i=0}^{ncols-1}p1_{ij}\right) * \left(\sum_{j=0}^{nrows-1}\sum_{i=0}^{ncols-1}p2_{ij}\right)}{n^2 * \left(\sum_{j=0}^{nrows-1}\sum_{i=0}^{ncols-1}p1_{ij}^2\right) - \left(\sum_{j=0}^{nrows-1}\sum_{i=0}^{ncols-1}p1_{ij}\right)^2}$$

(Equation 12–3)

$$b = \frac{1}{(nrows * ncols)} * \left(\sum_{j=0}^{nrows-1} \sum_{i=0}^{ncols-1} p2_{ij} - c * \sum_{j=0}^{nrows-1} \sum_{i=0}^{ncols-1} p1_{ij} \right)$$

(Equation 12–4)

After computing the optimum values of c and b, you can use these values in Equation 12-2 to find the minimum value of E for two pixel blocks. You then define your own criterion for the minimum value of E to determine when two regions are similar enough to be classified as the same block in the region dictionary. To use this new information, you must not only store the dictionary index for each region in the image, but you also must have the values of c and b to transform the intensity values to their proper levels in the final image. Equations 12-3 and 12-4 provide a solution to handling regions that are geometrically similar but have different intensities. The *RWFgraph_PixelBlock* member function *remapIntensity()* lets you remap the intensity values in a pixel block by passing a contrast and brightness value. Having found the optimum brightness and contrast settings to get the best match between two pixel blocks, let's tackle the problem of identifying similar regions of different scales and orientations.

A Question of Scale

All you need to do at this point is to be able to compare regions of different sizes by computing E between the two differently sized regions. The simplest way to do this is just to subsample the larger of the two regions to the same resolution as the smaller region. The simplest type of image resampling is called *nearest-neighbor* resampling. For instance, if one region is twice as large in both dimensions as the other, you simply take every other pixel both vertically and horizontally in the larger region. You would use the same approach for regions that are two, three, four, or however many times larger. You can generalize this approach to resample blocks with sizes that are noninteger multiples of one another. The function *rwf_PixelBlockResample()* shown in Listing 12-1 resamples an input pixel block to the same resolution of the passed-output pixel block.

Listing 12-1. The function *rwf_PixelBlockResample()* uses nearest-neighbor resampling to remap the input pixel block to the same resolution as the output pixel block.

```
// Copy the input block to the output block
// with nearest-neighbor resampling
void
rwf_PixelBlockResample(RWFgraph_PixelBlock &inp,
                       RWFgraph_PixelBlock &outp)
{
  int xin, yin;
  int xout, yout;
  float x, y, xfactor, yfactor;
  int ix, iy;
  RWFpixel pixel;

  // Get the input and output sizes
  // Make sure the output scans in the normal order

  inp.getSize(xin, yin);
  outp.getSize(xout, yout);
  outp.setScanningOrder(0, 0, 0);

  // These represent the increment in input coordinates
  xfactor = (float)xin / (float)xout;
  yfactor = (float)yin / (float)yout;

  // x and y are the input coordinates to get
  // the pixel from
  // RWFMISC_NINT() rounds a float to an int
  y = 0.0;
  for(int j=0; j < yout; j++) {
    x = 0.0;
    iy = RWFMISC_NINT(y);
    for(int i=0; i < xout; i++) {
      ix = RWFMISC_NINT(x);
      pixel = inp.getPixel(ix, iy);
      outp.setPixel(i, j, pixel);
      x += xfactor;
    } // End x loop
    y += yfactor;
  } // End y loop
}
```

322

As a side note, you can also implement other types of resampling algorithms that, for instance, average groups of pixels from the input pixel block to generate the output pixel block. The specific type of resampling you would use depends on a number of factors, including maximizing the speed of the algorithm (nearest-neighbor resampling is the fastest method) and the type of imagery being used. For the compression algorithms of this chapter, you may use any type of resampling method simply by changing the definition of *rwf_PixelBlockResample()*.

Now that you can resample one pixel block to the same resolution as another, you are almost ready to complete the region dictionary algorithm. One final addition is to take advantage of the scanning order to let you compare regions in different orientations. By cycling through the different scanning-order values, you can compare a pixel region to the eight possible orientations (90-degree rotations and reflections about the *x*- and *y*-axes) of the output-pixel region. This gives the algorithm a better chance of finding a match between similar regions.

To simplify the comparison operations, the *RWFgraph_PixelBlock* member function *compare()* returns the computed error value between two pixel blocks as well as the optimum values of *c*, *b*, (the contrast and brightness values) and the scanning order that generated the optimum value of the difference factor *E*. Using the *compare()* function, you can now easily scan an image to compare different regions for storage in the image dictionary. As discussed earlier, the simplest approach is just to divide an image into square regions, such as 8-by-8 squares, and compare each region to every other region to eliminate duplicates. The ones that remain are stored in the region dictionary along with a map of where to position each region to reconstruct the image. This map is called the *region map*. Each entry in the region map specifies the dictionary index, contrast, brightness, and scanning order that produced the minimum value of *E* for that region in the output image. For many types of images, the dictionary method can result in significantly less storage than storing the original image, and decoding the dictionary to reproduce the original image is quite simple and quick.

However, the dictionary method still has its limitations. For instance, we did not take advantage of being able to compare different-sized regions. This can be incorporated into the algorithm for constructing the dictionary, by initially dividing the image into larger regions and comparing them to smaller regions. If the regions match, then you store an additional scale factor that defines the ratio of sizes between the larger region and the smaller one. This makes the region map a little more complicated, as you now must contend with the possibility of having multiple-sized output regions. Even with this additional feature, the dictionary method does not really prove very satisfactory for a lot of images, primarily because you still must divide the image into fixed regions with fixed boundaries. There is, however, an alternative method based on the fractal techniques of Chapters 5 and 6. Amazingly, the fractal methods let you dispense with the image dictionary altogether, requiring you only to store the transformations from one image to its self-similar counterpart. To understand how this is possible, let's digress for a moment and re-examine the fractal figures of Chapters 5 and 6.

Image Generators

In Chapter 6, you saw how to define the Sierpinski Gasket using an initial triangle and three transformations. Using the *RWFaf_Object* class from Chapter 6, you can use any object as the initiator, not just an initial triangle. As we mentioned earlier, no matter what object you use for the initiator, the limit of the recursions (that is, if the recursion were carried out indefinitely) is always the Sierpinski Gasket. This property results from the fact that the individual generator transformations always reduce the size of the initiator. As the recursion continues, the initiator is reduced to a vanishingly small size, so the initial shape is of no consequence. A transformation with the property of always reducing the size of the initiator is said to be a *contractive* transformation, or equivalently, a contractive mapping. Figure 12-3 shows several examples of constructing a Sierpinski Gasket using different initiators, all resulting in the familiar final figure.

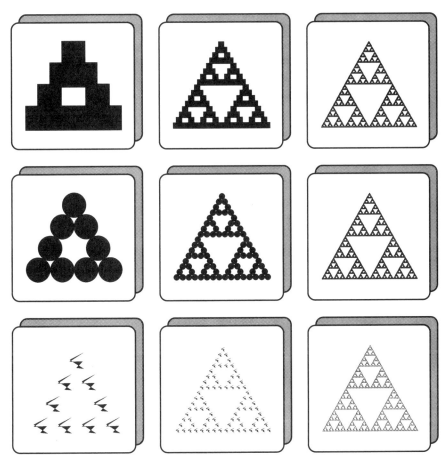

Figure 12-3. No matter what initiator you use for the Sierpinski Gasket, you ultimately end up with the same figure.

All self-similar fractal figures have the same limiting figure, regardless of the initiator. This property is known as the *Contraction Mapping Principle*. The mathematical details of this theorem are beyond the scope of this book, but you can find an excellent discussion in Chapter 5 of *Chaos and Fractals*, Springer-Verlag, 1992, listed in the bibliography. The Contraction Mapping Principle applies to all the fractal shapes you have seen so far, including the Sierpinski Gasket, Sierpinski Carpet, and Menger Sponge. To recreate any of these shapes, you only need the definition of the generator. You can then apply the generator to any initial shape that is convenient. The number of iterations needed to produce the final figure from an arbitrary initiator depends on the resolution of the screen and how contractive the transformation is (that is, does the transformation scale the object by half, one-third, two-thirds, or some other factor?). The point is that you do not need to know what the initiator is to reproduce the object, you only need to know what the generator is.

The recursive algorithm used in the code for the *generate()* member function of *RWFaf_Object* essentially constructed a series of transformations to apply to the initiator. At each recursion level, the current transformation was modified by applying the generator again. However, you can interpret this construction of the fractal object in another equivalent way. As usual, you start with the initiator shape. After the first recursion pass you have essentially constructed a new figure to replace the initiator. You then use this new figure as the initiator for the next pass. Each subsequent pass of the recursion uses the figure of the previous recursion level as the initiator for the next pass. So, you can interpret each recursive pass as if you applied the generators to the entire figure from the previous stage, rather than as if you built a series of transformations of just the initiator with which you started. This view of fractal figures as an iterative process that generates successive approximations to the actual fractal is at the heart of the fractal-image compression scheme described in this chapter. Using the iterative construction scheme will let you dispense with the region dictionary in the image-compression scheme.

One other property that directly results from the Contraction Mapping Principle is that a fractal figure is *invariant* with respect to the generator for the fractal. This means that if you apply the generators to the fractal figure, you get the exact same fractal figure again. So for a given set of generators defining a fractal object, the resulting fractal figure is unique. Conversely, if you find a set of contractive generators that map an object to itself, you have found the unique set of generators for the particular object. If you repeatedly apply these generators to a particular starting figure, you will ultimately end up with the unique fractal figure for those generators.

Your goal in the fractal-image compression scheme is simple: Given an image, you want to find a set of contractive generators that at least approximately map the image to itself; that is, leave the image basically unchanged. If you can find such a set of contractive transformations, then the Contraction Mapping Principle applies. The image is a fractal object that can be created from any starting image by successively applying the generators, just as any other fractal object. Your goal then is to find the contractive transformations that leave an image unchanged.

Image Transformations

Let's return for a moment to the original region method of compressing images. To construct the region dictionary for an image, you divided the image into equal-sized regions and identified which regions were similar enough to be considered the same region. A similar process applies in the fractal-image compression scheme. For our first implementation, you again divide the image up into equal-sized areas, say 8-by-8 pixel regions (the actual size is a completely arbitrary choice). For each image region, you scan the entire image to find a 16-by-16 pixel region that is most similar (E is a minimum between the two regions). So far, this sounds just like the original method. In this case, however, you do not divide the image into a fixed grid of 16-by-16 pixel regions. Instead, you examine every 16-by-16 pixel region of the image, stepping through the image one pixel at a time. Once you have found the most similar 16-by-16 region, you store the location, orientation (scanning order), and the brightness and contrast settings that map the larger region to the smaller region. These values define a transformation from the larger 16-by-16 pixel region to the 8-by-8 pixel region being processed. You identify the nearest 16-by-16 region for each 8-by-8 subpixel region of the image, which provides a transformation for each 8-by-8 region in the image. Figure 12-4 illustrates the process.

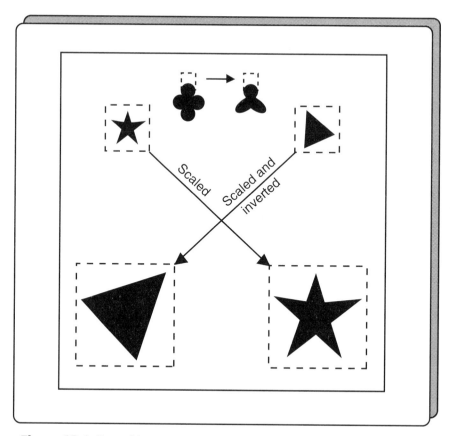

Figure 12-4. Fractal-image compression starts by identifying a mapping from larger regions of the image to smaller regions of the image. You must find a mapping for every subregion (8-by-8 pixel regions) to some larger region.

After processing all the subregions, you now have a transformation between every 8-by-8 subpixel region to a larger 16-by-16 pixel subregion in the image. Where does all this get you? Well, you now have a set of transformations that take larger regions of the image to smaller regions of the image. All these transformations are contractive by construction because they all map a larger area to a smaller one. Furthermore, the transformations were specifically made to map the entire image to itself, or at least make a close approximation by minimizing the errors in each transformation. Collectively, all these transformations define a generator for the image, which maps the entire image to itself.

Because the transformations are all contractive, the Contraction Mapping Principle applies. According to this principle, if you repeatedly apply these transformations to any starting image, you will ultimately find with the unique image the generators were derived from; that is, the image you wish to encode. So, you don't need the region dictionary at all! In fact, you can start with any image whatsoever, and through successive iterations of the generators, you'll end up with the encoded image. Figures 12-5 and 12-6 provide some examples of applying the fractal-encoded-image generators to a starting checkerboard pattern.

Original image   *Encoded image*

Figure 12-5. Decoding a fractally encoded image starting with a checker-board image.

Original image   *Encoded image*

Figure 12-6. Decoding another fractally encoded image.

The function *rwf_ImageEncode8x8()*, shown in Listing 12-2, encodes an image passed in a pixel block using the fractal-compression method. The block is evenly divided into 8-by-8 regions. For each subregion, the entire

image is scanned to find the best-fitting 16-by-16 subregion. The set of transformations are stored in a table of region-mapping structures defined by the class *RWFimage_RegionMap*.

Listing 12-2. The function *rwf_ImageEncode8x8()* returns a table of region maps that essentially define the generators for a simple fractal encoding. The function *rwf_ImageFindBestMatch()* finds the closest match for a given region.

```
class RWFimage_RegionMap {
public:
// Define the input region
int x_region, y_region; // Upper-left corner
int x_size, y_size;     // Dimensions of input region

// Maps to a larger region
int x_output, y_output; // Upper-left corner
int out_factor;         // Output region is always an
                        // integer multiple of input
int scan_order;
int b;   // Brightness offset
float c; // Contrast setting
float error; // Error term between the regions
};

// Define the table of transformations
typedef RWFlist_SimpleTable<RWFimage_RegionMap>
  RWFlist_RegionMapTable;

// This function produces a list of region maps
// to encode an image using fixed 8 x 8 subregions.
void
rwf_ImageEncode8x8(RWFgraph_PixelBlock &image,
                   RWFlist_RegionMapTable &rtable)
{
int xsize, ysize;
int ntable;
RWFimage_RegionMap rmap;
image.getSize(xsize, ysize);
rmap.x_size = rmap.y_size = 8;
rmap.out_factor = 2;
```

```
rtable.reset();  // Reset the table to 0 size;
ntable = 0;

for(int in_y=0; in_y < ysize-1; in_y += 8) {
  for(int in_x=0; in_x < xsize-1; in_x += 8) {
    rmap.x_region = in_x;
    rmap.y_region = in_y;
    rwf_ImageFindBestMatch(image, rmap);
    // Now save the settings in the dictionary for this
    // region
    rtable[n++] = rmap;
  } // End of x region loop
} // End of y region loop

} // End of function

void
rwf_ImageFindBestMatch(RWFgraph_PixelBlock &image,
                       RWFimage_RegionMap &rmap)
{
  static RWFgraph_PixelBlock in_region, out_region;
  int xsize, ysize;
  int in_xsize, in_ysize;
  float min_e;
  float b, c, e;
  int scan_order;

  image.getSize(xsize, ysize);
  in_region.setSize(rmap.x_size, rmap.y_size);
  in_region.getFromBlock(image,
                         rmap.x_region, rmap.y_region);
  xstep = rmap.out_factor * rmap.x_size;
  ystep = rmap.out_factor * rmap.y_size;
  out_region.setSize(xstep, ystep);
  out_region setScanningOrder(0);
  min_e = 1000000;

  // Now scan every region in the image
  for(int y=0; y < ysize - ystep; y++) {
    for(int x=0; x < xsize - xstep; x++) {
      out_region.getFromBlock(image, x, y);
```

```
        e = in_region.compare(out_region, c, b,
                              scan_order);
      if(e < min_e) {
        rmap.error = e;
        rmap.b = RWFMISC_NINT(b);
        rmap.c = c;
        rmap.scan_order = scan_order;
        rmap.x_output = x;
        rmap.y_output = y;
      }
    } // End of scan in x
  } // End of scan in y


} // Finished, best match is in rmap
```

New, Improved Fractal Encoding

You store or transmit region maps as the compressed form of an image. The main disadvantage of the fractal-compression method over the dictionary method is accuracy. There can certainly be cases where no larger region is similar enough to the smaller region to make a reasonable comparison. This problem is exacerbated in the method used by *rwf_ImageEncode8x8()* because fixed-sized subregions are always used. You can significantly improve upon the encoding method by using variable-sized regions. The basic idea is to start with fairly large regions, such as 64-by-64 areas, and look for the most similar larger region (once again, examining regions that are greater than the subregion by a factor of two). If the value of *E* between the two regions is within a certain predetermined threshold value, then mark the subregion as processed and add it to the region map table. If the threshold value is exceeded (there are no suitable similar regions), then divide the sub-region and redo the process on the smaller regions. Using this method, you make the encoding more efficient by allowing for the possibility of encoding larger areas with a single transformation. Figure 12-7 illustrates how the subdivision of regions is accomplished.

The function *rwf_ImageEncodeQuadTree()* implements the automatic subdivision algorithm. If a region must be subdivided, it is divided into four equal pieces (hence the name *quadtree*), as shown in Figure 12-7.

rwf_ImageEncodeQuadTree() initially divides the image into a grid of 64-by-64 pixel squares. Each initial square is then checked against all possible 128-by-128 regions of the image. If no suitable matches are found, then the square is subdivided and the process is repeated on the now 32-by-32 pixel regions. The subdivision then proceeds recursively until either the error criteria is met or the smallest region size (in our case, 8-by-8 pixel regions) is reached. Once either of these conditions is met, the region map for that particular portion of the image is added to the region map table.

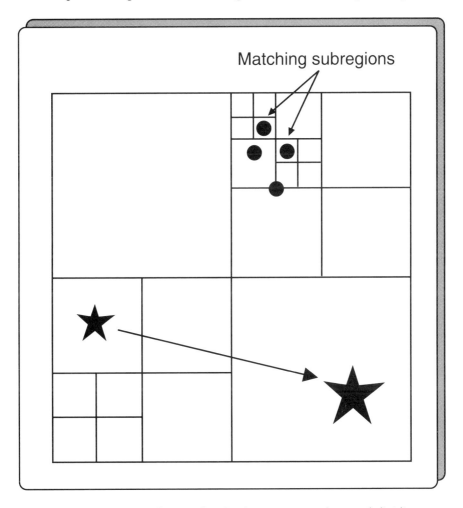

Figure 12-7. Instead of using fixed subregions, you keep subdividing a region until a suitably similar larger region is found, or you reach the smallest subregion allowed.

Decoding an Image

To complete the fractal-compression scheme, you need a decoding function that generates the image from a region map table. The function *rwf_ImageDecode()* generates the image. You tell *rwf_ImageDecode()* how many times to process the generator and what, if any, image should be used to start the iteration. (By default, the checkboard is used.) *rwf_ImageDecode()* begins by drawing the initial image on the screen. The region map is then scanned to map regions of the screen from one location to another. The remapping operation is performed by *rwf_ImageDecodeRegionTable()*, shown in Listing 12-3. A temporary buffer is used to store the image during the decoding operation. When all the transformations in the region map table have been processed, the buffer is written back out to the screen to prepare for the next pass. In effect, *rwf_ImageDecodeRegionTable()* does all the hard work, while *rwf_ImageDecode()* simply sets up the initial image and sets the number of times to process the generators.

Listing 12-3. The function *rwf_ImageDecodeRegionTable()* performs one pass of transforming an image with an image generator defined by a passed region map table.

```
void
rwf_ImageDecodeRegionTable(RWFlist_RegionMapTable &rtable,
                           RWFgraph_PixelBlock &out_image)
{
  static RWFgraph_PixelBlock in_region, out_region;
  RWFgraph_PixelBlock temp_image;
  RWFimage_RegionMap rmap;
  int out_xsize, out_ysize;
  int x_screensize, y_screensize;

  int n = rtable.size();
  out_image.getSize(x_screensize, y_screensize);
  temp_image.setSize(x_screensize, y_screensize);

  for(int i=0; i < n; i++)
    rmap = rtable[i];
```

```
        in_region.setSize(rmap.x_size, rmap.y_size);
        // Now get the region from the screen
        in_region.setScanningOrder(0);
        out_xsize = rmap.x_size * rmap.out_factor;
        out_ysize = rmap.y_size * rmap.out_factor;
        out_region.setSize(out_xsize, out_ysize);
        out_region.getFromBlock(out_image,
                                rmap.x_output,
                                rmap.y_output);
        // Now resample to the output size
        rwf_PixelBlockResample(out_region, in_region);
        // Rescale the intensities
        in_region.remapIntensity((float)rmap.c,
                                 (float)rmap.b);
        // OK, now copy the remapped region into
        // the temporary buffer
        in_region.setScanningOrder(rmap.Scan_order);
        in_region.copyToBlock(temp_image,
                              rmap.x_region, rmap.y_region);
    } // End of loop on region map table

    out_image.getFromBlock(temp_image,0,0);

} // Finished!
```

Fractal Flexibility

All the examples presented so far have stored the entire image in a single pixel block. This is the fastest approach if the image will fit into memory. All the functions are easily modified to work either directly from the screen or from a file by using *RWFgraph_PixelBlock* member functions, which allow *getFromFile()* or *getFromScreen()* to read from whatever source you desire. All the algorithms presented in this chapter function on an image of virtually any desired resolution.

An additional benefit of the fractal-image encoding technique is that it lets you decode the image to any desired resolution. The function *rwf_ImageDecodeRegionTable()* of Listing 12-3 assumes that you wish to decode the image to the same resolution as it was originally encoded. However, by the simple addition of a scale factor, you can decode the image to any desired resolution. The scale factor is simply the ratio between the desired output-image size and the original encoded image size. By simply scaling all the buffer sizes to match the desired output size, you can use the identical coding procedure. An overloaded version of *rwf_ImageDecode()* is provided on the disk that accompanies this book. This overloaded version lets you pass an explicit desired output-image size for decoding an image.

The region-mapping table can be reduced considerably in size for actual storage on disk by using only the minimum number of required bits for each entry. For instance, you only need three bits to store the scanning order, perhaps 10 bits for the *x*- and *y*-offsets that define the upper-left corner of the input and output regions (40 bits total), and 16 bits for storing the sizes of the regions (12 bits for the input region and only 4 bits for the output region scale factor). The intensity mapping can be reduced by using 6 bits for the brightness offset value and 6 bits for the contrast value (12 bits total). So, the entire region map can be stored using a total of 71 bits, or approximately 9 bytes. For the 8-by-8 pixel minimum subregion that requires 64 bytes of pixel storage (note that this subregion was used in this chapter), the worst condition stores a separate region map for each region. This results in a compression ration of better than 7:1. Using the quadtree algorithm, you can expect significantly better results by storing larger regions.

Presenting a Good Image

The program *icompres.exe* provides a demonstration of the encoding and decoding process of several selected images. An initial image is presented on the screen and then encoded. As each region of the image is processed, the region is marked with a white outline rectangle. After completing the encoding process, the image is then decoded, starting with the checkerboard background image. The program pauses between each decoding step to let you see the result of each stage. You'll note that the decoding is not perfect; that is, the resulting image is not identical to the starting image. This is because the encoding process almost never finds exact matches between regions. The resulting generators are therefore only approximations to the actual image generators. You can easily modify the program to read in different files, or turn it into an interactive demonstration that asks the file to decode and to encode parameters such as minimum region size and the threshold error level for region-to-region comparisons.

But be warned about using the encoding and decoding routines of this chapter: They may require a substantial amount of computing time, depending on the size of the image being processed. Recall that the encoding process requires scanning every possible larger subregion with a factor larger than the subregion being matched. If you are encoding 8-by-8 pixel subregions, for instance, you must scan every 16-by-16 pixel subregion to find the best match. For a 256-by-256 image, this requires 241-by-241-by-8 (all possible scanning orders) = 464,468 subregion compare operations for each 8-by-8 image subregion. Even with a reasonably fast computer, this can take a while to complete. This is why you use methods such as the quadtree approach, to reduce the total number of subregions that must be examined and consequently speed up the encoding process.

The decoding process can also require many iterations to converge to the final encoded image, depending on the overall structure of the image and the minimum error level used in the encoding process. In general, the decoding process takes much less time than the original encoding procedure. Through experimentation, you can find the optimum settings for the error-level threshold and region sizes for particular image types. In most cases, however, the encoding process will take some time to run, so be patient!

Using Fractal Compression

The basic techniques for fractal image compression as described in this chapter have been patented (U.S. Patent #5,065,447 and corresponding international patents) by Dr. Michael Barnsley, president of Iterated

Systems, Inc. in Atlanta, Georgia. Iterated Systems has graciously provided permission for the inclusion of the C++ source code presented in this chapter so you can gain a solid understanding of the basic concepts embodied by fractal image compression. To illustrate the improvements that can be obtained in actual practice, Iterated Systems, Inc. has provided some more refined examples of fractal encoding shown in color plates 15, 16, and 17. These color images have been encoded and then decoded using the same basic techniques as described in this chapter, using a more sophisticated search technique to find matching portions within an image, resulting in significantly better compression ratios and more accurate image reproduction.

Because all of the basic fractal compression techniques described in this chapter are patented, you must follow the rules for patented material, namely: No rights other than for examination of the principles of the technology as described previously are granted to you. Any use beyond that expressly permitted herein may constitute patent infringement and is prohibited. Additional rights may be obtained by the express written consent and grant of a license by Iterated Systems, Inc. If you wish to set up an image compression system based on fractal encoding of images, you should apply for a license to:

Licensing Dept.
Iterated Systems, Inc.
5550-A Peachtree Parkway
Suite 650
Norcross, Ga. 30092

Iterated Systems, Inc. can also provide you with the latest commercial implementations of fractal image compression technology.

From Compression to Chaos

You have seen how the fundamental self-similar structure of fractals leads to a method for finding self-similarity in virtually all images. The fractal-image compression scheme described in this chapter can be used on a wide range of images, which provides significant reductions in the amount of storage required for the image. With fractal-image compression, you describe an image as a series of contractive transformations from one portion of the image to another. This is essentially the same definition used for all the fractals you have seen in which we have described them as scaled copies of themselves. Using the Contraction Mapping Principle, you can reconstruct the image from any other image by simply iterating through the generators, just as you reconstruct the Sierpinski Gasket or any other fractal by successive iteration on any starting object. By taking advantage of the self-similarity found in many image types, you can describe the image in a new, more compact way than other types of compression methods can.

The fractal-compression algorithms shown in this chapter are only the beginning and certainly far from perfect. There are a number of ways you can improve these algorithms, including by using rectangular rather than square regions or by using nonrectangular regions such as triangles. You cannot expect that the similar features in most images will just show up along the vertical and horizontal axes.

The routines presented in this chapter can be generalized when you consider them as arbitrary region-to-region transformations. The shape of the regions is unimportant as long as every portion of the image has a contractive mapping to a larger portion of the image. You can also improve on the number of decoding passes required to reproduce the final image by starting with, for example, a reduced resolution version of the original image. Finally, you can handle the problem of regions that simply do not map well to any other larger portion of the image (E is always too large). By reintroducing the region dictionary, you can simply store those regions that do not map well. With the combination of the region dictionary and fractal compression, you can significantly improve accuracy and decoding speed at the cost of lower compression ratios. You can also handle color images by either treating them as separate red, green, or blue layers or by modifying the *compare()* function to measure distance in color space, rather than just differences in intensities. Many companies, such as Iterated Systems Inc. of Atlanta, Ga., are actively working to develop more practical and efficient algorithms for both the encoding and decoding processes. Fractal-image compression is still an area of very active research and study, and no standard method has yet emerged. Several references listed in the bibliography can provide more in-depth material on the topic.

The study of fractals has merged with another new discipline, the study of chaotic systems, or more simply, the study of chaos. *Chaotic systems* are simply those systems with output that is very sensitive to their input and those systems with specific behaviors that—over time—seem quite unpredictable even though the system is completely deterministic. In the next chapter, you'll see how the Contraction Mapping Principle applies to more general dynamic systems. Using the visualization methods of the previous chapters and armed with our knowledge about affine fractals, you will be able to examine and visualize more complex systems, and even make some successful "predictions" about the unpredictable world of nonlinear systems.

Chaos

I f you follow scientific literature at all, you've probably been inundated with the term *chaos* describing the behavior of a complex system. In short, the term *chaos* is used to describe any system that can be distinguished by the following two related behavioral qualities:

- the system output appears unpredictable (that is, it is difficult—if not impossible—to quantitatively predict how the system will evolve over time); and

- the output is very sensitive to the input values, namely, a very small change in the input values can produce radically different output values.

Chaotic systems abound, from predicting the weather, the stock market, or global economies to describing the behavior of nuclear reactions in a star or to describing complex molecular interactions. The study of chaotic systems is an attempt to find order in apparent disorder. Even if you cannot predict the exact behavior of a system, you might be able to put boundaries on how the output will behave or describe the long-term behavior. As you saw in Chapter 8, fantastically complicated outputs can result from very simple systems. If you were simply given some of the fractal images in this book, such as the Mandelbrot Set, you would be hard-pressed to describe the method for producing that image. However, now knowing that relatively simply equations can produce exotic results like the Mandelbrot Set, it is reasonable to think that a chaotic system might also be the result of relatively simple equations. Historically, you tend to think of complex behavior as resulting from complex rules. As the fractal images and objects of this book demonstrate, this is not entirely true in many cases. In this chapter, you'll be introduced to some of the techniques used to study chaotic systems, and you'll learn how the tools developed in the previous chapters provide ways of analyzing the complex behavior of such systems.

Nonlinear Dynamics

Actually, there is nothing particularly new about the study of chaotic systems except the term *chaos*. A chaotic system is a system described by nonlinear dynamics. Before the advent of modern computers, scientists avoided nonlinear systems simply because the analysis of such systems by hand is so tedious and awkward. All the so-called nice rules that apply to linear systems, such as uniqueness of solutions and independence of scale, break down for a nonlinear system. So, the tendency is to approximate a nonlinear system with a linear one. A typical approach is to break the problem down into operating regimes (restricting the input to the system to a particular range) and to describe the system in each regime with a different set of linear equations. For instance, you approximate the motion of a pendulum by assuming that the length of the pendulum is long compared to the length of the arc the pendulum travels through. This assumption results in a simple linear differential equation describing the periodic motion of the pendulum. If you violate this assumption, however, you must go back to the original nonlinear equation describing the motion of the pendulum and make a different approximation. Modeling a nonlinear system with a linear approximation in this manner works well in many instances, but it breaks down at the threshold between regimes. For instance, when the system breaks out of a particular mode (say, if you were to violently push the pendulum), this in turn violates the assumptions for which the linear approximations were developed.

The modern computer has vastly improved our ability to analyze non-linear systems. It is now possible to generate solutions for complex non-linear systems using numerical methods directly, running millions of iterations in a reasonable amount of time. However, while you can generate reams of numerical solutions, you often don't necessarily need all these solutions. In many cases, you simply *want* to predict the qualitative behavior of the system. In other cases, such as designing an airplane, you must be able to predict the qualitative behavior of a system.

You have already seen one method of analysis using plots of the Julia and Mandelbrot Sets for a nonlinear system, such as the systems in Chapter 8. Nonlinear dynamics involve feedback systems with output that is a non-linear function of the input. There are two basic ways of describing a non-linear system. The first and most common system description (in the mathematical and physical sciences) is a set of nonlinear differential equations:

$$x'(t) = dx/dt = f1(x,y,z,...)$$ *(Equation 13–1)*

$$y'(t) = dy/dt = f2(x,y,z,...)$$

$$z'(t) = dz/dt = f3(x,y,z,...)$$

(The ellipsis indicates the number of variables you may have.)

The second type of system is a *discrete feedback* system, in which the next state of the system is a function of the previous states of the system. You can describe such a system with equations in the form shown in Equation 13-2.

$$x_{k+1} = f(x_k, x_{k-1}, x_{k-2},...,x_0)$$ *(Equation 13–2)*

In Equation 13-2, x_k may be a single variable, a complex variable, or a vector variable containing as many different variables as are in the system being described. You have already seen several examples of nonlinear systems from Chapter 8, in which complex variables were used to represent a nonlinear system of two variables, x and y. The Julia and Mandelbrot diagrams are generated using a single equation in the form shown in Equation 13-2, in which the next complex value depends on the previous value. You'll primarily be interested in these type of feedback systems because they are the easiest to work with on the computer. However, because most systems you'll encounter are given in the form of Equation 13-1, you must come up with a way to recast such a set of equations into the form of Equation 13-2.

Equation 13-1 describes a system that is a continuous function of the parameter t, which usually denotes time. The simplest approximation is just to approximate the continuous system using short time steps. You start at some initial time t_0, and then approximate the output of the system for a short time step dt. For simplicity, let's consider a nonlinear system of a single variable, as described by the equation $x'(t) = dx/dt = f(x)$. A first approximation to the value at $x(t+dt)$ is simply:

$$\frac{dx}{dt} = \frac{x(t+dt)-x(t)}{dt} = f(x(t)) \qquad \textbf{\textit{(Equation 13--3)}}$$

Equation 13-3 is called *Euler's Method* and is one way of estimating the value of $x(t)$ using discrete time steps dt. Of course, the accuracy of this approximation depends on the behavior of $f(t)$. If $f(t)$ is relatively smooth, then Equation 13-3 is a reasonable approximation. If, however, $f(t)$ is not well-behaved, then Equation 13-3 will not be as good an approximation as you might like. You can improve on Equation 13-3 using a higher order approximation such as the *trapezoidal* or *Heun's Method*:

$$x(t+dt)=x(t)+ \frac{dt}{2}\left(f(x(t))+f(x(t)+dt*f(x(t)))\right) \textbf{\textit{(Equation 13--4)}}$$

For the purpose of this chapter, we'll just use Euler's Method for approximating a continuous system. But remember that there are many other numerical methods of approximating a set of differential equations. In fact, the book *Numerical Recipes in C* (Cambridge University Press, 1988) has many code examples that generate more precise discrete approximations of continuous systems. As you'll see, you can easily incorporate other numerical integration algorithms into the graphical routines presented in this chapter.

Using the Euler Method (or any other method), you can model a system as a feedback system. Starting with an initial value for all the variables at time $t=0$, you can compute values at successive times by iterating Equation 13-3 until the desired time is reached. As you saw in Chapter 8, it is not difficult to find amazingly complex structures even in relatively simple nonlinear equations, such as the equation $f(z) = z^2 + c$ that's used for the standard Mandelbrot Set. The Julia and Mandelbrot Sets provide one way of examining the structure of an iterated system. They essentially provide maps of stable starting values for the system of equations being studied. The following are some other ways you can visualize the structure of these equations:

◆ For a given starting input state: What is the long-term behavior of the system? Does the system output gravitate toward a single stable value, oscillate among several values, shoot off to infinity, or have any other predictable characteristics? Answering these questions will give you a description of the system's *stability*.

◆ How sensitive is the system to different starting states? If the initial input value is slightly altered, does the system reach the same long-term state or does it exhibit different behavior? Answering these questions will give you a description of the system's *sensitivity*.

These are generally difficult questions to answer precisely about a given system. However, this at least provides you with a method for learning how a system behaves.

Going Into Orbit

In Chapter 8, we were only interested in the question of whether a given initial value caused the system to "blow-up" (shoot off to infinity) or not. To answer the questions already posed about the stability and sensitivity of a system, you must look in more detail at how the system behaves for a given input. The most direct way to do this is to plot the orbit of various starting values. The *orbit* is just a plot of each system-output value at each iteration. Start with an initial position (increment $k=0$ or time $t=0$), iterate the system to generate x_1, plot x_1, and continue. Figure 13-1 shows sample orbits for the iterated equation: $z_{k+1} = z_k^2 + c$, with $c = 0$ and $c = 0.5 + 0.5i$. In each case, there are 100 starting points that are plotted for 100 iterations each. The interesting feature to observe in each case is where the points tend to cluster, which indicates where the output of the system is likely to tend toward. The set of output values to which the system tends is called *attractors* of the system. Once the system output is a value that lies on an attractor, all succeeding output values for any further iterations lie in the attractor forever. A given system may have a single point as an attractor, or it may have many different curves or sets of points as attractors. The attractors of a system are one way of defining the long-term behavior of the system.

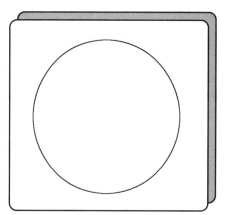 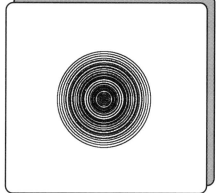

Figure 13-1. Plotting the orbits for random starting points both inside and on the unit circle for the system $z_{k+1} = z_k^2$.

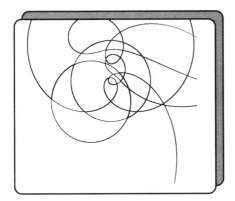 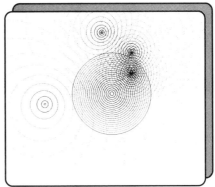

Figure 13-2. Plotting the orbits for random starting points both inside and on the unit circle for the system $z_{k+1} = z_k^2 + c$, with $c = 0.5 + 0.5i$.

For the $c=0$ case, the starting points are taken from random positions both on and inside the unit circle. You can easily analyze the results for the $c=0$ case. If the starting position is inside the unit circle, then the iteration will quickly move the point to the origin, resulting in the strong clustering of points plotted around the origin. For points on the unit circle, the iteration will leave those points on the unit circle, resulting in a clustering along the unit circle. The point at the origin is called an *attractive fixed point* because any time the system is in a state near the origin, the system will quickly move toward the stable value of zero at the origin. The region inside the unit circle is called the basin of attraction for the attractor at the origin. Any time the system reaches a state in the basin of attraction, the system will ultimately end up on the corresponding attractor.

The system $z_{k+1} = z_k^2$ also has the point at infinity as an attractor, because any starting point outside the unit circle will cause the system output to eventually become infinite. So, the region outside of the unit circle represents the basin of attraction for the point at infinity. The unit circle represents the boundary between the two attractors of the system. If the system starts out on the unit circle, it will remain there, continually moving around the unit circle (except in the special case that the starting value has a complex angle equal to 360 degrees $/ 2^n$ for some integer n, in which case the system will end up at the value one and remain there). However, if the system starting value has a length minutely different from one, then the system will tend toward infinity. Similarly, if the length is less than one, then the system will rapidly move toward the origin. The behavior of this system is analogous to a ball on top of a hill. The ball can be positioned to stay at the top of the hill, but the slightest motion will roll the ball roll down the hill to a more stable position.

Note that the value $z = 1$ is also a fixed point of this system, but it is not an attractive fixed point. For all practical purposes, nonattractive fixed points of a system can be ignored because it is virtually impossible for the system to ever reach such a state with nonattractive fixed points without starting off in it.

Figure 13-1 also illustrates how a sensitive dynamic system can be tricky to work with. A system with more than one attractor will always exhibit sensitive behavior at the boundary between the basins of attraction. Recall that the *complex* data type represents complex numbers in the form $x + yi$, using either *float* or *double* data types to store x and y. To illustrate the behavior of points on the unit circle, you might start by generating a set of random complex numbers normalized to have a length of one. If you then start iterating the system equation ($z_{k+1} = z_k^2$), you'll quickly find the points departing the unit circle and moving toward the origin or toward infinity. This occurs because the finite precision of the internal representation of floating-point values, and the subsequent loss of significant digits each time the complex value is squared. The behavior of this system is very sensitive to whether the starting values have a length greater or less than one. Although this is not truly a chaotic system, it does exhibit one of the main characteristics of such systems; that is, that the long-term behavior of the system is extremely sensitive to certain starting points. Instead of following the straightforward approach to plotting the orbits for points on the unit circle, we represented points on the unit circle simply by their angle with respect to the x-axis, and simply doubled the angle for each iteration. This approach guarantees that the orbits will remain on the unit circle. There are few real systems in which you can easily find such tricks to correct the resulting plots.

Figure 13-2 illustrates how easily things can get a little messier. If you compare this figure with those of the corresponding Julia Set from

Chapter 8, you'll see that Figure 13-2 starts to resemble the Julia Set. You might expect this because the points within the Julia Set always map to other points in the Julia Set under the transformation. In fact, the Julia Set can be used as a mask to filter out uninteresting starting values because points outside the Julia set always tend toward infinity. Figure 13-2 does not, however, provide a clear indication of the overall behavior of the system, other than it indicates the clustering toward the Julia Set as a whole. The entire Julia Set may—or may not—be an attractor for the system, and there may be one, several, or infinitely many different attractors for the system.

Strange Attraction

Attractors come in three flavors. The first type you have already seen, the attractive fixed point. The second is the *periodic attractor* in which the system settles down to points along a closed curve of finite length. Once the system reaches the periodic attractor, it always remains on the curve and simply moves to different points along the curve as the iteration progresses. The most common type of periodic attractor is the orbit of a planet around a star. Once the planet settles into an orbit, it will remain there, following an elliptical path around the central star.

An attractor that is neither a fixed point or periodic is called a *strange attractor*. Strange attractors are completely deterministic paths of infinite length. In other words, once the system reaches a state on the attractor, it remains on the attractor but never repeats the same state no matter how many iterations are computed. In most cases of interest, strange attractors are fractal curves. The Sierpinski Gasket, for instance, is the attractor for the series of transformations defining the gasket. The basin of attraction for the gasket is the entire plane. Any point in the plane will eventually move to a point on the gasket and remain on the gasket. The total gasket is unchanged by the transformations, but points on the gasket move to new positions on the gasket during each iteration. So, the orbit of a point under the Sierpinski Gasket transformations does not follow a simple path on the plane, but moves to different positions on the gasket indefinitely (the only exceptions being the points at the corners of the gasket).

The first notable case of a chaotic system was observed by Edward Lorenz in 1962 while he was developing a simplified mathematical model of airflow patterns in the atmosphere for predicting weather. He noticed a problem in the results of his model when he compared results generated by a computer program with results obtained using a calculator. After verifying the correctness of both calculations, he determined that the only difference between the two was in the initial data he entered. With the calculator, he only entered the initial values with three-decimal accuracy. The computer used data with six decimal accuracy. The radically different outputs from two sets of very similar input data graphically demonstrates the care that must be taken in working with nonlinear systems, even systems based on relatively simple equations.

The original Lorenz model uses the equations shown in Equation 13-5. With the Euler Method, you can easily convert the equation to a discrete iterative model using an appropriately small time step, *dt*.

$$x' = \sigma*(y\text{-}x) \qquad \qquad \textbf{\textit{(Equation 13–5)}}$$

$$y' = Rx - y - xz$$

$$z' = -Bz + xy$$

Lorenz used the parameters $\sigma = 10$, $R = 28$, and $B = 8/3$. Figure 13-3 shows a sample plot of the Lorenz attractor projected onto the $x\text{-}z$ plane. This plot is generated simply by iterating through the equation with a time step of $dt = .001$ and plotting the points (x, z) for each iteration. The actual attractor lies in three-dimensional space and, unlike Figure 13-3, the attractor never intersects itself in three dimensions and therefore defines a unique path in space. The structure of a strange attractor, like those of all fractal figures, can be quite complicated and difficult to characterize. By generating plots such as those of Figure 13-3, you can at least see that the system roams about the two central nodes, never straying very far from these regions. So although it is difficult to predict the exact behavior of the system (such as how many times the path circles one node before traversing over to wrap around the other node), you can at least bound the overall behavior and predict that it will be in either one of two main states, either circling one node or the other. This type of analysis is useful for describing the system. You can determine, for instance, what would happen if you varied the parameters of the system (in this case, σ, R, and B) in addition to the starting point.

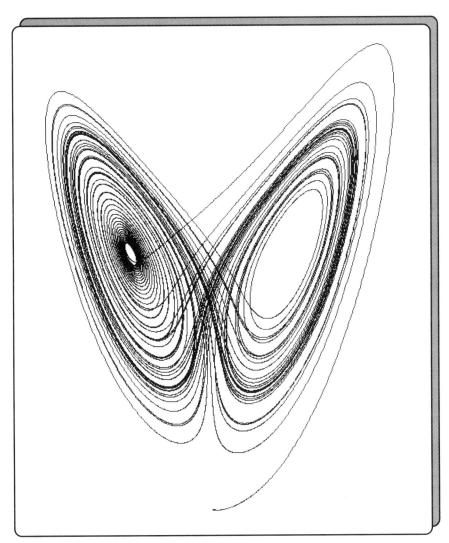

Figure 13-3. Sample plot of the Lorenz attractor in the *x-z* plane.

Generating plots such as Figure 13-3 is relatively easy using the derived class *RWFgraph_2DPlotObject*. This class is derived from the *RWFgraph_Object* class and is very similar to the *RWFgraph_ComplexObject* class of Chapter 8. In fact, it includes the same member functions as RWFgraph_ComplexObject plus a few additional functions for plotting more general types of functions, as shown in Table 13-1.

Table 13-1. Member functions for the *RWFgraph_2DPlotObject* class.

Member Function	Description
int getMinX(void)	Returns the minimum *x*-screen coordinate for the current setting of the screen window
int getMaxX(void)	Returns the maximum *x*-screen coordinate for the current setting of the screen window
int getMinY(void)	Returns the minimum *y*-screen coordinate for the current setting of the screen window
int getMaxY(void)	Returns the maximum *y*-screen coordinate for the current setting of the screen window
void setScreenWindow(int xmin, int ymin, int xmax, int ymax)	Sets the screen window for the complex object. By default, the screen window is set to the entire screen.
void getScreenWindow(int &xmin, int &ymin, int &xmax, int &ymax)	Gets the screen window for the object
void setWindow(float xmin, float ymin, float xmax, float ymax)	Sets the range of values in the *x*- and *y*-dimensions for the object
void getWindow(float &xmin, float &ymin, float &xmax, float &ymax)	Gets the current range of the *x*-*y* window for the object

Table 13-1. *continued*

Member Function	Description
void zoomWindow(float x, float y, double scale)	The point *(x, y)* becomes the center of the window. The current window scale is multiplied by scale.
void setPlotFunction(int (*pfunc) (RWFvec_Vector &curposition, RWFvec_Vector &xy, void *user_data))	Sets the function to plot. The plot performs a single iteration of the system equation. The user data structure passes whatever data the function might need to perform the computation.
void setInitialPoint(RWFvec_Vector &initial_position, void *user_data, int connect)	Sets the initial point to plot and the data structure for the plotting function. The connect flag indicates whether to connect successive *(x, y)* points with a line *(connect = 1)* or to draw them as individual points *(connect = 0)*.
void setNumIterations(long max_iterations)	Sets the number of iterations for plotting points
void setFirstIteration(long first_iteration)	The plotting function is called *first_iteration* times before starting to plot points. This lets the system settle down onto an attractor before starting the plot.

Unlike *RWFgraph_ComplexObject*, *RWFgraph_2DPlotObject* lets you plot functions of as many dimensions as you like. You must, however, provide a means for projecting the variables onto the two-dimensional screen of your display. You specify the function to plot with the *setPlotFunction()* member function. Your plotting function takes three arguments: a vector specifying the current position in the iteration, a two-dimensional vector containing the output *(x, y)* coordinates of points to plot on the screen, and a pointer to a user data structure that specifies other information your function might need, such as the time step. For example, the function to plot the Lorenz Attractor is shown in Listing 13-1.

Listing 13-1. The plot function for plotting the Lorenz Attractor in the *x*-*z* plane.

```
// Define the data for the Lorenz Attractor
class RWFchaos_LorenzData {
public:
  float sigma, b, r;
  float dt;

  // Constructor for default values
  RWFchaos_LorenzData(void)
    {sigma = 10.0; b = 8.0 / 3.0; r = 28.0; dt = 0.001;};
};


int
rwf_chaosPlotLorenzAttractor(RWFvec_Vector &xyz,
                    RWFvec_Vector &xy,
                    void *user_data)
{
  RWFchaos_LorenzData *ldata =
    (RWFchaos_LorenzData *) user_data;

  if(!ldata)
    return 0; // No valid data

  float x = xyz[0];
  float y = xyz[1];
  float z = xyz[2];
  float new_x, new_y, new_z;
  float dt = ldata->dt;

  // Now evaluate the next points using Euler's method
  new_x = x + dt*(ldata->sigma * (y - x));
  new_y = y + dt*(ldata->r*x - y - x*z);
  new_z = z + dt*((-ldata->b)*z + x*y));
```

```
        // Generate x-z plot
        xy[0] = x;
        xy[1] = z;

        // Update the coordinates for the next pass
        xyz[0] = new_x;
        xyz[1] = new_y;
        xyz[2] = new_z;

        // Everything is ok, return
        return 1;
    }
```

For the Lorenz Attractor, the user data structure *RWFchaos_LorenzData* defines the parameters for Lorenz equations and the time step for each increment. The passed three-dimensional vector is updated for each iteration. The plotting function returns either one (meaning the point is valid for plotting) or zero (indicating the point is not valid). For more sophisticated plotting, you could pass a three-dimensional viewing geometry definition in your user data structure and project the *(x, y, z)* coordinates onto the screen. You can create quite informative plots by adjusting the parameters in the passed user data structure. For instance, you can create a plot using one set of parameters, change the color with *setColor()*, and overlay another plot with the new parameters. With this method, you can, for example, track how the shape of the attractors and the positions of the nodes vary as a function of the system parameters.

The member function *setInitialPosition()* specifies the starting vector for the plot, the user data to use, and whether to draw the points as separately plotted points or to connect each new point with the previous point. The member function *setNumIterations()* determines the number of iterations to use. In all other respects, a *RWFgraph_2DPlotObject* object behaves like an *RWFgraph_ComplexObject* object.

A Population Explosion

Another example of chaotic behavior from relatively simple equations comes from the biological sciences. A common model for how a

population of competing individuals changes over time is given in Equation 13-6. The population p is a quantity between 0 (extinct) and 1 (all predators removed, leading to extinction on the next iteration when the food supply is exhausted), and the parameter r essentially specifies the strength of the competing forces as the population deviates from its optimum value of 0.5.

$$p^{k+1} = r*p^k*(1 - p^k) \qquad\qquad\qquad \textit{(Equation 13–6)}$$

r must range between 0 and 4 because whenever r is greater than 4 or anytime the population reaches the value of 0.5, it exceeds 1 on the next iteration, and consequently dies. This innocuous equation behaves well for values of r between 0 and 3. The population quickly settles down to a single stable value. For values of r greater than three, however, things change quickly.

To illustrate this phenomenon, you use a different kind of plotting method known as a Feigenbaum (named after the physicist Mitchell Feigenbaum) or a bifurcation diagram. A *Feigenbaum Diagram* is a plot of the attractors of a one-dimensional system (in this case, using p as the y-coordinate) versus the system parameters (in this case, the parameter r along the x-axis). Starting with an initial value of r, you evaluate the system for a number of iterations to reach stability, plotting all the points (r, p) during the iteration. You then increment r by a small amount and perform the iteration again, always starting with an initial value of $p = 0.5$. Figure 13-4 shows what happens as r is increased. For r less than 3, the system quickly settles down to a single stable state. At around $r = 3$, however, two attractive points appear, and the plot begins to diverge in two directions, creating two distinct branches (hence the name bifurcation diagram). For these values of r, the system oscillates between the two stable values for each iteration. As r increases, each branch subdivides again, and the subdividing continues until you have a indistinguishable mass of separate branches. For any particular value of r, the system simply moves from one branch to another for each iteration. Like the Lorenz Attractor, the behavior of the system becomes more and more unpredictable as r approaches 4.

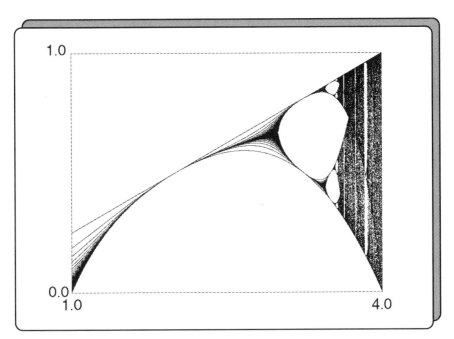

Figure 13-4. Feigenbaum diagram for the population equation. As the system parameter *r* approaches 4, the number of attractive fixed points increases exponentially.

You can generate a Feigenbaum Diagram using the plotting function shown in Listing 13-2. The member function *setFirstIteration()* specifies how many iterations you should perform before starting to plot values. This lets the system settle down to states on the attractor before starting to plot points, which helps ensure that you are only plotting points along the attractor.

Listing 13-2. Plotting function for drawing the Feigenbaum Diagram of the population equation.

```
// Define the data for the population equation
class RWFchaos_PopulationData {
public:
  float r, // Current r,

  // Constructor for default values
  RWFchaos_PopulationData(void)
    {r = 1.0};
```

```
};

int
rwf_chaosPlotPopulationFeigenbaum(RWFvec_Vector &pvec,
                                  RWFvec_Vector &xy,
                                  void *user_data)
{
  RWFchaos_PopulationData *pdata =
    (RWFchaos_PopulationData *) user_data;

  if(!pdata)
    return 0; // No valid data

  // Only one value is needed in the passed data
  // vector, representing the current population
  pvec[0] = pdata->r * pvec[0] * (1.0 - pvec[0]);
  // Ok, now plot (r, p)
  xy[0] = pdata->r;
  xy[1] = pvec[0];

  // All done, return
  return 1;
}
```

Feigenbaum Diagrams are another method of seeing how the behavior of a system is influenced by varying the system parameters. The Feigenbaum Diagram has a very complicated structure and is, in fact, a fractal figure. Figure 13-5 shows an expanded plot of the Feigenbaum Diagram, roughly starting from the point where the first splitting occurs. When properly scaled vertically and horizontally, Figures 13-4 and 13-5 show a very similar shape, indicating the fractal nature of the Feigenbaum Diagram. There is a great deal of subtle structuring in the Feigenbaum Diagram, making it similar in complexity and mathematical significance to the Mandelbrot Set. For instance, it turns out that the ratio of the branch lengths (measuring the branch length as the distance between the point where a branch starts and the point at which it splits into two more other branches) is a constant called, naturally enough, the Feigenbaum Constant. Furthermore, this constant is the same for many different types of iterators, not just the population equation used in this example. The intricate mathematics describing the structure of this object are beyond the scope of this book, but you can find more information and mathematical details in the references listed in the bibliography.

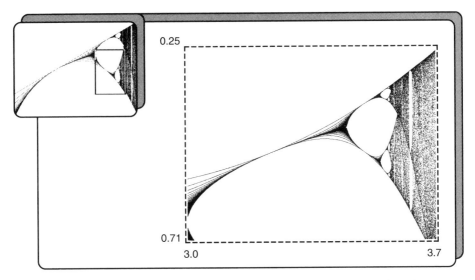

Figure 13-5. Expanded region of the Feigenbaum Diagram that depicts the top branch from the point where the first branching occurs. Note the striking similarity between this branch and the original figure. Each branch is similar to the entire figure when properly scaled.

The population equation was relatively simple to model because it only has one variable (the population p) and one system parameter r. Using the method shown in Listing 13-2, you can plot Feigenbaum Diagrams for many different types of functions to determine how the attractors of the system behave as a function of the system parameters. For the population equation, you can easily see that using parameters greater than three can result in quite unexpected and dazzlingly complex behavior.

Random vs. deterministic behavior

One final issue of concern in studying chaotic signals is trying to distinguish truly chaotic behavior from simple random noise. With a chaotic signal, there is still a clear structural relationship between successive points. Each iteration causes the system to follow a path along an attractor. With random noise, each successive point bears only a statistical relationship or, possibly, no relationship to the previous values. One simple way to graphically depict such dependencies is to create a plot of the current system output against the previous system output. Any dependence in the variables will show up as the plotted points tracing a curve, just like plotting any function as point *(x, f(x))* traces a graph on the display. Figure 13-6 shows an example of two functions; the first function is plotted as simple linear graphs on top, and then the second as points (x_k, x_{k-1}) on the bottom of the figure. The first function is the output of a random-number generator, whereas the second is the output of the population equation for *r = 3.95*. Although the line graphs appear similar, the two-dimensional plots show very different behavior, indicating the structure inherent in the second curve.

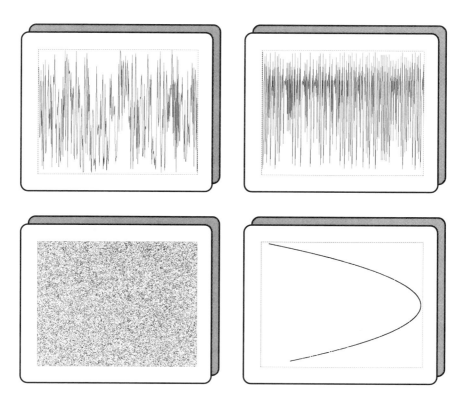

Figure 13-6. At the top of this figure, a graph shows the output of a random-number generator compared with a graph of the output of the population equation. The bottom portion of this figure shows the creation of a two-dimensional graph by plotting points as (x_k, x_{k-1}), clearly indicating the functions that generated the second data set.

Chaos as Science

The study of chaotic systems has grown rapidly during the past 10 years because of the discovery that you can, indeed, find order in apparently random behavior. In a way, chaos has changed the view of many scientists concerning observed complex behavior. As discussed at the beginning of this chapter, the general assumption was that a complex system was necessarily governed by complex rules that would be very difficult—if not impossible—to find. But by demonstrating exceedingly complex behavior in objects such as the Mandelbrot Set, the Feigenbaum Diagram, and the Lorenz Attractor that use very simple rules, many researchers now understand that a system does not need to be complex to exhibit complex behavior. If nothing else, chaos has motivated new ways of thinking about complex problems in virtually every scientific field. As you have seen in this chapter, the study of chaos also provides new tools for studying systems and, hopefully, quantifying and finding the underlying relatively simple rules that generate complex behavior.

This chapter has only scratched the surface of the many intricacies involved in studying complex, chaotic systems. The science of chaos is new and is therefore still rapidly evolving. The tools in this chapter give you some basic methods for exploring nonlinear systems, but we have by no means exhausted the available techniques. Starting with the graphical routines of this chapter, you can now build your own tools for studying complex behavior, and generate some fascinating figures in the process. By combining multiple plots, such as overlaying plots of the system attractors and using color to highlight different aspects of the plots, you can create images that are both beautiful to look at and useful analytical tools.

In the next and final chapter, we'll summarize how all the topics in this book fit together to provide a cohesive framework for visualizing the world around us. We'll then look at the potential for fractal techniques to solve many different types of problems that occur in apparently unrelated disciplines. Fractals and their many cousins are certainly not the only problem-solving tools you have available, but they can be particularly useful and effective for many types of previously intractable problems. You'll undoubtedly be working with fractals in one form or another in the future, so understanding what they can—and cannot—do will only help you in tackling your particular problems, creating your own fantastic art, forecasting the weather, and studying the chaos of everyday events.

The Future of Fractals

You have already seen a number of applications for fractals and their chaotic cousins throughout the previous chapters. The software provided on the disk that accompanies this book has been structured to make all the various fractal-modeling techniques more accessible and adaptable. Our emphasis has been on how the various fractal-generating techniques are related to one another. By exploiting this common basis using C++ hierarchical classes, you now have the ability to create a huge variety of fractal shapes and images with a surprisingly small amount of code. In this chapter, we'll look at some of the other potential applications for fractals, which are only now being experimented with. Additionally, you'll see some ways in which the techniques already presented can be improved upon to increase their overall usefulness.

The scientific and commercial applications for fractals outside computer graphics are only beginning to be explored. Fractals are quite appealing objects because they let you create a model of great complexity using very simple rules. Equally important, you hope that the reverse is also true. Given a complex phenomenon you want to analyze

and, perhaps, describe as the result of simple rules being repeatedly applied at different scales. Fractals are not the ultimate panacea for understanding all phenomena, but they can help in many different types of analysis. And they are a lot of fun to use as well!

Fractal Analysis

Today, you see fractals and chaos occurring throughout the popular scientific literature primarily because they offer the appealing hope that complex behavior can be broken down into much simpler pieces for further analysis. A similar scientific phenomenon occurred 200 years ago with the discovery of the Fourier series. The idea behind the Fourier series analysis is very elegant. You take a signal and model it as a sum of other signals, known as *basis functions* (the behavior of these functions is well understood). In the case of the Fourier-series analysis, you take some periodic signal and model it as a linear combination of sinusoids. If the system under study has a linear response and you determine the response of the system to a single sinusoid, then you can directly determine the response of the system to *any* linear combination of sinusoids and, consequently, to the particular input you are studying. Today, Fourier analysis is a standard part of any scientific or engineering education because it lets you to break complex signals into individual components that have known system response.

Many researchers are hoping that fractal analysis can offer the same kind of analytical ability as Fourier analysis. Instead of describing an object in terms of a "standard" set of basis functions, such as sinusoids, you describe the object as linear combinations of itself. All the affine fractals work this way, defining an object as infinite scaled copies of some set of initiators. Similarly, the image-compression techniques worked by defining an image as a collection of scaled, rotated, and translated copies of itself. So if you know the behavior of a system with respect to its smaller pieces, you can subsequently predict the response of the system to a more complicated combination of those pieces.

Chaotic biology

Many researchers in the biological sciences are trying to apply chaotic analysis to the study of complex behavior in areas ranging from determining how nerve impulses are created, transmitted, and received to modeling biorhythms in people and animals. There are many rhythmic elements—from your own heartbeat to annual bird migrations—that dominate the lives of most animals on our planet. Why do these rhythms arise at all, and what external factors influence the frequency and strength of these rhythms? Because a biological system, like yourself, is composed of so many complex interacting pieces, it is virtually impossible to create a complete model of such a system from first principles, that is, from the molecular level on up. Instead, you must take the approach of trying to isolate the primary influences for certain behavior and build up a simple model for that specific behavior.

Medical technology has reached the point where you can acquire extensive measurements of the electrical and mechanical activity going on in a person. For example, the electrocardiogram (EKG) lets you gather detailed real-time data about a heartbeat. A typical EKG tracing is a complex signal that gives you information about how the heart is working. As each set of individual valves open and close, they produce changes in the EKG signal. By comparing measurements of normal and abnormal hearts, you can build up a model that lets you use the EKG to predict abnormal behavior. Because your heartbeat is periodic, Fourier analysis is often used to analyze an EKG. However, chaos theory offers an interesting alternative analysis technique that can provide more information. Fourier analysis lets you identify periodic components in a signal. In the case of the heartbeat, Fourier analysis lets you see possible spurious components caused by heart abnormalities. However, modeling with a chaotic system may help decide why a particular abnormality causes the heart—and the corresponding EKG—to behave the way it does.

The graphical techniques for plotting the orbits and attractors of nonlinear systems is already being applied in many areas to gain further insight into the interaction between various parts of a system. By combining multiple measurements into a single plot, you can see the interaction as part of a whole, much as the plot of the Lorenz Attractor from Chapter 13 demonstrated the unexpected multiple nodes. Furthermore, given the data, you can easily use the methods of Chapter 13 to compare your set of equations modeling the system to the actual data. The many examples from chaos theory demonstrate the possibility that the interaction between complex systems does not necessarily require a complex model.

The other principal reason for using chaotic systems for biological models is to tackle the difficult problem of separating random influences from chaotic ones. All measurements are subject to noise. Whenever you get a measurement with a lot of unexpected features, the usual assumption is that the spurious features are the result of noise, or random processes. As you have seen, this may not always be the case, as the output of a chaotic system can often look very noisy. There is a great deal of research being conducted now on how to distinguish between a chaotic signal and a random one. So far, the current results are inconclusive as many methods have failed to properly separate test signals generated by random processes and chaotic equations. However, research is actively continuing because such techniques would be extremely useful in many different areas.

Fractal communications

One intriguing possible application for chaotic systems is in the area of communications. Extensive research in chaotic communications is currently being done at the U.S. Naval Research Laboratory. To understand this application, consider how AM radio works. The amplitude of a base, carrier-wave signal at a fixed frequence is modulated with another message signal, such as someone talking. The combined signal is broadcast, and the receiver extracts the original message by averaging the energy in frequencies near the known fixed carrier. FM radio works in a similar manner, except the carrier frequency is modulated instead of the carrier amplitude. These methods work well for public broadcasts, but they are not very useful for sending and receiving secure private broadcasts.

Instead of using a fixed-carrier signal, a chaotic-carrier signal makes an excellent choice for secure communications because of its unpredictability. If you can synchronize a sending and receiving chaotic system, then you can encode a message at one end by mixing the chaotic carrier and the message signal, and then decode the message on the other end by subtracting the chaotic component. To decode the message, the receiving system must have some means of generating the exact same chaotic signal the sending system used to encode the message. The sending system therefore sends two signals:

♦ the combined message and chaotic carrier; and

♦ a separate "drive" signal that instructs the receiver how to decode the message.

The drive signal is used on the broadcast end to generate the chaotic carrier. The receiving end has an identical chaotic system, and uses the drive signal to generate the same chaotic carrier. By requiring both ends to have the same system for decoding the drive signal, you ensure a reasonable level of security in the transmission. Generating the chaotic signal without knowing what particular chaotic system was used is usually extremely difficult.

Better Fractals

Although the fractal models presented in the previous chapters are quite flexible, there are still a number of ways in which they can be improved. The terrain model of Chapter 11, for instance, creates a model using an initial grid of points. One of the features of the modeling technique was that each grid cell can be independently processed; that is, the fractal fBM interpolation of height values only requires the heights at the four corners of the grid cell. There is, however, a slight problem. The edges of each grid cell are generated using one-dimensional fBM along the edges, and two-dimensional fBM for the interior points. This means that the interpolated values along the edges are functions only of the two corners defining the edge, and not of the surrounding points between grid cells. Figure 14-1 illustrates the problem, often called the *creasing* because it causes creases to appear in the final terrain image.

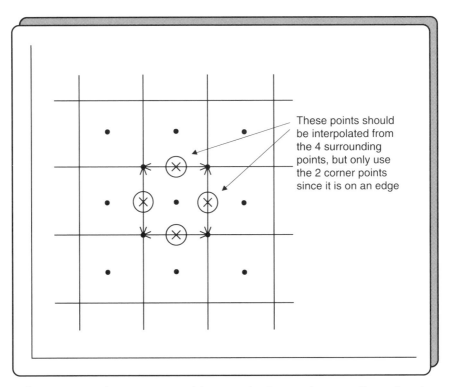

These points should be interpolated from the 4 surrounding points, but only use the 2 corner points since it is on an edge

Figure 14-1. The creasing problem results from using one-dimensional fBM for the edges between grid cells.

The creasing problem is very similar to the problem of curve fitting in computer graphics. If you want two curves to smoothly join together, you not only want them to match up to the same point, but you also want them to have matching derivatives at the point where they join, as shown in Figure 14-2. If the derivatives do not match, then the curves have a sharp cusp at the joining point. The creasing problem is essentially a three-dimensional version of this problem. Two adjacent grid cells are guaranteed to have a matching edge, but the two fBM interpolated surfaces may not be sloping in the same direction along the edge. Another way to look at the problem is that by using one-dimensional fBM along the edge, you have introduced a directional dependence that is not present when using two-dimensional fBM because both the x- and y-directions are weighted equally.

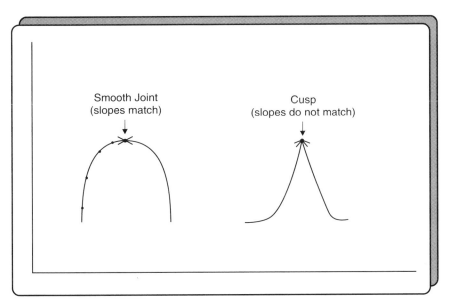

Smooth Joint
(slopes match)

Cusp
(slopes do not match)

Figure 14-2. The creasing problem for terrain modeling is similar to the curve-fitting problem of computer graphics. Two curves fit smoothly together when they meet at a common point and the slopes of the curves match.

The creasing problem is fundamental to the approach of using independent grid cells. Ideally, you would like to use the same two-dimensional fBM algorithm along the edges that are used for the interior points. You can, in fact, do this, but it requires using interpolated points from the neighboring grid cells, as shown in Figure 14-3. Once you require the use of neighboring grid cells, you lose the cell-to-cell computing independence you sought to gain. So as the old cliché goes, there are no free lunches. But there are alternative approaches that you can use to help reduce the creasing, including using nonrectangular tiles, as described by B. B. Mandelbrot in Appendix A of *The Science of Fractal Images* (Springer-Verlag, 1988).

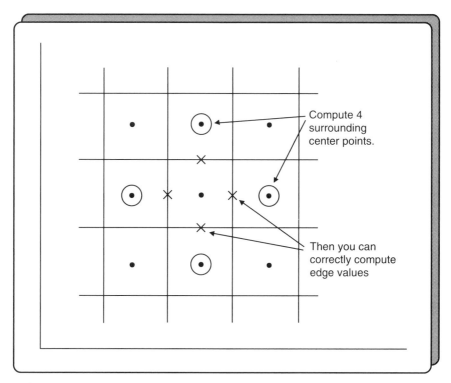

Figure 14-3. You can reduce the creasing problem by using computed midpoints from adjacent grid cells. However, you lose the ability to independently process grid cells. So in effect, you would have to save the data from all neighboring grid cells to process the current grid cell, which is a very impractical approach.

Volume Compression

Chapter 12 focused on the problem of static-image compression. However, the same techniques can be applied to objects other than those that are two dimensional. You could, for instance, compress a three-dimensional object just like an image by defining a collection of generators that map the object to itself. The encoding and decoding techniques are identical no matter how many dimensions are involved.

One practical application for three-dimensional fractal encoding is for storing volumetric data. A *volumetric* model is the three-dimensional equivalent of an image. Just as a raster image is divided into a two-dimensional grid of individual pixels, a volumetric model divides an object into a three-dimensional grid of *voxels*. Volumetric models are extensively used in medical imaging so three-dimensional Computer Aided Tomography (CAT) scans can produce accurate models of internal organs.

Storing a typical voxel-based model can require a lot of disk space. Whereas a 256-by-256 pixel image only requires 64 Kbytes of storage, a 256-by-256-by-256 voxel model requires 16 Mbytes of storage! In some applications, fractal encoding can provide tremendous compression ratios for three-dimensional voxel data. Implementing such an compression scheme is a straightforward enhancement of the routines described in Chapter 12. As volumetric data becomes more common, you can expect to see many people using fractal encoding and other compression techniques to cope with the vast amount of data.

Another way to exploit fractal encoding is to extend the technique to compress an entire sequence of images, such as a video clip, rather than just a single image. You can think of a series of frames as a stack of images, defining an object in three dimensions with time (frame number) as the third dimension. If the images are related, such as panning across a mountain scene, you would expect a lot of correlation between images. So you can consider defining a mapping from one region in an entire set of frames to other smaller regions in another set of frames. You must, of course, broaden your definition of a region to include the same area from multiple frames. However, the encoding process would basically be identical. You divide the frames as before, except now you must also consider the same area of each image across multiple (not necessarily all) frames in the motion sequence. The routines presented in Chapter 12 can be expanded to handle an encoding scheme of this sort by defining *compare()* member functions that compare multiple regions across multiple frames.

Similarly, the decoding process would generate a whole set of frames at one time by mapping one region in one set of frames to another region in another set of frames. Clearly, this technique is only practical if a given set of frames has a lot of similar regions from frame to frame, just as compressing an image requires reasonably self-similar regions within the same image. However, several companies are exploring the possibilities of this technique to reduce the storage requirements of animation clips in multimedia applications.

Fractal Fun

The terrain modeling presented in Chapter 11 encapsulates most of the useful features of fractals. Fractals describe small detailed structures as copies, albeit scaled, translated, and rotated of larger pieces of other objects. However, most real objects are not true fractals in the sense that they have the exact same structure at all scales, rather most objects share the same structure over some range of scale. The terrain-modeling approach of Chapter 11 gives you the ability to combine the global structure of actual measured terrain with a microstructure definable by fractals. Unlike the fractally encoded images of Chapter 12, the terrain model does not create this detail with scaled copies of the original map, but rather by using another approach based on terrain classes. The terrain model does, however, let you smoothly combine the two approaches (real and synthesized) together. Furthermore, you can easily extend the same techniques to model three-dimensional objects using volumetric-based models.

All the fractal routines are designed to let you change the model as you reach different scales. The action function lets your program decide what specific action to take as a function of the recursion level and therefore as a function of the current scale being processed. You can therefore alter the parameters of your model, such as changing the relative branch sizes or spacing as you reach smaller sizes or you change the model altogether by drawing leaves instead of branches, for instance. As you have seen, a fractal object does not have to be composed of one set of initiators or a constant set of generators. Those are just the easiest forms with which to start. Once you understand how to use the action functions, you'll see that there are an unlimited number of combinations you can try.

Adding new features is quite easy with the object-oriented library developed throughout the book. By constructing a logical class hierarchy, you can easily create new fractal objects and try new techniques without having to worry about the details of how objects are drawn or how the fractal algorithms are specifically implemented. The software is designed to let you freely experiment and play with the algorithms. C++ and object-oriented programming techniques, in general, make it easy to create such a set of software tools.

We hope you enjoy experimenting with the methods from all the chapters. For those of you interested in the more mathematical details concerning fractals, we highly recommend the following texts:

Peitgen, Heinz-Otto, and Dietmar Saupe. *The Science of Fractal Images*. Springer-Verlag, 1988.

Peitgen, Heinz-Otto, Hartmut Jürgens, and Dietmar Saupe. *Chaos and Fractals*. Springer-Verlag, 1992.

While we have shown you many examples of fractal objects throughout this book, there are infinitely many more than could possibly be shown in one or a hundred books. The routines in Chapters 5 through 9 can generate just about any fractal image or object you have ever seen and many you haven't seen. The following texts provide more examples of specific equations and generators to produce intriguing images:

Finlay, Mark. *Getting Graphic*. M&T Books, 1993.

Pickover, Clifford A. *Computers, Pattern, Chaos, and Beauty*. St. Martin's Press, 1990.

Stevens, Roger T. *Fractal Programming and Ray Tracing with C++*. M&T Books, 1991.

Stevens, Roger T. *Fractal Programming in C*. M&T Books, 1989.

Stevens, Roger T., and Christopher D. Watkins. *Advanced Graphics Programming in C and C++*. M&T Books, 1991.

Watkins, Christopher, Stephen Coy, and Mark Finlay. *Photorealism and Ray Tracing in C.* M&T Books, 1992.

Watkins, Christopher, and Larry Sharp. *Programming in 3 Dimensions: 3-D Graphics, Ray Tracing, and Animation.* M&T Books, 1992.

Functions

The following lists the various functions, chapter by chapter.

Functions Found In Chapter 3

All the member functions in this chapter are listed in the tables of the chapter. This section therefore lists just the classes found in the chapter.

Vector and Matrix Classes

```
RWFvec_VectorTemplate
```

Template class for homogeneous vectors. You can create a vector of any data type with a suitable *typedef* declaration.

`RWFvec_Vector`

Vector class of *float* variables. This class is used to store coordinate positions and direction vectors. It is defined as: *typedef RWFvec_VectorTemplate<float> RWFvec_Vector*.

`RWFmat_MatrixTemplate`

Template class for matrices. You can create a matrix of any data type with a suitable *typedef* declaration.

`RWFmat_Matrix`

Matrix class of *float* variables. This class is used to define affine transformations in homogeneous coordinates. This class is defined as: *typedef RWFmat_MatrixTemplate<float> RWFmat_Matrix*.

Graphic Object Classes

`RWFgraph_Object`

Base class for graphics objects. This class defines all the transformation operations and the virtual *draw()* function to display the object on the screen.

`RWFgraph_Point`

Graphics class representing a single point.

`RWFgraph_Line`

Graphics class representing a line segment drawn between two points.

`RWFgraph_Polyline`

Graphics class representing a connected series of points.

`RWFgraph_Polygon`

Graphics class representing a closed figure. The first point is repeated as the last point of the polygon.

`RWFgraph_Circle`

Graphics class representing a circle.

`RWFgraph_ViewingGeometry`

Defines the viewing geometry for rendering perspective views of three-dimensional objects.

Table Classes

`RWFlist_SimpleTable`

Template class for a table of objects. The subscript operator *[]* lets you access any element of the table. The table dynamically allocates space as you access larger indices.

`RWFgraph_ObjectList`

A class derived from both *RWFgraph_Object* and *RWFlist_SimpleTable*. This class lets you define a graphics object as a collection of other graphics objects.

`RWFlist_MatrixTable`

A table for storing multiple matrices. This class is used extensively with the fractal objects of Chapters 5 and 6.

Functions Found In Chapter 4

Demonstration program

```
pachinko.exe
```

This program demonstrates how a normal distribution arises by simulating a Japanese pachinko game.

Random-number generators

```
void rwf_randSrand(unsigned long seed)
```

Reinitializes the random-number generator with a new starting seed. *rwf_srand()* will always generate the same sequence for the same seed value.

```
float rwf_randRand(void)
```

Returns uniformly distributed random numbers in the range 0.0 to 1.0.

```
float rwf_randGaussian(void)
```

Returns standard, normal distributed random numbers. These numbers have a mean of 0.0 and a variance of 1.0.

```
float rwf_randExponential(void)
```

Returns exponentially distributed random numbers in the range from 0 to +infinity. This function is provided primarily as an example of how to generate those distributions with an integratable density function using *rwf_rand()*.

Random-number classes

```
class RWFrand_RandomVariable
```

A base class for providing random variables with a particular mean, standard deviation, and distribution. You must derive a random variable class with a particular distribution from this base class.

```
class RWFrand_UniformRV
```

A uniformly distributed random variable with the specified mean. For simplicity, the standard deviation specifies the limits of the random variable. That is, a *RWFrand_UniformRV* will return values from *mean − stdev to mean + stdev.*

```
class RWFrand_GaussianRV
```

A normally distributed random variable with the specified mean and standard deviation.

Functions Found In Chapter 5

Demonstration program

```
vonkoch.exe
```

Demonstration program that lets you explore how various combinations of generators and initiators can create different types of fractal curves.

Functions

```
RWFmat_Matrix rwf_graphLineToLineMatrix(RWFgraph_Line &line1,
              RWFgraph_Line &line2)
```

Computes the affine transformation to transform *line1* to *line2*.

```
void rwf_graphNormalize(RWFgraph_LineTable &lt)
void rwf_graphNormalize(RWFgraph_Polygon &poly)
void rwf_graphNormalize(RWFgraph_Polyline &poly)
void rwf_graphNormalize(RWFmat_MatrixTable &mt)
```

These functions normalize the passed generator, such that the endpoints of the generator match the unit line segment from (-0.5, 0.0) to (0.5, 0.0). This routine is especially useful when the generator is acquired from another source, such as digitizing from the screen.

```
float rwf_matGetGlobalScalingFactor(RWFmat_Matrix &matrix)
```

Finds the effective scaling factor of the passed matrix. If the matrix is part of a generator, the scale factor must be less than 1.0.

Class definitions and associated member functions

```
class RWFvk_BasicObject
```

A graphics-object class derived from the base class *RWFgraph_Object*. Because it is a derived graphics class, an *RWFvk_Object* has all the same member functions as any graphics object. Initiators and generators are defined by a series of line segments, normally as a polyline or polygon.

Public member functions for *RWFvk_BasicObject*

```
void setInitiator()
```

Various overloaded versions are provided to allow defining an initiator in several ways, either with a line-segment table, a single line segment, a polyline, or a polygon:

```
void setInitiator(RWFgraph_Line &line_seg)
void setInitiator(RWFgraph_LineTable &lt)
void setInitiator(RWFgraph_Polygon &poly)
void setInitiator(RWFgraph_Polyline &poly)
```

```
void setGenerator()
```

Several overloaded versions are provided to allow defining a generator in several ways, either with a line-segment table, a polyline, or a polygon:

```
void setGenerator(RWFgraph_LineTable &lt)
void setGenerator(RWFgraph_Polygon &poly)
void setGenerator(RWFgraph_Polyline &poly)


void setMaximumLevel(int max_level)
```

Sets the maximum recursion level for the object. The maximum recursion level is set to 4 pixels by default.

```
void setMinimumSize(float size)
```

Sets the minimum size in pixels at which to terminate the recursion. Once the size of the object being drawn is less than size, then the recursion is terminated. The default setting is 1 pixel.

```
class RWFvk_Object
```

A graphics-object class derived from the base class *RWFgraph_Object*. This class is the more general version of *RWFvk_BasicObject*. With this class, you may define an initiator as any collection of base objects, not just line segments. Because it is a derived graphics class, an *RWFvk_Object* has all the same member functions as any graphics object. *RWFvk_Object* has all of the same member functions as *RWFvk_BasicObject*.

Public member functions for *RWFvk_Object*

```
void setInitiator()
```

Several overloaded versions are provided to allow defining an initiator in several ways, either with a table of pointers to base objects, a single object, a polyline, or a polygon.

```
void setInitiator(RWFgraph_Line &line_seg)
void setInitiator(RWFgraph_Object *object)
void setInitiator(RWFgraph_LineTable &lt)
void setInitiator(RWFgraph_Polygon &poly)
void setInitiator(RWFgraph_Polyline &poly)
void setInitiator(RWFlist_ObjectPtrTable &otable);
```

If the objects in an object table are not unit-sized, then you may specify the size of each object either as a single value for all objects or as a matching table of sizes for each individual object. In most cases, you should avoid the use of nonunit-sized objects.

```
void setInitiator(RWFlist_ObjectPtrTable &otable, float size);
void setInitiator(RWFlist_ObjectPtrTable &otable,
                  RWFlist_SizeTable &size_table);
```

All the other member functions are identical to those in *RWFvk_Basic-Object*.

Functions Found In Chapter 6

Demonstration program

gaskets.exe

Demonstration program that lets you explore how various combinations of generators and initiators can create endless variations of the Sierpinski Gasket.

Functions

rwf_afSetLevel(int level)

Sets the last recursion level processed when an object is drawn. This function is generally used by the fractal-drawing algorithms using the reverse-drawing method. Regions are erased until this recursion level is reached. With the reverse-drawing method, only regions belonging to recursion levels above this level are left on the screen. The recursion level should be reset by a call of *RWFaf_setLevel(-1)*.

int rwf_afGetLevel(void)

Retrieves the last level set by RWFaf_setLevel().

void rwf_afDraw(RWFgraph_Object *object, int level)

The default-drawing routine for an RWFaf_Object type object. It simply calls the *draw()* method for the passed object.

void rwf_afFill(RWFgraph_Object *object, int level)

The default-filling routine for an *RWFaf_Object* type object. It simply calls the *fill()* method for the passed object.

```
void rwf_afDrawColorCycle(RWFgraph_Object *object, int level)
```

An alternate drawing function that cycles through the colors based on the passed recursion level. This routine is provided simply as an example of the kind of processing that might be performed in an action function.

```
void rwf_afDrawLastLevel(RWFgraph_Object *object, int level)
```

Same as *RWFaf_draw()* except that it only draws objects when the recursion level is greater than the last call to *RWFaf_setLevel()*.

```
class RWFaf_Object
```

A graphics object class derived from the base class *RWFgraph_Object*. Because it is a derived graphics class, an *RWFaf_Object* has all of the same member functions as any graphics object. This is the base class for all procedurally defined self-similar objects.

Public member functions for *RWFaf_Object*

```
void setInitiator(RWFlist_ObjectPtrTable &otable)
```

The initiator is defined by a table of pointers to base objects. For a Koch Curve, this would be a table of line segments. For a Sierpinski Gasket, this would be a one-element table pointing to an equilateral triangle. Derived classes usually provide overloaded versions of *setInitiator()* to make a more convenient definition appropriate to the particular object. If this function is explicitly called, then the previous initiator is deleted and replaced by the new initiator.

```
void setEraseInitiator(RWFlist_ObjectPtrTable &otable)
```

Defines the initiator for the *reverse* processing of the fractal object in which regions are removed from the object. The erase initiator is defined by a table of pointers to base objects, just as the main initiator is.

```
void setGenerator(RWFmat_MatrixTable &mtable)
```

A generator is defined as a sequence of matrices. Derived classes, such as *RWFvk_Object* class, define overloaded versions to provide a more convenient definition.

```
void setAction(void (*action)(RWFgraph_Object *object,
                   int level))
```

Sets the function to call when recursively generating the fractal object. Normally, the action function is one of the standard drawing functions for the initiator objects, but it may be any suitable function.

```
void process(void)
```

Starts the recursive processing of the fractal object. The action function is called whenever the recursion terminates.

```
void process_reverse(void)
```

Same as *process()*, except the action function is called at every recursion level to erase the objects specified by the erase initiator.

```
void draw(void)
```

Draws the object. When creating derived classes, this should be defined to set the appropriate action function and call either *process()* or *process_reverse()*.

```
void fill(void)
```

Fills the object. When creating derived classes, this should be defined to set the appropriate action function and call either *process()* or *process_reverse()*.

```
void setMaximumLevel(int max_level)
```

Sets the maximum recursion level for the object. The maximum recursion level is set to 4 pixels by default.

```
void setMinimumSize(float size)
```

Sets the minimum size in pixels at which to terminate the recursion. Once the size of the object being drawn is less than *size*, then the recursion is terminated. The default setting is 1 pixel.

Other Classes

```
class RWFsg_Gasket
```

A Sierpinski Gasket object, derived from *RWFaf_Object*. The constructor for the class automatically creates the appropriate initiator and generator for the Sierpinski Gasket.

```
class RWFsg_Carpet
```

A Sierpinski Carpet object, derived from *RWFaf_Object*. The constructor for the class automatically creates the appropriate initiator and generator for the carpet.

```
class RWFsg_ReverseGasket
```

A Sierpinski Gasket object, but drawn using the reverse-drawing method of erasing regions that do not belong to the gasket. This object is most useful for creating filled versions of the gasket and interactive demonstrations.

```
class RWFsg_ReverseCarpet
```

A Sierpinski Carpet object, but drawn using the reverse-drawing method of erasing regions that do not belong to the carpet. This object is most useful for creating filled versions of the carpet and interactive demonstrations.

Functions Found In Chapter 7

Demonstration program

```
night.exe
```

Demonstrates the use of both the tree fractals and the cratering fractals. Generates a night scene with trees silhouetted against a starry, moonlit sky.

Classes and member functions

```
class RWFaf_UserDataTable
```

A table of pointers to user-defined data structures. Because these are stored as void pointers, the data that each entry points to is *not* deleted when the table is deleted.

```
class RWFvk_HeightData
```

Defines the height modifying parameters for the standard Koch polyline generator. This is an example of a user-defined set of parameters to pass to the matrix-generating functions.

```
class RWFvk_Object
```

A new member function is provided to randomize Koch Curves.

```
void setRandomFunction(
    void (*ranfunc)(RWFgraph_Polyline &basepoly,int level,
                    void *userdata,
                    RWFgraph_Polyline &outpoly), void *data)
```

Defines a randomizing function to call along with a user-defined data structure that specifies how the polyline generator is to be altered. The randomizing function is passed the baseline generator for this object, the current recursion level, a pointer to a user-defined data structure, and an output polyline for the modified generator.

```
class RWFaf_Object
```

Several new member functions are provided to add controlled randomness to a fractal object.

```
void setGenerator(RWFaf_UserDataTable &udtable)
```

Define a generator as a table of pointers to a user-defined data structure. Each pointer is passed to a matrix-generating function defined with *setMatrixFunction()*.

```
void setMatrixFunction(int (*matrixfunc)(void *data, int level,
                          RWFmat_Matrix &gmatrix))
```

Sets the definition of a function that is called to set the generator matrix at each recursion level. The function is passed a pointer to the user-defined data structure for this generator, the current recursion level, and the matrix to set. The function returns a zero to indicate that this generator should be not be processed, or it returns a one.

```
class RWFtree_Object
```

Derived from *RWFaf_Object*, this class defines a default tree-branching structure. The object is drawn using the *process_reverse()* method, so every stage of the recursion is drawn.

```
class RWFtree_BranchData
```

Defines the branching parameters for a tree. This is an example of a user-defined set of parameters to pass to the matrix-generating functions.

```
class RWFtree_CraterObject
```

Derived from *RWFaf_Object*, this class defines a default generator for elliptically shaped craters. The object is drawn using the *process_reverse()* method, so each stage of recursion is drawn on the screen.

```
class RWFtree_CraterData
```

Defines the clustering parameters for a crater object. This is an example of a user-defined set of parameters to pass to the matrix-generating functions.

Matrix generating functions

```
void
rwf_vkRandomizeHeight(RWFgraph_Polyline &basepoly,
                      int level, void *rand_data,
                      RWFgraph_Polyline &outpoly)
```

Sample function for randomizing the height of the Koch Curve generator. This function would be passed as an argument to the *setRandomFunction()* member function for the *RWFvk_Object* class.

```
int rwf_treeFindBranchMatrix(void *data, int level,
                             RWFmat_Matrix &matrix)
```

Sample function for computing a generator matrix based on a passed *RWFtree_BranchData* structure. This function would be used in a *setMatrixFunction()* call for an *RWFtree_Object* or *RWFaf_Object class.*

```
int rwf_treeFindCraterMatrix(void *data, int level,
                             RWFmat_Matrix &matrix)
```

Sample function for computing a generator matrix based on a passed *RWFtree_CraterData* structure. This function would be used in a *setMatrixFunction()* call for an *RWFtree_CraterObject* or *RWFaf_Object class.*

Functions Found In Chapter 8

Demonstration program

```
julia.exe
```

An interactive demonstration that lets you roam around the Julia and Mandelbrot Sets for the transformation functions *f(z) = zpower + c*. You can set the scale and center in the complex plane, the maximum number of iterations and the exponent. The program also features color cycling to provide some interactive viewing of the encirclements of each set.

Classes and member functions

```
class RWFgraph_ComplexObject
```

A base class derived from the *RWFgraph_Object* class. This class provides several member functions that map a rectangular region of the complex plane to a rectangular window of the screen. The Julia Set class is derived from this base class.

```
int getMinX(void)
```

Returns the minimum *x*-screen coordinate for the current setting of the screen window.

```
int getMaxX(void)
```

Returns the maximum *x*-screen coordinate for the current setting of the screen window.

```
int getMinY(void)
```

Returns the minimum *y*-screen coordinate for the current setting of the screen window.

```
int getMaxY(void)
```

Returns the maximum *y*-screen coordinate for the current setting of the screen window.

```
void setScreenWindow(int xmin, int ymin, int xmax, int ymax)
```

Sets the screen window for the complex object. By default, the screen window is set to the entire screen.

```
void getScreenWindow(int &xmin, int &ymin, int &xmax, int &ymax)
```

Gets the screen window for the object.

```
void setWindow(float xmin, float ymin, float xmax, float ymax)
```

Sets the range of complex values for the object.

```
void getWindow(float &xmin, float &ymin, float &xmax, float &ymax)
```

Gets the current range of complex values for the object.

```
void zoomWindow(float x, float y, double scale)
```

The point (x, y) becomes the center of the window in the complex plane. The current window scale is multiplied by *scale*.

```
class RWFJulia_Object
```

An object derived from the *RWFgraph_ComplexObject* class for generating Julia Sets. The associated member functions let you set your own transformation function, stopping criteria, and action function. This class can also be used to generate the Mandelbrot Set for a transformation.

```
void setTransformation(
        complex (*tfunc) (complex &z, int level, void *tdata),
        void *transform_data)
```

Sets the transformation function to find the Julia Set. This function is passed the current value of z at the pixel, the current iteration level, and a pointer to an optional data set, which the transformation function may need for its calculations.

```
void setEscapeFunction(
        int (*efunc) (complex &z, int level, void *edata),
        void *escape_data)
```

Sets the escape function for the Julia Set. The escape function determines if the iteration should be terminated. It returns 1 if the passed z-value is a member of the escape set, and 0 otherwise. The escape function is passed the current value of z at the pixel, the current iteration level, and a pointer to an optional data set, which the escape function may need for its calculations. Normally, this data pointer is the same as the one passed to *setTransformation()*.

```
void setActionFunction(
        void (*afunc) (int i, int j, int level, int max_level,
              void *adata),
        void *action_data)
```

Sets the action function that performs the appropriate function (usually plotting a pixel) when the iteration terminates. This function is passed the (i, j) location of the current pixel, the current iteration level, the maximum iteration level, and a pointer to an optional data set, which the action function may need for its calculations. Normally, this data pointer is the same as the one passed to *setTransformation()*.

```
struct RWFJulia_zpowerdata
```

A sample data structure providing the exponent and offset used for the transformation *zpower + c*.

```
void RWFJulia_zpowerTransform(complex &z, int level,void *tdata)
```

A transformation function that computes $f(z) = z^{power} + c$. You must provide a pointer to a *RWFJulia_zpowerdata* structure with appropriate settings for *power* and the offset *c*.

```
int RWFJulia_zpowerEscape(complex &z, int level, void *edata)
```

This function determines when the *z*-value is a member of the escape set by comparing the magnitude of *z* with the *cutoff* value passed in the *edata* structure, which must point to a *RWFJulia_zpowerdata* structure.

```
void RWFJulia_drawColor(int i, int j, int level, int max_level,
                        void *action_data)
```

A sample action function for an *RWFJulia_Object* object. If the iteration terminated before reaching the maximum recursion level, then the pixel is colored to indicate at what iteration level it terminated. Otherwise, the pixel is colored 0.

```
Complex RWFJulia_MandelbrotTransform(Complex &z, int level,
                                     void *data)
```

A transformation function for generating the Mandelbrot Set. This function uses the *level* parameter to check if it is in the first iteration pass. If it is, then the passed *z* -value is saved as the offset *c* in the passed data structure, which must be a pointer to a *RWFJulia_zpowerdata* structure.

Functions Found In Chapter 9

Demonstration program

```
fbmdemo.exe
```

Demonstration program to illustrate how both one- and two-dimensional fraction Brownian motion (fBM) are generated. You also see how the controlling parameters of H, σ^2, and the choice of random-number generators affect the appearance of the fBM curves and surfaces.

Functions

```
void
rwf_fbm1DGenerate(float y1, float y2,
                  float (*random_func)(void),
                  float stdev, float level_scale, int nlevels,
                  float *values)
```

Generates one-dimensional fBM data from *y1* to *y2*. *random_func* is a pointer to the random-number generator to use. If you pass a *NULL*, then a Gaussian distribution is used. *stdev* determines the initial scale of the random variations. *level_scale* scales the standard deviation for each recursion level. *nlevels* sets the number of recursion levels processed. The passed *values* array must have enough room to contain at least $2^{nlevels} + 1$ *points*.

```
void
rwf_fbm2DGenerate(float corners[], float (*random_func)(void),
                  float stdev, float level_scale, int nlevels,
                  float **z)
```

Generates two-dimensional fBM data using the grid fBM algorithm. The *corners* array contains the initial *z*-values at the four corners of a square in the *x-y* plane. *random_func* is a pointer to a random-number generator you can use. If you pass a *NULL*, then a Gaussian distribution is used. *stdev* determines the initial scale of the random variations. *level_scale*

395

scales the standard deviation for each recursion level. *nlevels* sets the number of recursion levels processed. The passed two-dimensional *values* array must have enough room to contain at least *(2nlevels + 1)*(2nlevels + 1)* points.

```
void
rwf_fbm1DDiscreteGenerate(int class1, int class2,
                          float (*random_func)(void),
                          int nlevels, int *values)
```

Generates one-dimensional discrete fBM data for the transition from *class1* to *class2*. *random_func* is a pointer to the random-number generator you can use. If you pass a *NULL*, then a uniform distribution is used. The passed *values* array must have enough room to contain at least *2nlevels + 1* points.

```
void
rwf_fbm2DDiscreteGenerate(int corners[],
                          float (*random_func)(void),
                          int nlevels, int **classes)
```

Generates two-dimensional discrete fBM data using the grid fBM algorithm. The *corners* array contains the initial class values at the four corners of a square in the *x-y* plane. *random_func* is a pointer to the random-number generator to use. If you pass a *NULL*, then a Gaussian distribution is used. *nlevels* sets the number of recursion levels processed. The passed two-dimensional *values* array must have enough room to contain at least *(2nlevels + 1)*(2nlevels + 1)* points.

Functions Found In Chapter 10

Demonstration program

```
storm.exe
```

Demonstration program that lets you explore how to create various cloud scenes and simulated lightning.

Functions

```
void rwf_graphSortMatrices(RWFgraph_ViewingGeometry &vg,
                           RWFmat_Matrix &global_matrix,
                           RWFvec_Vector &ref_point,
                           RWFlist_MatrixTable &mtable,
                           RWFlist_SortingOrderTable &order)
```

Determines the appropriate drawing order for multiple transformed copies of an object with respect to the reference point of that object. The *order* array receives the designated drawing order. The matrix *global_matrix* left multiplies each matrix in *mtable*.

```
int  rwf_tree3DFindBranchMatrix(void *data, int level,
                                RWFmat_Matrix &bmatrix)
```

Generates the three-dimensional matrix for random branch generation. This function uses the same *RWFtree_BranchData* structure used by the two-dimensional version, *RWFtree_FindBranchMatrix()*.

```
int  rwf_tree3DFindCloudMatrix(void *data, int level,
                               RWFmat_Matrix &10bmatrix)
```

Generates the three-dimensional matrix for random cloud generation.

Classes

```
class RWFaf_3DObject
```

A graphics object class derived from the base class *RWFgraph_Object*. Because it is a derived graphics class, an *RWFaf_3DObject* has all the same member functions as any graphics object. This class has exactly the same member functions as *RWFaf_Object* and works in an almost identical manner, except that it expects three-dimensional rather than two-dimensional initiators and generators. This is the base class for all three-dimensional fractals with the desired action to draw the object on the screen.

```
class RWFgraph_Tetrahedron
```

A tetrahedron with unit height and its base centered at the origin.

```
class RWFgraph_Cube
```

A unit cube (each side is length one) with its base centered at the origin.

```
class RWFsg_3DGasket
```

A three-dimensional version of the Sierpinski Gasket.

```
class RWFsg_MengerSponge
```

A three-dimensional version of the Sierpinski Carpet.

```
class RWFtree_Cloud
```

Generates a fractal cloud using a default set of parameters. This class is derived from the *RWFtree_3DObject* class, so you can easily override the default values.

Functions Found In Chapter 11

Demonstration program

```
mountain.exe
```

Demonstration program that lets you explore how the various fBM parameters affect a simple model of a mountain.

```
mountree.exe
```

Demonstration program that creates the image shown in Color Plate 8, combining simulated terrain, trees, and clouds.

Functions

```
void
rwf_fbm2DGenerate(float corners[], long seeds[],
                  float (*random_func)(void),
                  float stdev, float level_scale, int nlevels,
                  float **z)
```

Generates two-dimensional fBM data using the grid fBM algorithm. The only difference between this and the version from Chapter 9 is that you pass an additional array of random-number seeds assigned to each corner. If you pass the same seed values at each corner, you'll always generate the same fBM values.

```
void
rwf_fbm2DDiscreteGenerate(int corners[],
                          float (*random_func)(void),
                          int nlevels, int **classes)
```

Generates two-dimensional discrete fBM data using the grid fBM algorithm. The only difference between this and the version from Chapter 9 is that you pass an additional array of random-number seeds assigned to

each corner. If you pass the same seed values at each corner, you'll always generate the same fBM values.

Classes

```
class RWFgraph_GridElement
```

A simple class used to store the data for each cell in a *RWFgraph_Grid* object. Currently, only an elevation and class value are used, but you can easily add more attributes to describe more complex grid databases.

```
class RWFgraph_Grid
```

A graphics object class derived from the base class *RWFgraph_Object* and from *RWFmat_Matrix*. This class stores a matrix of *RWFgraph_GridElement* objects that define elevations and classes for each point in the grid.

```
class RWFfbm_ClassTableElement
```

Stores the color, initial standard deviation, and fractal parameter *H* to use for each class in a grid object. Each entry of an *RWFlist_ClassTable* is an *RWFfbm_ClassTableElement*.

```
class RWFlist_ClassTable
```

A table of *RWFfbm_ClassTableElement* entries. Using this table, you can define the color, initial standard deviation, and fractal dimension for each class stored in an *RWFgraph_Grid*. A *RWFlist_ClassTable* lets you assign different attributes to different classes so you can make snow appear white, water blue, grass green, and so on.

Member functions for class *RWFgraph_Grid*

```
void setPixelSize(float x_size, float y_size)
```

Sets the size of each cell in the grid. The default size is one for both *x* and *y*.

400

```
int findScanningOrder(RWFgraph_ViewingGeometry &vg)
```

Determines the correct scanning order to draw grid cells in back-to-front order for the passed viewing geometry. The returned value ranges from one to eight. This routine is primarily used by the *draw()* member function to ensure the correct scanning order.

```
void setMaximumRecursion(int max_level)
```

Sets the maximum recursion level to use when subdividing grid cells with the fBM algorithm. The default maximum recursion level is five (32-by-32 subdivision of each grid cell).

```
void setRecursionLevel(RWFgraph_ViewingGeometry &vg)
```

Sets the recursion level for subdividing each grid cell. The computed recursion level will not exceed the value set by *setMaximumRecursion()*.

```
void setClassTable(RWFlist_ClassTable &ctable)
```

Sets a class table from which to retrieve the color, initial standard deviation, and fractal dimension for each class within the grid.

Functions Found In Chapter 12

Demonstration program

```
icompres.exe
```

Demonstration program that lets you see how an image is encoded and then subsequently decoded.

Functions

```
void rwf_PixelBlockResample(RWFgraph_PixelBlock &inp,
                            RWFgraph_PixelBlock &outp)
```

Resamples the input pixel block inp to the same resolution as the output pixel block outp, using nearest-neighbor resampling.

```
void rwf_ImageEncode8x8(RWFgraph_PixelBlock &image,
                        RWFlist_RegionMapTable &rtable)
```

Creates an *RWFlist_RegionMapTable* to define the fractal transforms for an image. The entire image is stored in the passed pixel-block image. This function uses a fixed grid of 8-by-8 pixel subregions for the image.

```
void rwf_ImageFindBestMatch(RWFgraph_PixelBlock &image,
                            RWFimage_RegionMap &rmap)
```

This function finds the best matching region of the size specified in *rmap*. The entire image is scanned to find the one with the minimum difference between the input and output regions. The elements of *rmap* are then set to values for the matching output region.

```
void rwf_imageEncodeQuadTree(RWFgraph_PixelBlock &image,
                             RWFlist_RegionMapTable &rtable,
                             float max_error, int min_size)
```

Encodes an image using the quadtree method of recursively dividing regions until the error criteria is met (error is less than *max_error*) or the minimum size is reached (region size less than *min_size*).

```
void rwf_imageDecode(RWFimage_RegionMap &rtable,
                     RWFgraph_PixelBlock &out_image, int npasses)
```

Decodes an image based on the passed region map table. The decoding starts with a simple checkerboard image with the final result drawn on the screen. The passed *xsize* and *ysize* values define the original resolution of the image. The argument *npasses* defines the number of iterations of decoding to perform.

```
RWFpcx_File *rwf_pcxOpen(char *filename)
```

Opens the passed filename as a PCX format file. If the file name is not opened, then a NULL pointer is returned.

Classes

```
class RWFgraph_PixelBlock
```

A class holding a rectangular array of 8-bit pixels. The member functions for this class are listed in Table 12-1.

```
class RWFpcx_File
```

Defines a handle to a PCX-format image file. The member functions for this class are as follows:

```
void getSize(int &x, int &y)
```

Returns the dimensions of the PCX file.

```
void readBlock(RWFgraph_PixelBlock &pblock, int &x, int &y)
```

Reads in a rectangular region from the PCX file into *pblock*. Any pixels outside the actual file are set to zero.

```
class RWFimage_RegionMap
```

A class defining a mapping from an smaller input region to a larger output region.

```
class RWFlist_RegionMapTable
```

A table of *RWFimage_RegionMap* objects.

Functions Found In Chapter 13

```
class RWFgraph_2DPlotObject
```

A graphics class derived from *RWFgraph_Object*. This class lets you plot an iterated multidimensional function to create scatter diagrams (plotting individual points) or line graphs. You must provide a function that generates two-dimensional *(x, y)* points from the multidimensional data. The member functions for this class are described in Table 13-1.

```
int rwf_chaosPlotLorenzAttractor(RWFvec_Vector &xyz,
                                 RWFvec_Vector &xy,
                                 void *user_data)
```

A sample plotting function for plotting the Lorenz Attractor. The *user_data* structure must be a *RWFchaos_LorenzData* structure that defines the coefficients for the Lorenz equations and the time step for the plot.

```
int rwf_chaosPlotPopulationFeigenbaum(RWFvec_Vector &pvec,
                                      RWFvec_Vector &xy,
                                      void *user_data)
```

A sample plotting function to generate a Feigenbaum Diagram for the population equation. The *user_data* structure must be a *RWFchaos_PopulationData* structure that defines the population-equation attributes to plot.

Installing the Software

Directories

The disk that accompanies this book contains all the source, Borland C++ project, and executable files stored in two compressed *zip* files: *source.zip* and *exec.zip*. These files are decompressed using the utility *pkunzip.exe*, also provided on the disk. You should copy the entire contents of the disk to a suitable subdirectory on your hard drive, such as *c:\rwf*. Once you have copied the contents of the disk, you decompress the files by typing:

```
c:
cd \rwf
install
```

The *install.bat* file will decompress both *zip* files. You'll need approximately 2 megabyte of free disk space to store all the source and executables. Once the files are decompressed, you may delete both *zip* files from your hard drive.

405

In addition to the C source files and executables, there are two other files: *makefile* and *links*. These two files are used by *make* to compile all the modules and link each demonstration program to produce executable programs. The executable files (designated by the extension *.exe*) for all the demonstration programs described in each chapter are provided on the disk, so you don't have to make them. You may run any of these programs simply by typing the desired program name from the DOS command prompt.

The file *makefile* is provided as an example of how to compile and link your own programs. The *makefile* can also be used to rebuild all the demonstration programs. The *makefile* is currently set up for the Borland C++ version 3.1 compiler and libraries. If you have Borland C++, you can create all the demonstration programs simply by changing to the directory where the files were copied and typing *make*:

```
c:
cd \rwf
make
```

The *makefile* currently assumes that you have installed Borland C++ onto your C: drive in the standard directories. You'll need approximately 1 megabyte of additional hard-disk space for all the object files (*.OBJ* extension) produced when the modules are compiled. The *makefile* is shown in Listing B-1.

Listing B-1. The *makefile* to create the demonstration programs.

```
all: PACHINKO.exe VONKOCH.exe GASKETS.exe NIGHT.exe JULIA.exe \
     FBMDEMO.exe STORM.exe MOUNTAIN.exe MOUNTREE.exe \
     ICOMPRES.exe

# Set your library and include directories here
LIB_DIR = c:\borlandc\lib
INC_DIR = c:\borlandc\include

CFLAGS = -ml -2 -f287 -G -O2 -V -vi--I$(INC_DIR) -c
```

```
CC = bcc
LINK = tlink /L$(LIB_DIR)

#All of the modules listed here must be linked in for each
#of the demonstration programs

COMMON_OBJ = \
     RWFGRAPH.obj RWFMAT.obj                                       \
     RWFRAND.obj  RWFVK.obj    RWFAF.obj    RWFSG.obj    \
     RWFTREE.obj  RWFJULIA.obj                                     \
     RWFFBM.obj   RWF3D.obj    RWFGRID.obj                \
     RWFIMAGE.obj RWFCHAOS.obj RWFMISC.obj

pachinko.exe  : $(COMMON_OBJ)
vonkoch.exe   : $(COMMON_OBJ)
gaskets.exe   : $(COMMON_OBJ)
night.exe     : $(COMMON_OBJ)
julia.exe     : $(COMMON_OBJ)
fbmdemo.exe   : $(COMMON_OBJ)
storm.exe     : $(COMMON_OBJ)
mountain.exe  : $(COMMON_OBJ)
mountree.exe  : $(COMMON_OBJ)
icompres.exe  : $(COMMON_OBJ)

.obj.exe:
     $(LINK) cOL $*.obj @links $*.exe, , graphics emu mathl cl

.cpp.obj:
     $(CC) $(CFLAGS) $*.c
```

If your compiler includes directories or libraries that are installed in a different directory, then you must specify where *make* should look for them by changing the symbols *INC_DIR* (include directories) and *LIB_DIR* (library directories) to the appropriate locations. If you are using a different compiler, you'll need to make the appropriate changes to *makefile* for your compiler's version of *make*. You must also provide the correct command line for the compiler by changing the definition of the *CC* symbol and the *LINK* symbol of *makefile*.

To link a program of your own creation, you must link with all the modules specified by the symbol *COMMON_OBJ* (shown in Listing B-1). If you're using the Borland project files, then you must include all the modules as part of the project. Project files for each of the demonstration programs included on the disk. However, these project files assume that library directories are included and are standard.

A complete listing of the disk's contents and the individual *zip* files is shown in the following series of tables.

Files on the disk

File	Description
PKUNZIP EXE	Decompresses the files
INSTALL BAT	Runs *pkunzip* on the two compressed files
SOURCE ZIP	All C source files and Borland project files
EXEC ZIP	Executable copies of all demonstration programs

Files for make

LINKS

MAKEFILE

README   Last minute changes or enhancements

Demonstration Program Source Files (*source.zip*)

Program source file	Program described in
PACHINKO CPP	Chapter 4
VONKOCH CPP	Chapter 5
GASKETS CPP	Chapter 6
NIGHT CPP	Chapter 7
JULIA CPP	Chapter 8
FBMDEMO CPP	Chapter 9

STORM CPP	Chapter 10
MOUNTAIN CPP	Chapter 11
MOUNTREE CPP	Chapter 11
ICOMPRES CPP	Chapter 12
PLATE1 CPP	Chapter 5
PLATE2 CPP	Chapter 5
PLATE3 CPP	Chapter 5
PLATE4 CPP	Chapter 6

Module Source Files (*source.zip*)

Source file	Module described in
RWFGRAPH CPP	Chapter 3
RWFVEC CPP	Chapter 3
RWFMAT CPP	Chapter 3
RWFRAND CPP	Chapter 4
RWFVK CPP	Chapter 5
RWFAF CPP	Chapter 6
RWFSG CPP	Chapter 6
RWFTREE CPP	Chapter 7
RWFJULIA CPP	Chapter 8
RWFFBM CPP	Chapter 9
RWF3D CPP	Chapter 3 and 10
RWFGRID CPP	Chapter 11
RWFIMAGE CPP	Chapter 12
RWFCHAOS CPP	Chapter 13

Header Files (*source.zip*)

Header file	Classes/functions described in
RWFMISC HPP	n/a
RWFGRAPH HPP	Chapter 3
RWFVEC HPP	Chapter 3
RWFMAT HPP	Chapter 3
RWFLIST HPP	Chapter 3
RWFRAND HPP	Chapter 4

RWFVK HPP	Chapter 5
RWFAF HPP	Chapter 6
RWFSG HPP	Chapter 6
RWFTREE HPP	Chapter 7
RWFJULIA HPP	Chapter 8
RWFFBM HPP	Chapter 9
RWF3D HPP	Chapter 3 and 10
RWFGRID HPP	Chapter 11
RWFIMAGE HPP	Chapter 12
RWFCHAOS HPP	Chapter 13

Project Files (*source.zip*)

PACHINKO PRJ

VONKOCH PRJ

GASKETS PRJ

NIGHT   PRJ

JULIA   PRJ

FBMDEMO PRJ

STORM   PRJ

MOUNTAIN PRJ

MOUNTREE PRJ

ICOMPRES PRJ

Demonstration Program Executables (*exec.zip*)

PACHINKO EXE

VONKOCH EXE

GASKETS EXE

NIGHT   EXE

JULIA   EXE

FBMDEMO EXE

STORM   EXE

MOUNTAIN EXE

MOUNTREE EXE

ICOMPRES EXE

Bibliography

Barnsley, Michael. *Fractals Everywhere*. Academic Press, 1988.

Barnsley, Michael, and Lyman P. Hurd. *Fractal Image Compression*. A.K. Peters Ltd., 1993.

Foley, James D., Andries van Dam, Steven K. Feiner, and John F. Hughes. *Computer Graphics: Principles and Practice*. 2d ed. Addison-Wesley Publishing, 1990.

Hoel, Paul G., Sidney C. Port, and Charles J. Stone. *Introduction to Stochastic Processes*. Houghton Mifflin Company, 1972.

Ladd, Scott Robert. *Applying* C++. M&T Books, 1992.

Ladd, Scott Robert. *C++ Components and Algorithms*. M&T Books, 1992.

Lippman, Stanley B. *A C++ Primer*. Addison-Wesley Publishing, 1989.

Mandelbrot, Benoit B. *Fractals: Form, Chance, and Dimension*. W.H. Freeman and Company, 1977.

Mandelbrot, Benoit B. *The Fractal Geometry of Nature*. W.H. Freeman and Company, 1977.

Oualline, Steve. *C Elements of Style*. M&T Books, 1992.

Peitgen, Heinz-Otto, Hartmut Jürgens, and Dietmar Saupe. *Chaos and Fractals*. Springer-Verlag, 1992.

Peitgen, Heinz-Otto, and Dietmar Saupe. *The Science of Fractal Images*. Springer-Verlag, 1988.

Peitgen, Heinz-Otto, and Peter H. Richter. *The Beauty of Fractals*. Springer-Verlag, 1986.

Peitgen, Heinz-Otto, et al., *Fractals for the Classroom: Strategic Activities*. 2 vols. Springer-Verlag, 1991.

Peterson, Ivars. "Basins of Froth: Visualizing the 'chaos' surrounding chaos." *Science News* 142, No. 20 (November 14, 1992): 329–330.

Peterson, Ivars, and Carol Ezzell. "Crazy Rhythms: Confronting the complexity of chaos in biological systems." *Science News* 142, No. 10 (September 5, 1992): 156–159.

Pickover, Clifford A. *Computers, Pattern, Chaos, and Beauty*. St. Martin's Press, 1990.

Press, William H., Brian P. Flannery, Saul A. Teukolsky, and William T. Vetterling. *Numerical Recipes in C*. Cambridge University Press, 1988.

Prusinkiewicz, P., and A. Lindenmayer. *The Algorithmic Beauty of Plants*. Springer-Verlag, 1990.

Schröder, M. *Fractals, Chaos, Power Laws*. W.H. Freeman and Company, 1991.

Siegal, Charles. *teach yourself... C*. MIS:Press, Inc., 1991.

Sprott, Julien C. *Strange Attractors*. M&T Books, 1993.

Stevens, Al. *teach yourself... C++*, 3rd Edition. MIS:Press, Inc., 1992.

Stevens, Roger T. *Fractal Programming in C*. M&T Books, 1989.

Stevens, Roger T. *Fractal Programming and Ray Tracing in C*. M&T Books, 1990.

Stevens, Roger T. *Advanced Fractal Programming in* C. M&T Books, 1990.

Watkins, Christopher D., Stephen B. Coy, and Mark Finlay. *Photorealism and Ray Tracing in* C. M&T Books, 1992.

Watt, Alan. *Fundamentals of Three-Dimensional Computer Graphics*. Addison-Wesley Publishing, 1989.

Wegner, T., and M. Peterson. *Fractal Creations*. Waite Group Press, 1991.

Wegner, T., Bert Tyler, Mark Peterson, and Pieter Brandehorst. *Fractals for Windows*. Waite Group Press, 1992.

Woodroofe, Michael. *Probability With Applications*. McGraw-Hill, 1975.

Index

Symbols

+= operator (C++ language) 54-55

μ (mean) 111

σ *See* Standard deviation

σ² (variance) 108, 111

A

action_func function 145, 150

Affine fractals, multidimensional 256-262

Affine transformations, 26, 66, 199

    computation of 71-73

    nonlinear transformations vs. 200-201

    with two-dimensional figures 146-147

AM radio 366

Arrays 94

Attractive fixed points 347-348

Attractors 346-355

    definition of 346

    fixed-point 347-348

    periodic 349

    strange 349-355

Average value *See* Mean

B

Back-face removal 263

Barnsley, Michael 33, 337-338

Basis functions 364

Bifurcation diagrams (Feigenbaum
    Diagrams) 356-359

Biology, use of fractal analysis in 365-366

Boundaries between different classes,
    in terrain 303-304

Brightness, matching 321

Brown, Robert 230

Brownian motion 230-231. *See also*
    Fractional Brownian motion

    fractal nature of 234-236

    mathematics of 231-233

C

Cantor, Georg 18-20, 27, 28

Cantor Sets 20-25, 223

    Sierpinski Gasket and 148-149, 157

Carpenter, Loren 281

CAT (Computer Aided Tomography)
    scans 371

C (computer language) 37, 41

C++ (computer language) 37-62

    advantages of 40-42

    class definitions in 46-47

    constructors and destructors in 47-49

    function overloading in 49-50

    header files 42-46

    #ifdef directive 59

    macros in 58-59

    module files 42

    naming conventions for 61-62

    object-oriented programming in 38-42

    overloaded operators in 51-54

    references 54-55

    static variables 56-57

    templates 60-61

    virtual functions in 50-51

Central-limit theorem 107

Chaos and chaos theory 34-35, 341-362

    attractors 346-355

    Feigenbaum diagrams 356-359

    Lorenz attractor 350-351, 354-355

A Library of Technical References from M&T Books

Getting Graphic: Programming Fundamentals in C and C++
by Mark Finlay

This book teaches the fundamentals of graphics programming. It shows C and C++ programmers how to plot points on a screen, draw geometric shapes, design 3-D figures, and more. This book/disk package is filled with sophisticated and usable source code examples and sample graphic images. *Getting Graphic: Programming Fundamentals in C and C++* is a perfect introduction to the exciting world of graphics. 500 pp.

Book/Disk	$39.95	#2829

Level: Beginning-Intermediate

Strange Attractors: Creating Patterns in Chaos
by Julien C. Sprott

Learn to create spectacular fractal images with this complete book/disk package. It explains a new technique for generating a class of fractals called strange attractors. Step-by-step instructions lead you through the creation of a program that produces an endless number of patterns and musical sounds. Contains more than 350 examples of computer art plus an interactive disk and 3-D glasses. Included with the book is source code in BASIC, C, C++, and VisualBASIC for Windows. 426 pp.

Book/Disk	$39.95	#2985

Level: All

A Library of Technical References
from M&T Books

Photorealism and Ray Tracing in C
by Christopher Watkins and Stephen Coy

C programmers interested in computer graphics...look no further! This is the book that puts the tools in your hands to produce photorealistic, 3-D images on PCs. Includes section on ray tracing, plus tips for producing sample images as well as creating original designs. Source code on MS/PC-DOS disk for reproducing and customizing sample images. Includes eight pages of full-color graphics. 476 pp.

Book/Disk $44.95   #2470

Level: Intermediate

Fractal Programming and Ray Tracing with C++
by Roger T. Stevens

Finally, a book for C and C++ programmers who want to create complex and intriguing graphic designs. This book thoroughly explains ray tracing, discussing how rays are traced, how objects are used to create ray-traced images, and how to create ray tracing programs. A complete ray tracing program, along with all of the source code, is included. Contains 16 pages of full-color graphics. 444 pp.

Book/Disk $39.95   #1180

Level: Intermediate

A Library of Technical References
from M&T Books

PageMaker 5 By Example
Windows Edition
by Webster & Associates

Become a PageMaker pro quickly and easily with this hands-on guide to using PageMaker 5 for Windows. It fully explains the new features and functions of this latest version. You'll find detailed information on everything from PageMaker basics to advanced techniques. Includes exercise disk that contains an animated tour of design basics, a glossary of terms, and an image viewer. 576 pp.

Book/Disk $34.95   #2977

Level: Beginning - Intermediate

Programming in 3 Dimensions:
3-D Graphics, Ray Tracing, and Animation
by Christopher D. Watkins and Larry Sharp

Required reading! This one is for all computer graphics enthusiasts who want a detailed look at 3-D graphics and modeling. Also features discussions of popular ray tracing methods and computer animation. Includes eight pages of full-color graphics. Provides C source code and numerous examples. MS/PC-DOS disk contains sample source code. A must! 512 pp.

Book/Disk $39.95   #2209

Level: Intermediate

1-800-488-5233

A Library of Technical References
from M&T Books

Advanced Fractal Programming in C
by Roger T. Stevens

Programmers who enjoyed our best-selling *Fractal Programming in* C can move on to the next level of fractal programming with this book. Included are how-to instructions for creating many different types of fractal curves, including source code. Contains 16 pages of full-color fractals. All the source code to generate the fractals is available on an optional disk in MS/PC-DOS format. 305 pp.

Book/Disk $39.95   #0974

Level: Intermediate

Advanced Graphics Programming in C and C++
by Roger T. Stevens and Christopher D. Watkins

This book is for all C and C++ programmers who want to create impressive graphic designs on IBM PCs or compatibles. Through in-depth discussions and numerous sample programs, you will learn how to create advanced 3-D shapes, wire-frame graphics, solid images, and more. All source code is available on disk in MS/PC-DOS format. Contains 16 pages of full-color graphics. 560 pp.

Book/Disk $39.95   #1733

Level: Intermediate

A Library of Technical References
from M&T Books

Applying C++
by Scott Robert Ladd

Intermediate level programmers . . . this is your next book! Learn how to design and maintain clean, efficient C++ applications and do it by using the very tricks, techniques and strategies of the industry's acknowledged C++ gurus. You want to get around language limitations? Solve problems in the real world? Find out what works and what doesn't? Get inside this volume and discover the keys to object-oriented programming design, C++ tricks and traps, interfacing with MS-DOS, planning and implementing C++ libraries and applications, building a spreadsheet and much more. Includes complete source code disk. 544 pp.

Book/Disk $34.95   #2624

Level: Beginning-Intermediate

C++ Components and Algorithms
by Scott Robert Ladd

It's true: experienced C programmers always need the kind of comprehensive tools that can help them develop and maintain powerful C++ applications. This excellent volume is where you can find them—all of them! Memory management, indexed files using B-Trees, mathematical programming, adaptive algorithms and more. The in-depth discussions and numerous source code examples are geared toward an understanding of C++'s inner workings. The programs and classes presented are compatible with various C++ compilers, making them valuable to a wide audience of C programmers. All source code included on disk in MC/PC-DOS format. 512 pp.

Book/Disk $39.95   #2276

Level: Advanced

1-800-488-5233

Accessory Disk Contents

Directions for installing the *Real-World Fractals* diskette:

1. Insert the diskette into your 3.5" floppy drive.

2. Install the software with the following commands:

    ```
    C:>cd \
    C:>mkdir rwf
    C:>copy b:*.* c:\rwf
    C:>cd \rwf
    C:>install
    ```

3. The demonstration programs are ready to run. A complete description of the contents of the diskette and how to compile the modules yourself may be found in Appendix B of the text.

4. The default display resolution is 800x600. If your VGA or SVGA card does not support this resolution, you may set the display resolution to another setting with the following command:

    ```
    C:>setmode
    ```

5. Be sure to read the README file for the latest information and program updates.